Additional Praise for *On Account of Race*

"Lawrence Goldstone's book *On Account of Race* is a careful and brilliant analysis of the effort of the Southern states to deprive the African American population of the right to vote after Reconstruction ended in 1877. There was no disguise of their purpose and no restriction on the method they used. From the grandfather clause or poll taxes or literacy tests, whatever could be used to block African Americans from voting was openly and emphatically applied. The white population was simply determined to keep the ballot box for themselves. Goldstone shows how the courts refused to interfere in any way with this program. Even such noteworthy judges as Justice Oliver Wendell Holmes approved the effort. The book carefully examines the campaign, which lasted almost one hundred years until the Voting Rights Act of 1965."

—LEON FRIEDMAN, Joseph Kushner Distinguished Professor
of Civil Liberties Law at Hofstra University

"In a book both reasonable and readable, Lawrence Goldstone effectively challenges the convenient mythology that racial segregation was a policy reflecting merely the isolated prejudices of the southern American states in the post–Civil War era. His main focus is the U.S. Supreme Court and the peculiar, absurdly twisted logic across a series of critical cases by which the justices undermined the Fourteenth and Fifteenth Amendments, systematically legitimating Jim Crow. The lesson is clear: that voting and other basic rights, unless broadly defended, can rest on fragile foundations indeed."

—RONALD KING,
professor of political science at San Diego State University
and coauthor of *Removal of the Property Qualification
for Voting in the United States*

ON ACCOUNT OF RACE

On
ACCOUNT
of
RACE

THE SUPREME COURT,
WHITE SUPREMACY,
AND THE RAVAGING OF
AFRICAN AMERICAN VOTING RIGHTS

LAWRENCE GOLDSTONE

COUNTERPOINT
Berkeley, California

Library of Congress Cataloging-in-Publication Data
Names: Goldstone, Lawrence, 1947– author.
Title: On account of race : the Supreme Court, white supremacy, and the ravaging of
    African American voting rights / Lawrence Goldstone.
Description: Berkeley : Counterpoint Press, 2020. | Includes bibliographical references
    and index.
Identifiers: LCCN 2019037734 | ISBN 9781640093928 (hardcover) | ISBN
    9781640093935 (ebook)
Subjects: LCSH: Race discrimination—Law and legislation—United States—
    History—19th century. | Race discrimination—Law and legislation—
    United States—History—20th century. | African Americans—Suffrage—History—
    19th century. | African Americans—Suffage—History—20th century.
Classification: LCC KF4755 .G65 2020 | DDC 342.7308/73—dc23
LC record available at https://lccn.loc.gov/2019037734

Jacket design by Sarah Brody
Book design by Jordan Koluch

COUNTERPOINT
2560 Ninth Street, Suite 318
Berkeley, CA 94710
www.counterpointpress.com

Printed in the United States of America
Distributed by Publishers Group West

10 9 8 7 6 5 4 3 2 1

To Nancy and Lee

Courts of law will give the sense of every article of the constitution that may from time to time come before them. And in their decisions they will not confine themselves to any fixed or established rules, but will determine, according to what appears to them, the reason and spirit of the constitution. The opinions of the supreme court, whatever they may be, will have the force of law; because there is no power provided in the constitution that can correct their errors or control their adjudications. From this court there is no appeal.

—"BRUTUS," writing against ratification
of the Constitution, January 31, 1788

CONTENTS

ON ACCOUNT OF RACE

Introduction

ON MARCH 7, 1965, 600 MEN AND WOMEN SET OUT from a church in Selma, Alabama, on a planned fifty-four-mile march to the state capital in Montgomery. They were led by two black men: John Lewis, the twenty-five-year-old son of an Alabama sharecropper, and Hosea Williams, who had a master's degree in chemistry and had been wounded in action in World War II while serving in General George S. Patton's Third Army.

In Montgomery, they intended to present Governor George Wallace with petitions demanding that African Americans be guaranteed the same constitutionally protected right to vote that whites in Alabama regularly and easily exercised. In Selma, only about 300 of the more than 15,000 eligible black voters had been allowed to register.

When the marchers reached the crest of the Edmund Pettus Bridge—which spanned the Alabama River and had been named for a Confederate general who had also been a Grand Dragon of the Alabama Ku Klux Klan—they saw dozens of white-helmeted state troopers waiting for them on the other side. The troopers were slapping nightsticks in their hands; whips and tear gas canisters hung from their belts; gas masks were at the ready. The Dallas County sheriff, Jim Clark, and his deputies, some on horseback, waited behind the troopers. Dozens of jeering white spectators waving Confederate flags were on the scene as well.

John Cloud, a major in the state police, spoke through a bullhorn and demanded that the marchers turn back. He gave them two minutes. Lewis, the leader of the Student Nonviolent Coordinating Committee, and Williams, of the Southern Christian Leadership Conference, were determined not to back down. They were equally insistent that the protest be peaceful, at least on their end. They instructed the marchers to kneel and pray and to not fight back if attacked.

And attacked they were, almost immediately. Viciously, and with fury and hate. Lewis and his fellow marchers were tear-gassed, beaten with nightsticks—Lewis suffered a fractured skull—whipped, and run down by horses. Many were spat on as they lay injured on the ground.

There had been any number of incidents of white brutality across the South, but this one was filmed by reporters for the entire world to see. On the ABC network, the television premiere of *Judgment at Nuremberg*, about the trials of Nazi war criminals, was interrupted so that millions could witness the horrible violence in Selma for themselves. The incident was soon dubbed "Bloody Sunday," and within days, demonstrations against Southern racism were held in more than eighty U.S. cities.

Finally, after decades of denial, the government acted. On March 15, President Lyndon Johnson appeared before a special joint session of Congress and told the assembled senators and representatives:

> The harsh fact is that in many places in this country men and women are kept from voting simply because they are Negroes. Every device of which human ingenuity is capable has been used to deny this right. The Negro citizen may go to register only to be told that the day is wrong, or the hour is late, or the official in charge is absent. And if he persists, and if he manages to present himself to the registrar, he may

be disqualified because he did not spell out his middle name or because he abbreviated a word on the application.

And if he manages to fill out an application he is given a test. The registrar is the sole judge of whether he passes this test. He may be asked to recite the entire Constitution, or explain the most complex provisions of state law. And even a college degree cannot be used to prove that he can read and write. For the fact is that the only way to pass these barriers is to show a white skin . . .

What happened in Selma is part of a far larger movement which reaches into every section and State of America. It is the effort of American Negroes to secure for themselves the full blessings of American life. Their cause must be our cause too. Because it is not just Negroes, but really it is all of us, who must overcome the crippling legacy of bigotry and injustice.

And we *shall* overcome.

Two days after the president spoke, the Senate majority leader, Democrat Mike Mansfield, and the minority leader, Republican Everett Dirksen, together introduced a bill to guarantee voting rights to African Americans. A similar bill was soon introduced in the House of Representatives. Over ferocious opposition by Southern congressmen, the bill passed in both houses. On August 6, 1965, President Johnson signed the Voting Rights Act into law.

The 1965 Voting Rights Act has been widely considered the single most effective piece of civil rights legislation ever produced in the United States. The law banned literacy tests and many of the other contrivances used in Southern states to deny the vote to men and women of color. Harking back to post–Civil War legislation of the 1870s, it allowed the federal government to send election supervisors to any state or county where discriminatory practices existed as of the 1964 presidential election, or where voter turnout or registration for that election had fallen below 50 percent of the voting age population. These were called "special coverage areas," and in these locations, local and state governments would be required to obtain permission from the federal government before making any change to their election laws or voting procedures.

The law was an enormous and immediate success. In Selma, eight days after President Johnson signed the bill, federal officials helped 381 African Americans register to vote, more than had been able to sign up in Dallas County for sixty-five years. By Election Day 1965, 8,000 new black voters helped turn Sheriff Clark out of office and into a mobile home salesman. African American voter registration exploded in every state that had been a part of the old Confederacy—nowhere more than in Mississippi, where in March 1965, only 6.7 percent of eligible African Americans had been registered. By November 1988, that number had jumped to 74.2 percent.

With increased participation in the electoral process, men and women of color, after more than a century, were elected to high public office, and have represented the nation in both houses of Congress and even in the White House. John Lewis was elected to Congress in Georgia, where he has remained ever since. African Americans by the thousands have served in state and local government.[1] Thanks largely to the Voting Rights Act, the promise of America, it seemed, had tentatively begun to be kept.

But the only reason a Voting Rights Act had been necessary in the first place was a series of Supreme Court decisions that began during Reconstruction and ended just after the turn of the twentieth century, in which the nine justices of the nation's highest tribunal had allowed, or more accurately mandated, white supremacist governments in the South to strip black Americans of that very right, a right that two constitutional amendments had been enacted specifically to safeguard. The measures that the Voting Rights Act delineated to ensure equal access to the ballot box were much the same as those the post-Reconstruction Court had declared unconstitutional, oblivious to a series of very public pronouncements by Southern whites that their intention had been "to get the nigger out of politics." In the guise of a strict reading of the text, and with sham neutrality, Supreme Court justices rewrote the Constitution to fit the racial attitudes of the day—and their own. In doing so, the justices allowed popular sentiment and their own notions of racial superiority to overwhelm the promise of equality under the law.

The effect was devastating. With the vacuum created by black disfranchisement, African Americans were helpless to prevent the horrors of Jim Crow from being sucked in to fill it. People of color, most either former slaves or their descendants, had endured beatings, whippings, and destruction of their property, and had even lost their lives in the attempt to secure a right that had been guaranteed to them under the Constitution, but denied by state and local officials. They fought desperately to prevent their right to vote from being systematically rescinded, only to see the Supreme Court uphold the most transparent laws enacted to drive them back into bondage.

There is no act more fundamental to democratic government than casting a vote. The ability to do so openly and fairly is considered to a great degree synonymous with freedom; the inability synonymous with subjugation or slavery. That the Supreme Court of the United States was the instrument by which millions of black Americans were denied this most basic privilege of citizenship is a national tragedy, the only occasion in United States history in which a significant group of citizens who had been specifically granted the right to vote had it then stripped away.

Until now.

On June 25, 2013, the Supreme Court, in a 5–4 decision, ruled in *Shelby County, Alabama v. Holder* that the formula for determining which states and localities would be designated "special coverage areas" was unconstitutional, because after almost fifty years, conditions had improved so much that the formula no longer represented reality. Unless the federal government could demonstrate that these rules were still required, wrote Chief Justice John Roberts in his majority opinion, which was joined by Justices Scalia, Thomas, Kennedy, and Alito, it was a violation of the rights of states and localities to require them to get permission before they could change their election laws. That "states' rights" had been the rationale under which earlier courts had allowed white supremacists to rob black Americans of their access to the political process was no longer germane.

"Our country has changed," Chief Justice Roberts wrote. "While any racial discrimination in voting is too much, Congress must ensure that the legislation it passes to remedy that problem speaks to current conditions."

Justice Ruth Bader Ginsburg wrote a strong dissent, in which she was joined by Justices Breyer, Kagan, and Sotomayor. She agreed that racial discrimination at the ballot box in the states that still required preclearance had decreased, but that was precisely because the law had remained in place. "Throwing out preclearance when it has worked and is continuing to work to stop discriminatory changes," she argued, "is like throwing away your umbrella in a rainstorm because you are not getting wet."

If the requirement was eliminated, the dissenters predicted, discrimination might well begin again. And so it has. According to the Brennan Center for Justice,

> The decision in *Shelby County* opened the floodgates to laws restricting voting throughout the United States. The effects were immediate. Within 24 hours of the ruling, Texas announced that it would implement a strict photo ID law. Two other states, Mississippi and Alabama, also began to enforce photo ID laws that had previously been barred because of federal preclearance.[2]

Other states have followed suit. In July 2017, in Georgia, 600,000 people, 8 percent of the state's registered voters, were purged from the rolls and required to reregister; an estimated 107,000 of them simply because they hadn't voted in recent elections. In 2018, the state blocked the registration of 53,000 state residents, 70 percent of whom were African American.

Voter ID laws and other restrictions that fall most heavily on the poor, African Americans, and Latinos have been initiated in a number of other states, not all in the South. Polling locations have been closed, early voting restricted, and registration rules made stricter; all, critics insist, to suppress the votes of certain classes and races. In some states, the same sort of "exact match" rules that President Johnson cited in his speech to Congress have been reinstituted.

But perhaps the most pernicious effect of *Shelby County v. Holder* is the renewed perception, among those who would discriminate, that the Supreme Court is their ally. As a result, they have become emboldened and, in many cases, have perpetrated abuses of power that would have been unthinkable with a different roster of justices.

On March 28, 2018, for example, in Tarrant County, Texas, forty-three-year-old Crystal Mason, an African American mother of three, was sentenced to five years in prison for voter fraud. Her crime was going to her local church to vote in the 2016 presidential election and, when she was told that her name did not appear on the voting rolls, casting a provisional ballot under her own name for Hillary Clinton. The vote was never counted. What she had never been told was that because she was on federal probation for tax fraud, her name had been stricken from the rolls and her right to vote suspended. Although the prosecutors, conservative Republicans, never accused her of intent in violating the law, they asked for the maximum sentence, which the judge, another conservative Republican, agreed to. Then, in addition to the five-year sentence from the state judge, at the request of federal prosecutors, Ms. Mason was forced to first serve a ten-month federal sentence for violating the terms of her supervised release. In Iowa, by contrast, a white woman, Terri Lynn Rote, who attempted to vote twice for Donald Trump, was fined $750 and received one year of probation.

In just one more example, in October 2018, a bus rented by a nonpartisan voter outreach group, in which dozens of black senior citizens were being driven to the polls, was stopped by Georgia officials and the seniors ordered off because, according to Jefferson County Administrator Adam Brett, the bus ride constituted "political activity."[3]

Whether these and similar modern transparencies will ultimately be ruled antithetical to the constitutional guarantees that Americans claim to hold so dear, or be upheld with same "states' rights" justifications that ushered in one of the most shameful periods in American history, will depend once more on the will and honor of the Supreme Court. In so deciding, the justices on the high bench will be issuing nothing short of a practical definition of American democracy.

★ ★ ★

The Supreme Court occupies a unique place in American government: it
is the only institution specified in the Constitution whose members are
not elected.[4] While describing its existence as an afterthought would be
an overstatement, its inclusion in the Constitution was grudging.

In 1787, most Americans did not want a federal court system at
all, and certainly not one that had any real power. In a new nation that
did not have sufficient funds to afford a modern army and navy, any
money spent to pay judges or build courthouses was thought wasted. Far
more important was the fear of judicial tyranny. Opponents of national
courts—and there were many—were certain a national judiciary would
quickly claim powers that were supposed to be reserved to the states. In
addition, most Americans cringed at the thought that citizens of one
state would be forced to stand in judgment before citizens of another—in
effect, foreigners.

As a result, Article III of the Constitution, which lays out the powers
and responsibilities of the federal courts, is by far the shortest of those
that define the three branches of government, consisting of only three
sections and six short paragraphs. It is also the most vague. While there
was mention of a "Supreme Court," Article III did not say exactly how
many judges would sit on it. Nor did the delegates lay out in detail what
powers the Supreme Court would have—whether or not, for example,
it would be allowed to pass on the constitutionality of laws enacted by
Congress and signed by the president—nor how courts other than the
Supreme Court would be organized, or whether they would even exist at
all. It was left to Congress to decide these questions after the Constitution was in place.

Even so limited, during the fight for ratification, the creation of a
national judiciary was one of the topics of greatest debate. In New York,
where ratification was very much in doubt, Alexander Hamilton, in *Federalist 78*, sought to assure skeptics that the Court would be the "people's"
branch of government, protecting ordinary citizens from encroachments

on their liberty by tyrants who might potentially occupy the legislature or the presidency. "It is far more rational," he wrote, "to suppose that the courts were designed to be an intermediate body between the people and the legislature, in order, among other things, to keep the latter within the limits assigned to their authority." He also assured his fellow citizens that the judiciary would be "beyond comparison the weakest of the three departments of power."

History has demonstrated that Hamilton could not have been more incorrect. Beginning with Chief Justice John Marshall in *Marbury v. Madison*, which established the very power of judicial review that Article III had omitted, the Supreme Court has carved out for itself—with justices who never face the voters and serve for life—a role that is often more dominant than either Congress or the president. Nor has the Court, through most of its history, been the people's branch of government, particularly if those people happened to be black.

This was never more true than in the decades after the Civil War, when the Supreme Court, always claiming strict adherence to the law, regularly flexed those judicial muscles and chose, in decision after decision, to allow white supremacists to re-create a social order at odds with legislation that Congress had passed, the president had signed, and the states had ratified.

For more than a half century afterward, black Americans were forced into segregation and once again regularly beaten, raped, and even murdered with no recourse at all to a legal system that had been created to protect them. As a result, African Americans came to realize that without a Supreme Court willing to come out from behind the camouflage of legal somersaults to demand enforcement of the laws protecting citizens' rights, even constitutional amendments are hollow and meaningless.

Like the slave era that preceded it, Jim Crow remains a wound on the national conscience, one that most Americans would like to consider closed, dismissing such reprehensible behavior as simply a regrettable episode of our distant past.

But to ignore the past is to risk the future.

Overthrow

B Y AUGUST 1898, ALEX MANLY, A THIN, HANDSOME man, only thirty-two years old, had made himself into a remarkable American success story. He was a respected community leader in Wilmington, North Carolina, owned and edited *The Daily Record*, the city's most widely read newspaper, served as the deputy registrar of deeds, and taught Sunday school at the Chestnut Street Presbyterian Church. Although he was the grandson of Charles Manly, a former governor of North Carolina, Manly's achievements were in no way a result of family connections.

That was because his grandmother, Corinne, had been one of Charles Manly's slaves.

Although he was light-skinned, with features that could easily be taken for white, Alex Manly never forgot his African American identity. In fact, *The Daily Record* was billed as "The Only Negro Daily Paper in the World." What made Manly's achievements more unusual was that by 1898, virtually all of the gains made by African Americans during

Reconstruction had been swept away, and white supremacists had once again taken control of state governments across the South.

But Wilmington, then North Carolina's largest city, was an exception, a thriving port on the Atlantic coast that was also an outpost of racial harmony. More than 11,000 of its 20,000 residents were African American—former slaves or their descendants—and black men owned a variety of businesses frequented by members of both races, from jewelry stores to real estate agencies to restaurants to barber shops. Although the mayor and city council remained almost entirely white, there were black police officers and firemen.

African Americans voted Republican, then the party of equal rights, and exerted a good deal of influence in Wilmington. Democrats, however, the party of white supremacy, had for decades controlled the state house in Raleigh. But in 1894, North Carolina's Populist Party, a group of mostly small farmers, almost all of whom were white, had tired of the Democratic ruling elite and joined with black Republicans to attempt to force Democrats from state government.

Although almost all the whites in this coalition continued to believe in the racial inferiority of African Americans, they needed the black vote to defeat their enemies. And defeat them they did. In the November 1894 elections, Fusionists, as they called themselves, took control of the general assembly and the state supreme court, and won in most of the state's congressional districts. Although once again the vast majority of new officeholders were white, some black men were elected to local and state office, by then almost unheard of in the South. Once in power, Fusionists made it easier for blacks and poor whites to vote, imposed taxes to fund public education, and passed a number of laws that favored small farmers and businessmen over large financial interests.

Democrats were enraged at these changes, but nearly all of their anger focused on the measures that improved voting prospects for blacks. The Fusionists were again successful in 1896, even adding the governorship to its trophy case, when Daniel Russell, a Wilmington native, was elected to that office. Democrats were determined to win it back.

As the 1898 elections approached, Daniel Schenck, a leading Democrat, warned, "It will be the meanest, vilest, dirtiest campaign since 1876. The slogan of the Democratic Party from the mountains to the sea will be but one word—nigger."[1] One of main Democratic campaign themes was that if their party were not returned to power, there would be an epidemic of attacks by black men on white women.

To stoke those fires, a statewide Democratic newspaper, *The News and Observer*, reprinted an August 1897 speech by Rebecca Latimer Felton, a Georgia suffragette, who would later become the first woman to serve in the United States Senate. "If it requires lynching to protect woman's dearest possession from ravening, drunken human beasts," she had told an enthusiastic white audience, "then I say lynch a thousand negroes a week."

Alex Manly had generally avoided controversy, but the accusation in *The News and Observer* that black men preyed on white women was too much. Manly, whose very existence was due to a white man preying on a black woman, responded with an editorial in which he charged white lynch mobs with murdering African American men because white women had *chosen* to become romantically involved with them. "Meetings of this kind go on for some time," he wrote,

> until the woman's infatuation or the man's boldness brings attention to them and the man is lynched for rape. Every Negro lynched is called a 'big, burly, black brute,' when in fact many of those who have thus been dealt with had white men for their fathers, and were not only not 'black' and 'burly' but were sufficiently attractive for white girls of culture and refinement to fall in love with them, as is very well known to all.[2]

It is difficult to imagine an accusation that could enrage white supremacists more.

Manly's editorial was reprinted across the South, accompanied by thinly disguised calls for violence against him. Typical was an article in the *Jacksonville Times*, which read,

> Last week the editor of the *Daily Record* of Wilmington, the only ne-
> gro daily printed in the state, published the following slander about
> the white women of the south. Strange to say the wretch has not been
> lynched, but poses before the people as one of the grand achievements
> of republican rule and a hideous example of one of the many that have
> come to the surface since white supremacy was relegated to the rear by
> selfish politicians.[3]

The editorial and the fact that Wilmington had so many successful African Americans made the city perfect for Democrats to inflame
white rage as the November election approached. When South Carolina senator "Pitchfork Ben" Tillman visited his neighboring state
to campaign for white rule, he thundered to a cheering crowd, "Why
didn't you kill that damn nigger editor who wrote that? Send him to
South Carolina and let him publish any such offensive stuff, and he
will be killed." (Tillman had acquired his nickname for threatening
to stick a pitchfork into President Grover Cleveland, who he called "a
bag of beef.") Sprinkled through Tillman's audience were men dressed
in red shirts, paramilitaries who had been active in Mississippi and
South Carolina since the 1870s, but who had only recently formed up
in North Carolina.

At a rally on the night of November 7, 1898, the eve of the election,
Alfred Waddell addressed a Red Shirt rally. Waddell was a former Confederate cavalry officer who had served three terms in Congress before
losing his seat in 1878 to Daniel Russell, who at the time was a Republican. He told the Red Shirts, "You are Anglo-Saxons. You are armed and
prepared, and you will do your duty. If you find the Negro out voting, tell
him to leave the polls, and if he refuses, kill him, shoot him down in his
tracks. We shall win tomorrow if we have to do it with guns."[4]

With Red Shirts and other armed white men roaming the streets, Democrats regained all they had lost, winning in Wilmington by 6,000 votes, where they had lost by 5,000 votes only two years earlier. Fraud was everywhere. Ballot boxes were stuffed so openly with phony votes for Democrats that in some districts the number of votes for Democratic candidates exceeded the total number of registered voters. In one precinct, for example, although only thirty Democrats were registered, 456 Democratic votes were reported out. Another precinct, with only 343 registered voters, reported out 607 votes, almost all for Democrats. And where the white Democratic vote was inflated, Red Shirts made certain the Republican vote, especially among African Americans, was suppressed. One predominantly black precinct reported only ninety-seven votes, although 337 Republicans had registered. The Red Shirts were so brazen that they met the train carrying Governor Russell, who was returning home to vote, and threatened to lynch him. Russell, almost 300 pounds, ran through the train and hid in a baggage car to escape.

Although Democrats had achieved almost total victory across North Carolina, triumph had only increased their thirst for revenge, especially in Wilmington, where Alex Manly's editorial and a thriving black community remained irresistible targets. In addition, since many local officials had not been up for reelection in 1898, Fusionists remained a power in city government.

On the morning of November 9, one day after the election, Waddell again called a meeting of Red Shirts. He waved in front of him a "White Declaration of Independence," which insisted that the American Constitution "did not anticipate the enfranchisement of an ignorant population of African origin." The Founding Fathers "did not contemplate for their descendants a subjection to an inferior race."[5]

The following morning, Waddell, "his white hair flowing in the light breeze," led an armed band of more than one hundred armed men on a procession to Alex Manly's newspaper office. Manly was not there, so they stormed inside, poured kerosene on all the printing equipment, and set it ablaze. Soon, the wooden building was consumed in flames and totally gutted.

The soaring flames seemed only to make the rampaging mob more furious at black residents of Wilmington, even those who lived peacefully and were not at all involved in politics.

And so, the shooting began.

Rev. Charles S. Morris, a Wilmington pastor, gave an eyewitness account in a speech to the International Association of Colored Clergymen in Boston in January 1899.

Nine Negroes massacred outright; a score wounded and hunted like partridges on the mountain; one man, brave enough to fight against such odds, who would be hailed as a hero anywhere else, was given the privilege of running the gauntlet up a broad street, where he sank ankle deep in the sand, while crowds of men lined the sidewalks and riddled him with a pint of bullets as he ran bleeding past their doors; another Negro shot twenty times in the back as he scrambled empty handed over a fence; thousands of women and children fleeing in terror from their humble homes in the darkness of the night, out under a gray and angry sky, from which falls a cold and bone chilling rain, out to the dark and tangled ooze of the swamp amid the crawling things of night, fearing to light a fire, startled at every footstep, cowering, shivering, shuddering, trembling, praying in gloom and terror: half clad and barefooted mothers, with their babies wrapped only in a shawl, whimpering with cold and hunger at their icy breasts, crouched in terror from the vengeance of those who, in the name of civilization, and with the benediction of the ministers of the Prince of Peace, inaugurated the reformation of the city of Wilmington the day after the election by driving out one set of white officeholders and filling their places with another set of white officeholders—the one being Republican and the other Democrat. All this happened, not in Turkey, nor in Russia, nor in Spain, not in the gardens of Nero, nor in the dungeons of Torquemada, but within three hundred miles of the White House.[6]

The killing did not end until the following day. Two dozen African Americans were officially reported murdered, but scores more may have been killed and their bodies dumped into the river. One local historian, Harry Hayden, an eyewitness, insisted more than 300 had died.

While African Americans were either slaughtered or ran in terror to hide in the nearby woods, Waddell and his men invaded City Hall and informed the mayor, the aldermen, and the police chief, all Fusionists, that they must either resign on the spot or be shot down. All complied, and by late afternoon, November 10, 1898, Wilmington had a new government, led by Mayor Alfred Waddell. Those local officials lucky enough to not be murdered, both black and white, were marched to the train station, some with nooses around their necks, and told they would be killed if they ever returned. None did.

Although the white press would later term the events in Wilmington a "race riot," it was in fact the only violent overthrow of a local government in United States history.

Harry Hayden, interviewed later by reporters, insisted that he and his fellows were not thugs. "The men who took down their shotguns and cleared the Negroes out of office yesterday were . . . men of property, intelligence, culture . . . clergymen, lawyers, bankers, merchants. They are not a mob. They are revolutionists asserting a sacred privilege and a right."[7] North Carolina authorities evidently agreed, since no one was punished for the crimes and Waddell and his fellow Democrats were allowed to remain in the jobs they had seized by force.

As for the terrified black citizens who had been forced to flee to the woods and sleep without blankets in a cold rain, only a few attempted to sneak back to town to gather some possessions before leaving Wilmington for good. In all, more than 2,000 African American men, women, and children fled the city, most of them, like Reverend Morris, never to return. Those who remained would live in total subjugation for the rest of their lives.

The victors, proud and triumphant, posed for a group picture in front of Alex Manly's burnt-out newspaper office, which was later reproduced in newspapers and magazines across America. But they had failed in one of their main objectives—to lynch Alex Manly. Years later, Manly's son Milo described how his father escaped.

> A German grocer who knew my father got in touch with him, and said, "Look, you've got to get out of town . . . This gang, there's all these people out there, but they've lined it up that nobody can leave the vicinity of this area, with this cordon, unless they have a certain password." He said, "Now, if it ever got known that I gave you the password, they'd kill me. But I know you. I trust you. I want you to get out of here." He gave my father the password. My father come up the line. They stopped him. "Where are you going?" He said—named a town up there. "What are you going up there for?" "Going to buy some horses. There's an auction up there." Or something like that. "Oh, all right." He gave the password. "Okay, but if you see that nigger Manly up there, shoot him." And they gave him two rifles. That's right. Off away he went.[8]

North Carolina authorities, appalled at the events in Wilmington, vowed to make certain such an incident could never take place again. The following year, the state legislature passed an amendment to the North Carolina constitution with provisions making it almost impossible for any African American to vote in the state.

I

Who Votes?

THE ROAD TO THE SUPREME COURT'S ADJUDICATION OF voting rights was neither straight nor clear. As fundamental as the right to vote appears to be, as a legal or even a political matter, it is anything but. From the moment of its founding, this nation's leaders, and its judges, have been wrestling with the issue of suffrage. The solutions and rules they applied, which have vastly changed over the course of American history, have reflected, and continue to reflect, the manner in which they viewed American democracy.

In the summer of 1787, when the fifty-five delegates to the Constitutional Convention in Philadelphia were pounding out rules for a new government, one of the most important questions was who should be allowed to vote and for what offices. If government was to be by the consent of the governed, as most everyone believed, just how was that objective to be realized? While it was relatively easy to identify the governed, what was not clear was which among them would be allowed to give their consent. Women, slaves, convicts, children, and Native Americans were out of the question, of course, but what other requirements should there be in order that a man—almost always a white man—be allowed to participate in government?

There were no clear rules, but the delegates seemed to agree that the franchise should be limited to those "with a stake" in the government they were choosing. But even that notion had a hazy first derivative. Large property owners certainly qualified, but did small farmers eking out a subsistence existence on a tiny plot of land? Or tenant farmers? What about those whose wealth did not include real property? Then there were the professionals—lawyers and doctors—and other service workers, all the way down to common laborers. What was their "stake" in the government?

The only other rule the delegates seemed to agree on was that a vote should be given freely and intelligently. The fear that a voter who was not sufficiently independent or sufficiently learned would cast a ballot, either for someone he was told to or someone not in the best interest of government, was widespread. Literacy, then, seemed to be a requirement, as was financial independence. And a voter should certainly be a resident of wherever it was he voted, but for how long and under what circumstances was unclear. What almost no one favored was universal suffrage, or anything close to it.

Although defining "property" remained thorny, very few of the delegates, all men of some sort of property themselves, favored allowing those who were not property holders to help choose the nation's leaders. They did not always admit it publicly, however. James Madison, who would later write in *Federalist 52*, "The definition of the right of suffrage is very justly regarded as a fundamental article of republican government," had a very different view in August 1787. In a Convention session, which was kept secret from the public, he said, "Viewing the subject in its merits alone, the freeholders [that is, landowners] of the country would be the safest depositories of republican liberty."[1]

In Virginia's ratification debates, Madison would go further in making the case for limited suffrage.

In future times, a great majority of the people will not only be without landed, but any other sort of property. These will either combine, under the influence of their common situation—in which case the rights of property and the public liberty will not be secure in their hands—or, what is more probable, they will become the tools of opulence and ambition; in which case there will be equal danger on another side.[2]

John Adams, then the nation's chief diplomat in London, was not present at the Convention, but had previously made his views known. In a letter written only six weeks before he would sign the Declaration of Independence, Adams expressed a firm conviction that those without property should not be allowed to vote. "Such is the frailty of the human heart, that very few men who have no property have any judgment of their own," he wrote. "They talk and vote as they are directed by Some Man of Property, who has attached their Minds to his Interest."[3]

Alexander Hamilton, the only delegate from New York to sign the Constitution, was the most insistent that only men of real property could be trusted to vote in the best interests of the nation. In a 1775 pamphlet, "The Farmer Refuted," Hamilton cited the great English legal theorist William Blackstone, who insisted that those "under the immediate dominion of others"—workers—or "persons of indigent fortunes"—the poor—could not be trusted to "give his vote freely, and without influence of any kind, then, upon the true theory and genuine principles of liberty."[4] At the Convention, Hamilton, during a six-hour speech in which he proposed a system of government very much like a monarchy, added,

All communities divide themselves into the few and the many. The first are rich and well born; the other, the mass of the people. The voice of the people has been said to be the voice of God; and however generally this maxim has been quoted and believed, it is not true in fact. The people are turbulent and changing; they seldom judge or determine right. Give therefore to the first class a distinct, permanent share in the government.[5]

Those favoring restricted suffrage had a problem, however. The revolution that had granted Americans sovereignty and the Constitution that would cement what would later be called "privileges and immunities of citizenship" was steeped in the Lockean concept of "natural rights," and what right could be more natural than that of choosing the people who would make the laws under which one must live? But granting the vote to what many in the convention considered rabble seemed to guarantee the descent that Madison described later, or worse.

There were those who saw less risk in widespread suffrage. One of the few who favored universal voting rights—at least among adult white males—was Thomas Jefferson, who in 1787 was representing the United States in Paris, and so also did not attend the Constitutional Convention. Jefferson had written in a 1776 letter, "I was for extending the rights of suffrage (or in other words the rights of a citizen) to all who had a permanent intention of living in the country. Take what circumstances you please as evidence for this, either the having resided a certain time, or having a family, or having property, any or all of them."[6] In a 1789 letter, he added, "Wherever the people are well-informed, they can be trusted with their own government; that whenever things get so far wrong as to attract their notice, they may be relied on to set them to rights."[7]

At the Convention, of those few delegates who did favor an expansion of voting rights beyond real property owners, the most prominent was Benjamin Franklin, by then eighty-one years old and gout-ridden. Almost sixty years earlier he had penned a short anecdote, still famous as "Franklin's jackass," which jabbed at those who thought property owners were the only qualified voters.

Today a man owns a jackass worth 50 dollars and he is entitled to vote; but before the next election the jackass dies. The man in the meantime has become more experienced, his knowledge of the principles of government, and his acquaintance with mankind, are more extensive, and he is therefore better qualified to make a proper selection of rulers— but the jackass is dead and the man cannot vote. Now gentlemen, pray inform me, in whom is the right of suffrage? In the man or in the jackass?[8]

In the end, there seemed no path through the thicket, no set of rules that should apply across the nation. As a result, the Convention delegates chose to treat voting in the same manner as other intractable problems—the makeup of the federal judiciary, for example. They dodged the issue entirely. For the House of Representatives, Article I, Section 2 simply reads that it "shall be composed of Members chosen every second Year by the People of the several States," without specifying which people, except that qualifications would be the same as those for "the most numerous Branch" of a state's legislature. Senators were to be chosen entirely by state legislatures—which was changed to popular vote in 1913 by the Seventeenth Amendment—and the president would be chosen by "electors," equal to a state's total number of congressmen, chosen once again according to rules adopted by individual state governments. Other than "guarantee[ing] to every State in this Union a Republican Form of Government," in Article IV, no further reference to the right to vote appears in the text of the Constitution.

Although most Americans had been tacitly left out of the voting process entirely, this was not a feature that Federalists wanted to publicize during ratification. Since the proceedings had been secret, with no record published until long afterward, those campaigning for ratification could say anything they pleased about what had transpired in Philadelphia. (Slave owners, for example, would portray Northerners as far more amenable to slavery as an institution than they had been during the debates.)

In New York, with ratification very much in doubt, Hamilton, Madison, and John Jay collaborated on the *Federalist*, eighty-five essays that portrayed the Constitution as vital to the future of both the state and the nation. In *Federalist 52*, Madison, in addition to terming the right to vote "fundamental," wrote further,

> It was incumbent on the convention, therefore, to define and establish this right in the Constitution. To have left it open for the occasional

regulation of the Congress would have been improper for the reason just mentioned. To have submitted it to the legislative discretion of the States, would have been improper for the same reason; and for the additional reason that it would have rendered too dependent on the State governments that branch of the federal government which ought to be dependent on the people alone.

In fact, almost none of this was true. The right to vote was left almost entirely "to the legislative discretion of the States," and they could and would exercise that power as they saw fit until after the Civil War, when the right to vote began to come under the authority of the Constitution with the enactment of the Fourteenth and Fifteenth Amendments.

In the meantime, suffrage was a muddle. Even a philosophical definition was lacking. Was voting a "natural" right, a "political" right, or a "constitutional" right? These distinctions were not academic. Just which of them should be adopted would prove crucial when voting rights cases came before the Supreme Court in the wake of the Reconstruction amendments. In addition, with no definition or statement in the Constitution, suffrage seemed to fall squarely under the aegis of the Tenth Amendment, which stated, "The powers not delegated to the United States by the Constitution, nor prohibited by it to the States, are reserved to the States respectively, or to the people."

★ ★ ★

Because the Founders had been unwilling to take on the issue, voting across the thirteen states, and in all new states admitted to the Union, often varied as much as the states themselves. The only requirement common to all of the original thirteen, except New Hampshire, was that a voter needed to be a property holder—in most cases showing he owned land, but in some only that he paid taxes. Some states excluded certain religions—Jews or Catholics—while others charged a fee to vote. Some states excluded immigrants. Every state denied the franchise to slaves and Native Americans.

As a result, at the time of the first presidential election, which took place from Monday, December 15, 1788, to Saturday, January 10, 1789— Congress did not establish a national election day, "the Tuesday after the first Monday in November," until 1845—only six out of every one hundred Americans were eligible to vote.

In some cases, that six included African Americans. After ratification, while no state allowed a slave to vote, the voting rights for free men of color who met a state's property requirement were surprisingly widespread. They could vote by law in Maryland, Massachusetts, Pennsylvania, and New Hampshire, and were not specifically restricted from voting in Connecticut, New York, New Jersey, Delaware, Rhode Island, and, surprisingly, North Carolina. The only states legally barring blacks from voting were Virginia, South Carolina, and thinly populated Georgia.

Because each state was free to make its own rules, a number of quirks worked their way into the system. One of the oddest was in New Jersey, where the 1776 state constitution granted all "persons" who met the property requirement the right to vote. As a result, to the horror of many men, widows and other women who owned property regularly cast ballots.

In 1790, Pennsylvania, with a new constitution, took the immense step of eliminating the property requirement. It did, however, require that a voter have paid state or county tax within two years before an election, except for the sons of qualified voters twenty-one or twenty-two years old. That same year, Congress began to define national citizenship, which would also impact access to the ballot box. The 1790 Naturalization Act allowed free white immigrants "of good character" to become United States citizens, provided they lived in the nation for two years and in their state of residence for one. Immigrants of color and Asians were excluded. In 1795, the residence requirement was extended to five years, and in 1798 to fourteen. In 1802, under President Thomas Jefferson, who wished to encourage small farmers to immigrate, the residence requirement was returned to the five-year standard, where it remains today.

In the wake of Pennsylvania's action, other states began to expand suffrage, and certain trends became manifest. By the first decades of the nineteenth century, some uniformity began to appear in voting regulations across the nation. Property restrictions were steadily eliminated in the original states, and most newly admitted states allowed adult men without property to vote as well. By the 1820s, only three states—Rhode Island, Virginia, and North Carolina—still had landholding requirements. Each of those was repealed in the ensuing decades. By 1856, both religious and property-holding requirements had been eliminated in every state in the Union, although six states continued to require that voters also be taxpayers.

But there were new restrictions as well. In 1807, for example, at the same time it granted the vote to all adult white males regardless of property holdings, New Jersey ended voting by women. Most of the narrowing, however, was for men of color. In 1792, Delaware stripped the vote from free black men, and in 1799, when Kentucky joined the Union, it did as well. Tennessee broke the trend when it was granted statehood in 1796, allowing every free male twenty-one or older to vote, but it instituted a race restriction in 1834. Ohio restricted the vote to white men when it joined the Union in 1803, as did Connecticut in its new constitution in 1818. In 1821, New York removed its property requirements for whites, but kept them in place for men of color. In 1842, Rhode Island removed a property requirement for native-born citizens only. While newly admitted slave states of Louisiana, Mississippi, Alabama, Florida, and Missouri did not even consider allowing free African Americans to vote, neither did free states California, Illinois, Indiana, Michigan, Iowa, and Oregon. Many states that had allowed black voting—Maryland, New Jersey, Delaware, and North Carolina—either outlawed African American voting or passed laws that achieved the same end. By 1860 only Maine, Vermont, Massachusetts, New Hampshire, and Wisconsin opened the ballot to men of color.

Since there were no national standards, there were no grounds for appealing voting restrictions to the federal judiciary. Free Americans of color, then, as the war that would define whether or not, as Thomas Jefferson wrote, "all men were created equal" became terrifyingly close, had little or no say in deciding whether the statement would be true or false.

Two Amendments ...

I N EARLY 1864, AS THE CIVIL WAR APPROACHED ITS THIRD
bloody anniversary and the eventual defeat of the Confederacy began to seem assured, the United States—and Abraham Lincoln—at
last decided to deal with slavery. The Constitution had allowed it, the
Supreme Court in *Dred Scott v. Sandford* had reinforced it, and Lincoln's
Emancipation Proclamation of January 1863 had prolonged it by not
freeing slaves in any state that had remained in the Union.

It took until January 1865, but then, over strong opposition from the
Democratic Party, the House of Representatives, on its second try, passed
by the required two-thirds vote a new amendment to the Constitution—
the Thirteenth—which would abolish, once and for all, in every corner
of the nation, the practice of human slavery. (The Senate had approved
the amendment in April 1864.) Although the president plays no official
role in amending the Constitution, Lincoln had persuaded, flattered, and
threatened reluctant congressmen to obtain the required majority. In December 1865, with the Confederacy a memory and President Lincoln

dead, the amendment was ratified by the required three-quarters of the state legislatures and became law.

But the end of slavery did not mean the beginning of racial equality. The task of integrating four million newly freed slaves into the fabric of free society was, under any circumstances, a nigh impossible task—no society in history had ever been faced with such a challenge. In post–Civil War America, achieving such a goal—the nature of which many in the country already defined differently—would be made that much more difficult by the presence of Abraham Lincoln's successor, Democrat Andrew Johnson of Tennessee.

Johnson was hardly the right man for a task that demanded incisive intellect, a keen sense of proportion, a flair for problem solving, a deft political hand, sensitivity to injustice, and, most importantly, racial tolerance. He seemed to be guided by two fundamental principles, each of which would frame his program of what became known, at least in the North, as Reconstruction.

The first was a profound and abiding racism. His antipathy to slavery was not as a moral evil, but that it facilitated an arrogant landed aristocracy, a "slaveocracy" as he put it. From poor origins himself, the epitome of the self-made man, Johnson loathed the planters, with their ostentatious wealth and airs of social superiority. But he loathed black people every bit as much and had no intention of allowing them to pollute white Christian society. He said in a speech to Congress:

> If anything can be proved by known facts, if all reasoning upon evidence is not abandoned, it must be acknowledged that in the progress of nations negroes have shown less capacity for government than any other race of people. No independent government of any form has ever been successful in their hands. On the contrary, wherever they have been left to their own devices they have shown a constant tendency to relapse into barbarism . . . I repeat the expression of my willingness to join in any plan within the scope of our constitutional authority which promises to better the condition of the negroes in the south, by en-

couraging them in industry, enlightening their minds, improving their morals, and giving protection to all their just rights as freedmen. But the transfer of our political inheritance to them would, in my opinion, be an abandonment of a duty which we owe alike to the memory of our fathers and the rights of our children.[1]

The second, a perfect complement to the first, was a commitment to federalism, a belief that the central government's authority over the states was severely limited. Except in those functions specifically prescribed by the Constitution, states should be free to act in whatever manner they pleased. Although states could no longer countenance slavery, nothing in the Constitution prevented a state from enacting laws that were blatantly discriminatory and allowed the white population to maintain virtually the same degree of control over African Americans that they had before 1860.

These laws, called Black Codes, mandated such contrivances as forced labor contracts, binding a worker to an employer on pain of criminal penalty or forfeiture of a year's back wages; forbidding African Americans to carry knives or guns; setting sunup to sundown working hours; allowing corporal punishment of workers; and creating standards for vagrancy that would apply to virtually every black agricultural worker not tied to a white employer. Strict racial segregation would also be enforced in schools, public buildings, and cemeteries.

Johnson also believed, as had Lincoln, that secession was illegal. The Civil War, therefore, had been a police action, not a war with a foreign power. As such, the eleven states of the Confederacy had never left the Union. "It is clear to my apprehension," he wrote in a letter to Congress,

that the States lately in rebellion are still members of the national Union . . . The 'ordinances of secession' adopted by a portion (in most of them a very small portion) of their citizens, were mere nullities . . . Were those States afterwards expelled from the Union by the war? The direct contrary was averred by this government to be its purpose, and was so understood by all those who gave their blood and treasure to aid in its prosecution. It cannot be that a successful war, waged for the preservation of the Union, had the legal effect of dissolving it.[2]

This notion was hardly outrageous. In 1862, since secession was not recognized, the fifty-seven seats in the House of Representatives that had been granted to the eleven Confederate states (out of 241 total) were kept on the roster, but they remained empty since no one had been sent to fill them.

If the states had never left, it followed then that they would not need to petition for readmission and could just fill those congressional seats, which is precisely what Andrew Johnson thought they should do. With the Black Codes in place, and no federal voting guidelines or guarantees in the Constitution, it seemed certain that those seats would be filled almost entirely by white secessionist congressmen elected by white supremacist voters.

And there would be more white secessionist congressmen than there had been in 1861. The Apportionment Act of 1862, which had assigned those fifty-seven of the 241 seats in the House of Representatives to the eleven states that had seceded, had been based on the old three-fifths rule, which counted three out of every five slaves when determining a state's congressional delegation. By ending slavery, however, the Thirteenth Amendment rendered that formula extinct. Since there were no longer "other persons" (as slaves had been termed), any future apportionment had to be based on a full counting of African Americans—an additional 1.6 million people, which translated into thirty-seven seats. The South, "as a result of *losing* the Civil War," would gain apportionment and "be entitled to an *increase* in membership in the House of Representatives and the Electoral College."[3]

Republicans in Congress saw things differently. By seceding, Southern states had abrogated the terms under which they had joined the Union and nullified whatever privileges the Constitution had bestowed. They might apply for readmission, certainly, but under the terms dictated by the government of the United States, from which they were, at that moment, excluded. In addition, the sin of slavery needed to be atoned for, and that would hardly be achieved by coddling the very men and women who had perpetrated the bloodiest war in the nation's history. For most Northerners, America's two most urgent priorities were the care of the millions of returned or returning war veterans, and the integration, in some fashion, of nearly four million newly freed slaves into the main-stream of American life.

The question was how, and under what terms? For a radical segment of the Republican Party, led in the House of Representatives by Thad-deus Stevens of Pennsylvania and in the Senate by Charles Sumner of Massachusetts (who, for his abolitionist stance, had once been beaten nearly to death by a cane-wielding South Carolina congressman on the Senate floor), this meant nothing less than to remake the South to a new set of political, socioeconomic, and especially moral specifications. The abolition of slavery was not enough. The nation must banish all traces of racial discrimination. African Americans in the conquered South must be granted full and equal citizenship with whites, and, for the first time, be sent to school, hold public office, sit on juries, own businesses, and walk or ride freely in any state in America.

To pay for this vast array of social programs, Radicals insisted that the United States confiscate the assets of Confederate leaders, applying any cash proceeds to the payment of the war debt, the pensioning of Union soldiers, and distribution of land to freedmen. Stevens's plan was to nationalize any estates whose lands exceeded 200 acres or were worth $10,000 or more. Each adult freedman would then be given "40 acres and a mule," an ex-pansion of the program William Tecumseh Sherman had initiated during the war. Of the remaining acreage, which would be worth approximately $3.5 billion, Stevens wanted $300 million invested in 6 percent government bonds, with the interest applied to pensions of war veterans and their depen-dents; $200 million used to reimburse Union loyalists for property damages; and the remaining $3 billion applied to pay down war debt.[4]

To Stevens and his fellow Radicals, equality for the freedmen tran-scended party or politics; it was a paramount ethical issue, one that would define the very character of the United States. Without redress for the evils of slavery and the successful integration of the freedmen into American society, the United States would remain a damned nation. Stevens proclaimed,

> We have turned or are about to turn loose four million slaves without a hut to shelter them or a cent in their pockets. The infernal laws of slavery have prevented them from acquiring an education, understanding the commonest laws of contract, or managing the ordinary business of life. This Congress is bound to provide for them until they can take care of themselves. If we do not furnish them with homesteads, and hedge them around with protective laws; if we leave them to the legislation of their late masters, we had better have left them in bondage.[5]

Their first skirmish with an equally intractable president took place in December 1865, when, with Johnson's encouragement, the eleven former slave states did indeed send representatives to Congress. Each one was white, as had been just about every voter who elected them; a former Confederate; and determined to protect the Black Codes. One of these would-be congressmen was Alexander Stephens, former vice president of the Confederacy. While the white Southerners waited to take their seats, the men in charge of both the House of Representatives and the Senate refused to call their names during the roll call. Thaddeus Stevens told them that they were from "conquered provinces" and not entitled to sit in Congress. The Southern delegates trudged out, leaving Andrew Johnson furious.

Underlying this conflict was the Radicals' intention to subordinate the Tenth Amendment to a new definition of federalism. In vanquishing the Confederacy, the national government had vastly increased both its size and its power over individual states. Washington was suddenly in a position to exercise unprecedented authority over state governments, particularly in those states that would be reconstituted as a condition for readmission to the Union.

Even before the war ended, eager reformers, both church and lay, had moved from North to South, preparing to launch perhaps the greatest experiment in social engineering ever attempted. They would teach, feed, and organize the freedmen. Not only would they integrate millions of erstwhile slaves into society as full and equal citizens, but they would forge and hammer the entire fabric of the plantation economy into a new, progressive, egalitarian order. It was this process that Radicals intended to protect and encourage.

To do so, on April 9, 1866, overriding Andrew Johnson's veto, Congress passed "An Act to protect all Persons in the United States in their Civil Rights, and furnish the Means of their Vindication."

The new law gave the federal government jurisdiction over state social policy for the first time. It was aimed unapologetically at Black Codes, and provided substantial guarantees for the rights of freedmen, starting with the most fundamental right of all: "All persons born in the United States and not subject to any foreign power, excluding Indians not taxed, are hereby declared to be citizens of the United States." Also guaranteed were right of contract, access to the legal system, and the right to employment for all citizens, black and white, and to "full and equal benefits of all laws and proceedings for the security of person and property."[6] Denial of any of these rights became a federal crime, enforceable according to federal law, in federal courts. With the exception of the removal of jurisdiction to federal courts, the bill's guarantees were pretty much in line with what a majority of the nation thought was fair. Democrats, of course, particularly in the South, demurred, complaining that the bill was a gross violation of states' rights, and a violation of the principles under which the United States was founded.

What was missing was a guarantee of the right to vote, which, had it been included, would have doomed the bill to failure. The prospect of hundreds of thousands of illiterate, socially and politically backward black men flooding to the polls was anathema to Democrats and moderate Republicans alike, and was even too radical for most Radicals. "When was it ever known that liberation from bondage was accompanied by a recognition of political equality?" asked one. "According to the laws of development and progress, it is not practicable . . . as soon as the state was organized and left to manage its own affairs, the white population, with their superior intelligence, wealth, and power, would unquestionably alter the franchise in accordance with their prejudices."[7] The speaker was no conservative, but rather William Lloyd Garrison, publisher of *The Liberator* and the man who termed the United States Constitution "a Covenant with Death and an Agreement with Hell" for its failure to end slavery in America.

Charles Sumner favored a literacy requirement for African Americans, a restriction that, even if applied without contrivance (as opposed to the approach Southern states took later), would guarantee that only a tiny portion of the black population would qualify to vote. Even Thaddeus Stevens, the ultimate firebrand, was hesitant to allow freedmen immediate access to the voting booth. Nor could those few in favor of granting the franchise to African Americans point to their more emancipated status in the North, since only five Northern states extended the franchise to blacks.

But, as anyone who could count was also aware, the days of considering the philosophical niceties of African American suffrage had ended in December 1865 with the ratification of the Thirteenth Amendment. Some formula for readmitting the Confederate states into the United States— assuming they ever had left—was certain to be developed, as were conditions for allowing former Confederates to take their places as citizens.

Enfranchising freedmen was therefore a matter of necessity rather than morality. If blacks were counted for apportionment but could not themselves go to the polls, white Democrats would dominate in the South and wield a good deal more power in Congress than they had before the war. So, in addition to integrating four million former slaves into society, even moderate Republicans realized that it was equally important to find a way to reintegrate eleven states and their white secessionists into that same society, all the while not threatening Republican control of Congress and eventually the presidency. At the very least, readmission on both an individual and state level would require acquiescence to the Radical program, including civil equality for African Americans and the willingness to grant the vote to a sufficient number to ensure Republican Party dominance. To lessen the Democratic vote, Radicals had no qualms about also taking the vote away from whites. Anyone who had fought for or abetted the rebels, as they saw it, had forfeited the privileges of citizenship, including the right to vote.

But there were complications. Andrew Johnson's veto of the Civil Rights Act—which he insisted was on the basis of states' rights—demonstrated to Republicans that the mandates embodied within it might well be transitory, subject to the whim of whoever sat in Congress or the White House. Thus Republicans, now moderate as well as Radical, saw the necessity of situating these principles in a place where Johnson, who was scheduled to remain in office until early 1869, and the Democrats could not get at them.

Transplanting the Civil Rights Act into the Constitution, however, was an extreme step, one that would engender fierce debate and many rounds of horse-trading. Spearheading the effort was John Bingham, a congressman from Ohio and one the nation's great champions of equal rights. Bingham's goal, he said later, was "a simple, strong, plain declaration that equal laws and equal and exact justice shall hereafter be secured within every State of the Union."[8] In addition, he intended that with this amendment, the "privileges and immunities" of citizenship guaranteed in the Bill of Rights, which had originally only applied to federal law, would now be binding on the states.

The draft that emerged from a joint congressional committee seemed to do just that and, for the first time, enabled sweeping federal power over the states, a direct challenge to the Tenth Amendment.

Section 1, which flowed directly from Bingham's pen and from which reams of jurisprudence have emanated, was essentially an enhancement of the Civil Rights Act:

> All persons born or naturalized in the United States, and subject to the jurisdiction thereof, are citizens of the United States and of the State wherein they reside. No State shall make or enforce any law which shall abridge the privileges or immunities of citizens of the United States;

nor shall any State deprive any person of life, liberty, or property, without due process of law; nor deny to any person within its jurisdiction the equal protection of the laws.

The second section went to the heart of the pragmatics of black voting.

When the right to vote at any election for the choice of electors for President and Vice President of the United States, Representatives in Congress, the Executive and Judicial officers of a State, or the members of the Legislature thereof, is denied to any of the male inhabitants of such State, being twenty-one years of age, and citizens of the United States, or in any way abridged, except for participation in rebellion, or other crime, the basis of representation therein shall be reduced in the proportion which the number of such male citizens shall bear to the whole number of male citizens twenty-one years of age in such State.

Thus, any state that chose to deny freedmen the right to vote would lose the bonus representation that had accrued to them through their non-voting black population.

The third section barred former Confederates from serving in state or national government, the criteria being broad but vague, and capable of being set aside, on a case-by-case basis, by a two-thirds majority of both houses of Congress. The fourth section voided any claims against the United States for loss of slaves or other Confederate property, and the fifth empowered Congress to pass legislation to enforce any of the other provisions.

Significant in both the gist and the wording of the amendment was the enforcement role of the courts and the reliance Congress had placed on the federal judiciary as the avenue through which those whose civil rights had been violated might seek redress. For the first time in American history, laws enacted by state legislatures that were seen to be racially discriminatory could be overturned in federal court. By investing the judiciary with this guardianship role, whichever party was dominant in Congress would no longer be relevant. Civil rights enforcement would have been constitutionally removed from partisanship.

After bouncing back and forth for months, the House endorsed a Senate version of the amendment on June 13, 1866, in a strict party-line vote of 120–32. The mood was as much relief as exhilaration. *The New York Times* observed, "The adoption by the House of the proposed Constitutional Amendment, as modified by the Senate, will, we trust, terminate all irritating discussion on the question of reconstruction."[9] The *Hartford Courant* added, "The amendment has been cleansed of Mr. Stevens' obnoxious ideas and is in good shape . . . Let Connecticut be the first state to ratify it."[10] Connecticut was indeed first, but the amendment needed to be ratified by three-fourths of the states.

Once more the question of the legality of secession became paramount, since the pool of states from which the three-fourths would be drawn was not clear. Andrew Johnson's view that the secessionist states were still part of the Union had been repudiated by Congress when Southerners were denied their duly apportioned seats by this very same Thirty-Ninth Congress in 1865. Yet to ignore the eleven states entirely seemed equally unpalatable. When Thaddeus Stevens proposed limiting ratification to Northern states, even his fellow Republicans balked.

Computing the three-fourths with Andrew Johnson's white supremacist governments in place in the South, however, presented what seemed an unconquerable obstacle to ratification. Once the amendment was ratified, Southern states would be faced with two extremely distasteful options: accept black voters and gain representation but risk that the added representatives would be Republicans or, even worse, Negroes; or deny freedmen the vote and accept diminished influence. There seemed only two alternatives under which Southern state legislatures would accept the Fourteenth Amendment: either make ratification a precondition for readmission to the Union, or change the legislatures.

Compounding the problem was the fervent opposition of Democrats, Northern as well as Southern, and fear, even among some Republicans, of such a drastic increase in the power of federal government. As a result, as the 1866 elections approached, in which Democrats were projected to make significant gains—perhaps even to take back Congress—only a woeful five states had ratified the amendment.

But the projections were wrong. Perhaps it was the nation's growing distaste for Andrew Johnson, but Republicans secured enough seats to maintain veto-overriding two-thirds majorities in both houses of Congress. Even more surprising was that after the election, many previously antipathetic congressmen seemed to change their positions on black suffrage simply to avoid identification with Johnson.[11]

Although the Fourteenth Amendment received a boost in support—fourteen more states ratified in the first three months of 1867—there was still no clear path to enactment. Most Southern state legislatures had rejected it out of hand (except Tennessee, which to Andrew Johnson's frustration had ratified in July 1866), and they had little incentive to change their view. Without them, the amendment was doomed. The solution was clear. If one could not persuade sitting governments to ratify the amendment, it would, as the Radicals had insisted, be necessary to change the governments.

The first step was the passage, in early March 1867, of "An Act to Provide for the More Efficient Government of the Rebel States," dubbed almost immediately the "Reconstruction Act." Its opening sentence read: "Whereas no legal State governments or adequate protection for life or property now exists in the rebel States of [all secessionist states were listed, except Tennessee]; and whereas it is necessary that peace and good order be enforced in said States until loyal and republican State governments can be legally established: Therefore . . ."[12] The "therefore" was a division of the ten secessionist states into five military districts, each commanded by no less than a brigadier general, and a direction to those commanders to "protect all persons in their rights of person and property, to suppress insurrection, disorder, and violence, and to punish, or cause to be punished, all disturbers of the public peace and criminals." A commander was authorized to empower civil courts or, if he chose, military tribunals to deal with offenders. Only death sentences were subject to review, and those by the president.

Section 5 of the law required each of the ten states to "form a constitution . . . in conformity with the Constitution of the United States in all respects." State constitutions were to be drafted by "male citizens, twenty-one years old and upward, of whatever race, color, or previous condition."[13] The resulting document would then need to be approved by Congress. When a state's constitution had been approved and a legislature formed, the state would be required to ratify the Fourteenth Amendment. Ratification thus became a *de jure* condition for readmission to the Union.

Although the law appeared to insist on color-blind male suffrage, there was no prohibition on states demanding certain qualifications for the franchise, as long as those qualifications were applied evenhandedly to all applicants. Literacy, lineage, poll taxes: all of these would be permissible under the law, as they would be under the Fourteenth Amendment. Of course, any attempt to skirt past the intent of this law, to disfranchise potential voters based only on race, would, so its sponsors believed, be given short shrift by the federal courts.

Andrew Johnson vetoed the bill virtually the moment it arrived at his desk. (He had complained to a newspaperman that whites "were being trodden under foot to protect niggers."[14]) Just as quickly, Congress overrode the veto.

After the Fortieth Congress was seated on March 4, 1867, work began immediately on a supplement to the Reconstruction Act designed to ratchet up pressure on both the secessionist states and the president. Within three weeks, both houses had passed a bill requiring that by September 1, 1867, the commanding general of each of the five military districts register every male twenty-one or over who was not disqualified from voting under Section 3 of the Fourteenth Amendment to vote on whether or not to hold a constitutional convention. The bill further laid out specific rules of how these conventions would be elected, and the procedures for having new state constitutions drafted and approved. Significantly, the entire process was to be overseen by the army, so that no artificial impediments to registration might be erected. Implicit in the bill was that, for the first time, African Americans—the men at least— would have unfettered access to the ballot box.

Predictably, Andrew Johnson vetoed the measure and both houses promptly overrode the veto, the House by a vote of 114–25 and the Senate by 40–7. Congress did not even give Johnson the courtesy of a hearing. "Not a word of debate; merely the reading of the [president's] message, the recording of the yeas and nays, and the business ends."[15]

The second Reconstruction Act flung open the door to legal equality. Across the South, Union Leagues, sometimes called Loyal Leagues, were organized, usually with the help of sympathetic whites, for the express purpose of initiating African American men into the political process. Black men registered to vote by the thousands and asserted their civil and property rights, and adults and children of both sexes attended schools sponsored by either the government's Freedmen's Bureau or private agencies.

With virtually all black men registering as Republicans, thousands of former "rebels," all Democrats, denied suffrage, and the army supervising the elections of constitutional convention delegates, the results were assured. New constitutions were drafted and then approved by Republicans. The Johnson-appointed governments were kicked out, replaced by Republican-controlled state legislatures that represented only a small minority of the white population, but almost every black voter.

The Fourteenth Amendment was, as required for readmission into the Union, ratified under these new state constitutions and thereby incorporated into the United States Constitution. As a result of the Reconstruction Acts, the prospect of the additional seats in the House of Representatives the South received being filled by Democrats seemed to have been eliminated. As *The New York Times* reported on July 10, 1868, the day after official ratification of the Fourteenth Amendment, the measure

settles the matter of suffrage in the Southern States beyond the power of the rebels to change it, even if they had control of the government.

Its potent provision is that where any portion of the citizens of a state
are denied the right of suffrage for any cause but crime, duly established, said citizens will not be counted in the basis of representation.
If South Carolina concludes to return to a white man's government, she
reduces her representation from five to two.[16]

Thousands of black Americans went to the polls, voting for the first
time, and, newly empowered, both freedmen and free-born, they soon
realized that they not only could vote for those seeking elective office, but
could seek elective office themselves. Throughout the old Confederacy,
more than 2,000 people of color would hold office during Reconstruction.[17] Almost 200 of these would be on the federal level, including two
senators, fourteen representatives, eleven United States deputy marshals,
three treasury agents, and two ambassadors. There were also African
American postmasters, census takers, land office agents, customs officials, and timber agents. On the state level, more than 800 served in the
legislature, and 300 were elected as delegates to constitutional conventions. There were militia officers, secretaries of state, superintendents of
education, state treasurers, land commissioners, and one deputy physician in a lunatic asylum. One man, P. B. S. Pinchback, served as governor
of Louisiana, if only for a few days.

The social fabric in much of the South began to change. It was not
uncommon for blacks and whites to work together, especially on the local
level. In some cases, they sent their children to same schools; in others,
they served on town boards. Cities like Wilmington were not the rule,
but nor were they specks in a vast ocean. For a time, Reconstruction,
fragile though it was, seemed, just possibly, on the verge of creating not
only a new South, but also a new America.

But there were many Southern whites who had no intention of ced-
ing or even sharing political power with people of color, no matter what
it said on a piece of paper.

3

Power in Black and White

The Klan

I N DECEMBER 1865, AT ALMOST THE VERY MOMENT THAT the Radical Republicans were refusing to seat congressmen from the defeated Confederate states, a group of six young Confederate war veterans, most college educated, met in Pulaski, Tennessee, a few miles north of the Alabama border. The town had been named after Kazimierz Pułaski, the Polish nobleman who had died heroically fighting for the Americans in the Revolutionary War. These six men would spark a revolution of a far different sort.

They had not met with that goal in mind, however. They were simply interested in having some fun by dressing up in elaborate disguises, inventing a series of secret passwords and oaths of allegiance, calling each other by a series of odd names, and then galloping around town after dark engaging in pranks. They named the group Kuklux, evidently from the Greek word "kuklos," which means "ring" or "circle," although there had been a group in ancient Greece with a similar name that called itself

"Circle of the Moon." "Klan" seemed to have been added simply because they liked the sound.

From the first, the targets of their "jokes" were local black residents. One of their early efforts involved a member of the group dressing in a white sheet and a frightening mask and then riding up to the home of a black family after midnight and demanding water. He would then seem to drink from the well bucket, but would actually be pouring the water into a rubber tube hidden beneath his robe. He would demand more and more water until the black man watching him could not believe anyone could drink that much. The white man would thank the black man, say that he had not had a drink since he died on the battlefield at Shiloh, and gallop off into the darkness.

This all seemed great fun until the white men realized that the freedmen genuinely believed that the ghosts of dead Confederate soldiers were galloping through the countryside. They also found out that they reminded the freedmen of slave patrols that rode at night before the Civil War, looking for runaways or any slaves that strayed out of their tumbledown cabins without permission. Beatings and whippings would follow.

Word spread quickly that freedmen were terrified of these strange "night riders," and new "Klan" groups popped up throughout the South. The outings soon turned more sinister. It was not long before the "Kuklux" began to use the terror that their rides provoked to "keep the freed slaves in line." The whippings and beatings of the slave patrols became common.

In April 1867, just after Congress passed the Reconstruction Acts and the United States Army was sent as an occupying force into the South, a call went out to all the Klan chapters—there were now dozens— to send representatives to Nashville, Tennessee. At this meeting, what had been a loose-knit group of individual chapters became a disciplined organization, with rules, leaders, and a military-like chain of command. At the top of that chain would be the Grand Wizard. Chosen for the job was one of the most feared and respected of all the Confederate soldiers, a legend, the "Wizard of the Saddle," General Nathan Bedford Forrest. The title "Grand Wizard" was chosen because of Forrest's nickname.

Forrest had enlisted in the Confederate army as a private and risen to general in less than two years. He was a brilliant horseman, a fearless fighter, ruthless with a saber or pistol, but most of all, he possessed perhaps the most brilliant military mind in the nation. Union General William Tecumseh Sherman described him as "the most remarkable man our civil war produced on either side," whose men "could travel one hundred miles in less time than ours can travel ten." Ulysses Grant called him "that devil Forrest."

There were times when Forrest's cavalry seemed to be attacking in two or three places at once. He would strike at an opponent's weakness, then move to a different weak spot when the first was reinforced.

Forrest was preternaturally tough. At the Battle of Shiloh, where he was the last man wounded, he led a charge toward Union troops and found himself alone and surrounded in their midst. He fired his revolvers until they were empty and then slashed with his saber at the troops trying to pull him off his horse. Soon he was hit with a musket ball that lodged in his spine, an incredibly painful injury. Using his free hand, he grabbed a Union soldier by the shirt collar and pulled him off the ground, using the man as a shield as he rode through the enemy troops to safety. One week later, with no anesthesia to be had, an army surgeon removed the musket ball from Forrest's spine.

But Forrest was also a participant in one of the war's greatest atrocities. In April 1864, Forrest attacked Fort Pillow in Henning, Tennessee, where a large part of the defending Union force were African American soldiers. Although Forrest later denied it, eyewitnesses, including those in Forrest's own command, insisted that after the Union garrison surrendered, he ordered all the black soldiers massacred. A Confederate soldier wrote to his sister,

> The slaughter was awful. Words cannot describe the scene. The poor, deluded negroes would run up to our men, fall upon their knees, and

with uplifted hands scream for mercy, but they were ordered to their feet and then shot down. I, with several others, tried to stop the butchery, and at one time had partially succeeded, but General Forrest ordered them shot down like dogs and the carnage continued. Finally our men became sick of blood and the firing ceased.[1]

No criminal charges were ever filed against Forrest or any of his men.

Under Forrest's leadership, the Kuklux, as it was still known, quickly began to function as a guerrilla army, patrolling those areas of the South where either United States troops could not easily reach or there weren't enough people to justify stationing a unit there. Whipping and beating soon gave way to killing and the burning of homes. But to many white residents, the Klan became the force of law where the detested Yankees could not function. And that meant controlling the black population.

Mary Polk Branch was the widow of a Confederate general, a plantation owner, a member of the best Southern gentry, and a first cousin to James L. Polk, the eleventh president of the United States. In 1912, she wrote the story of her life, *Memoirs of a Southern Woman*, in which she recounted stories of the Klan.

Then came Reconstruction days. It would have been very different if the negroes had been left to themselves, and not listened to the "carpetbaggers" who swarmed over the South, but by them they were incited to lawlessness and insult.

What could be done? There was no law! The Kuklux filled the needed want, and by thorough superstition awed the negroes into better behavior.

I have looked out in the moonlight, and seen a long procession wending their way slowly on the turnpike, in front of my house. Not a sound could be heard from the muffled feet of their horses, as in single file they moved in speechless silence—a spectral array clothed in white. No one knew who they were, whence they came, and what their object, but the negroes soon knew; and if there were excesses in their new-found liberty, crimes committed by them, they knew there would be a speedy retribution by these spectral visitants.

They effected a great good, but as good is often attended with evil, lawless men, who did not belong to the regular organization, disguised themselves as Kuklux.

For instance, on my brother Lucius's plantation, one night he was aroused by negroes from the quarter, calling at his window, begging him to get up; that there was, "A company of Kuklux at the quarter." He went at once, and demanded what they wanted. They said: "One of the negroes on the place has done a great deal of mischief, and we have come to whip him." My brother said: "I know him to be a good negro, and you cannot whip him." "But we must!" "You cannot," said my brother. "If you do it will be over my dead body, for I am his natural protector." "Well, General, your life is too valuable to be given for this negro's, so, as we do not wish to kill you, we will go."[2]

But sometimes the Klansmen did not go, as in an eyewitness account by Thomas Burton. Burton, born a slave in Kentucky in 1860, was sent to school with the help of John Fee, a white minister and founder of Berea College, and eventually became a doctor practicing in Indiana. Berea College accepted students of all races, as did Reverend Fee's congregation. In 1872, while a young Thomas Burton sat in church, he watched as Reverend Fee paid the price for his decency.

The sermon had commenced when a mob of sixty men with pistols and guns surrounded the house. One came in and said to Mr. Fee, "There are men here who wish you to stop and come out." He replied, "I am engaged in the exercise of a Constitutional right and a religious duty; please do not interrupt me," and preached on. The man went out, and soon two others returned and demanded that he come out. He preached on. They seized him and dragged him out, no resistance being made. Men with a rope swore they would hang him to the first tree unless he would promise to leave the county and never return. He replied, "I am in your hands; I would not harm you if you harm me; the responsibility is with you; I can make no pledge; duty to God and my country forbid." They swore they would duck him in the Kentucky River as long as life was in him unless he would promise to leave the county. He said: "I am a native of the State. I believe slavery is wrong. I am acting for the good of my country and all her people. You will know my motives at the judgment." He had proceeded but a few moments when one exclaimed, "We didn't come here to hear a sermon; let us do our work." They stripped Robert Jones naked, bent him down, and gave him thirty-three lashes with three sycamore rods. He was so injured that he could not walk the next day; but he made no pledges and did not leave. They said to Mr. Fee, "We will give you five hundred lashes if you do not leave the county and promise never to return." He knelt down and said, "I will take my suffering; I can make no pledge." Later two lawyers were engaged to prosecute in behalf of him and Jones. The mob swore they would give five hundred lashes to any lawyer who would prosecute the cases. The grand jury never inquired into it. This is one of many such mobs through which Rev. John G. Fee went in those days.[3]

Through terror and intimidation, the Klan in some areas operated as a shadow government, or as some called it, "the Invisible Empire." They could not have much effect in the cities or in other areas where the army was a constant presence, but in the countryside, they could prevent newly freed black citizens from exercising the civil rights that the Radical Republicans in Congress had fought so hard to gain for them, the most important of which was the right to vote.

It is difficult to appreciate the degree to which white Southerners loathed the sight of African Americans casting ballots in free elections. Frank Alexander Montgomery, who had been a lieutenant colonel in the First Mississippi Cavalry, wrote that the Reconstruction Acts, by allowing freed slaves to vote, "filled to overflowing the cup of bitterness the south was called upon to drink." Montgomery, who would later serve both as a member of the Mississippi legislature and a federal circuit court judge, thought it

> impossible to conceive that the ingenuity of hate could have devised anything which would have so humiliated the white people of the state as this cruel and unnecessary act, by which the former slave was placed upon a political equality with his master, in many cases superior to his master, for often the slave could vote while the master could not ... The negroes stood in a long line, patiently waiting each till his turn should come, and had no more idea what he was doing or who he was voting for than 'the man in the moon' had.[4]

As always, Southerners thought themselves reasonable rather than bigoted.

> The people of the north did not understand the character [of] the negro; to them, or the vast majority, he was a white man with a black skin, while we of the south knew him to be not only an alien race, but so vastly inferior that no fit comparison now occurs to me. Whatever traits of character he had which raised him from a condition of barbarism he owed to his association with the white man, and to-day it is well known that if he were even now removed from this association he would relapse into the lowest grade of humanity.

The Klan took specific aim at the Loyal Leagues. To white Southerners, these were "secret political organizations among the colored people, and were generally organized and presided over by their white allies. Meetings were usually held at night in some out-of-the-way place, and were harangued by white Republican speakers. These organizations solidified the black vote, for there was a league in every community, and every colored man was a member."[5]

The Klan's reputation in the countryside as a terrorist organization out of the reach of law spread dread among black residents. Often, Klan members needed simply to show up to keep black men from the voting booth. In many cases, they did not specifically have to break any laws.

> If a party of white men, with ropes conspicuous on their saddlebows, rode up to a polling place and announced that hanging would begin in fifteen minutes, though without any more definite reference to anybody, and a group of blacks who had assembled to vote heard the remark and promptly disappeared, votes were lost, but a conviction on a charge of intimidation was difficult. Or if an untraceable rumor that trouble was impending over the blacks was followed by the mysterious appearance of bodies of horsemen on the roads at midnight, firing guns and yelling at nobody in particular, votes again were lost, but no crime or misdemeanor could be brought home to any one.[6]

Klan terror achieved some notable success. In the presidential election of 1868, in eleven counties in Georgia, each with a majority of black voters, not a single vote was reported for Grant and the Republicans.[7] That same year, when the Reconstruction state constitution was up for a vote in Mississippi, "It was charged by the Republicans . . . that whites terrorized the negroes by the Kuklux method, and either kept them away from the polls or intimidated them into voting against the Constitution."[8]

Although there could be no specific measurement of the degree to which the Klan and similar white supremacist groups that it spawned suppressed black voting, that it was cutting into Republican majorities was obvious. Although Republicans took back the White House, Ulysses Grant besting New York's Horatio Seymour, the results in the Southern states could not help but be worrisome for Republicans. Democrats closed the gap in South Carolina, North Carolina, and Alabama, and won in Georgia, Louisiana, Kentucky, and Maryland. Virginia, Mississippi, and Texas had not yet returned to the Union, and Florida's three electoral votes were awarded to Grant, although no election had been held. Without African American votes, and if the former Confederates whose voting rights had been taken away had been allowed to cast ballots, Grant would likely have lost the popular vote. Democrats also gained twenty seats in the House of Representatives, although Republicans retained a clear majority, added seats in the Senate, and made big advances in state legislatures.

That white Republicans needed both the black vote and to maintain control in the South was apparent. Without either, their power in government and in many cases their jobs would disappear. By 1868, however, much of white America was losing its taste for the money and effort required to support Reconstruction.

With Democrats on the rise and Reconstruction on the wane in the old Confederacy, the Fourteenth Amendment was not going to be enough. There needed to be another, one that would place black Americans' right to vote beyond the ability of Southern state governments, even under Democratic control, to eliminate or restrict it.

4

...and a Third

Equal Rights Comes to the Ballot Box

B UT THERE COULD BE NO DELAY. THE RECONSTRUCTION governments could not survive without the army to back them up, and the army would not remain in the South forever. Radicals had based their initiatives on the assumption that with time, white Southerners would grow accustomed to sharing power with African Americans; that freedmen would assimilate sufficiently that their presence in government, schools, theaters, and business would gain at least tacit acceptance. The rise of the Klan and other terror groups, and the enthusiasm with which they had been greeted, had tempered that hope, if not destroyed it. Reconstruction could only continue with equal access to the ballot box, and once the army withdrew, the only way black Americans would be able to ensure that access was through the federal court system.

Proponents had made several attempts to ensure voting rights during the drafting of the Fourteenth Amendment, but each had failed. John Henderson, a senator from Missouri, had introduced an amendment that read, "No state, in prescribing the qualifications requisite for electors therein, shall discriminate against any person on account of color or race."[1] Charles Sumner had tried to include "no denial of rights, civil or political, on account of color or race."[2] Finally, the Radicals gave up. When the committee issued its report, it read,

> The committee were of the opinion that the States are not yet prepared to sanction so fundamental a change as would be the concession of the right to suffrage to the colored race. We may as well state it plainly and fairly, so that there shall be no misunderstanding on the subject. It was our opinion that three-fourths of the States of this Union could not be induced to vote to grant the right of suffrage, even in any degree or under any restriction, to the colored race.[3]

In addition, the second section of the amendment, which threatened Southern states with loss of House seats, had never been enforced, nor did it appear that it ever would be. In December 1868, Andrew Johnson, by then a lame duck president, pardoned everyone who had been either directly or indirectly associated with the Confederacy, thus rendering Section 3 of the Fourteenth Amendment moot.

There had been some victories. One month after the 1866 Republican landslide, Congress enacted a bill, over Johnson's veto, enfranchising blacks in the District of Columbia. In January 1867, a bill was passed that enfranchised the African Americans living in the federal territories. Congress passed another bill requiring blacks to vote in Nebraska in order for it to be granted statehood. Still, the trends were clear. And so, after the 1868 elections, "Supporters of universal suffrage for blacks realized that time was short for their efforts to accomplish their goal in the form of the Fifteenth Amendment."[4]

The process began during the Fortieth Congress, when on March 7, 1868, Senator Henderson introduced a proposed amendment, which read, "No State shall deny or abridge the right of its citizens to vote and hold office on account of race, color, or previous condition."[5] A similar proposal was introduced in the House. It became clear early on that most congressmen would only support a measure that broadly defined the goal and did not address some of the tactics that might be employed to disfranchise black voters, such as literacy tests, poll taxes, or property holding. In the House, John Bingham tried to persuade his colleagues to include more specific wording, as did Charles Sumner in the Senate. Bingham's original proposal would have banned literacy tests, a poll tax, education requirements, or property ownership as reasons for denying someone the right to register to vote. It was rejected.

Sumner's proposal was even more extreme, consisting of five sections, the first of which forbade denying or abridging the right to vote, or the right to hold office, "under any pretence of race or color"; the second mandated fines and prison sentences for violators; the third mandated similar fines and prison sentences for anyone refusing to register a potential voter on the basis of race or color; the fourth gave federal courts jurisdiction; and the fifth gave a wronged person the right to sue and collect damages.[6] Sumner could not even garner ten votes in support.

Debate continued for the remainder of 1868, with Bingham and Sumner mustering sufficient allies to prevent a watered-down version from being adopted in either chamber. But in the 1868 elections, when Democrats picked up twenty House seats, part of those gains was due to increased popularity in Northern states, many of which did not allow black men to vote. Waiting until the Forty-First Congress was seated in March 1869 suddenly seemed like an unacceptable risk. So, in January 1869, the draft amendments, weaker than equal rights advocates proposed, finally reached the floor of both houses for final debate.

Bingham still did not give up. On January 29, he replied to a colleague who told him he was wasting the House's time.

> Sir, I have stood here the advocate of impartial suffrage when gentlemen who now put themselves forward as its special friends were on the other side of the question. It has been the rule of my political life.

I never could see the propriety, under the Constitution of the United States, of any state disenfranchising any free citizen of the Republic by reason of his color from exercising this great privilege of freedom.[7]

The following day, he offered an amended version.

No State shall make or enforce any law which shall abridge or deny to any male citizen of the United States of sound mind and twenty-one years of age or upward the exercise of the elective franchise at all elections in the State wherein he shall have actually resided for a period of one year next preceding such election, (subject to such registration laws and laws prescribing local residence as the State may enact,) except such of said citizens as shall engage in rebellion or insurrection, or who may have been, or shall be, duly convicted of treason or other infamous crimes.

Bingham's proposal was defeated 160–24, with 38 not voting. Sumner offered his version once more and it was defeated 46–9.

Although the House reported out an abbreviated version, "The right of any citizen of the United States to vote shall not be denied or abridged by the United States or any State by reason of race, color, or previous condition of slavery of any citizen or class of citizens of the United States," Sumner had more luck in the Senate. Their draft read, "No discrimination shall be made in any State among the citizens of the United States in the exercise of the elective franchise or in the right to hold office in any State on account of race, color, nativity, property, education, or creed." But the House rejected the Senate's draft overwhelmingly, and a conference was called. In the meantime, the clock was ticking. There were only three weeks to pass the amendment before Democrats, allied with reluctant Republicans, might be in a position to block it.

After some back and forth, a final version was agreed to. It was identical to the first Senate version, which had read, "The right of citizens of the United States to vote and to hold office shall not be denied or abridged by the United States or any State on account of race, color, or previous condition of servitude," except "and to hold office" was eliminated. Some senators bristled at the office-holding guarantee being eliminated, but it was that or nothing. On February 26, 1869, just one week before the new Congress would be sworn in, both houses approved the amendment and sent it on to the states. Although John Bingham grudgingly went along, Charles Sumner abstained, unable to bring himself to support such a lukewarm proposition.

It took almost an entire year, but in early February 1870, the required twenty-eight states had ratified, and the Fifteenth Amendment became law. This included nine of the eleven Confederate states that still, for the moment, had Republican legislatures. Never again, proponents proclaimed, would a person be legally denied the right to vote because of the color of his, and eventually her, skin.

Weakened language or no, the ratification of the Fifteenth Amendment was met with a sense of triumph in many quarters. To inscribe in the Constitution a guarantee that color or race could not be a bar to the ballot box seemed to many the *coup de grace* to racial inequality. William Lloyd Garrison, whose view of black suffrage had changed, gushed over four million human beings transferred from "the auction block to the ballot box."[8] In the North, African Americans rejoiced. "In Boston, about 3,000 blacks, including the veterans of the 54th and 55th Massachusetts regiments, participated in the procession held in Boston Public Park. In Detroit, blacks carried portraits of Abraham Lincoln, Ulysses S. Grant, and John Brown, and sang verses which rang, 'The ballot-box has come, now let us all prepare to vote/With the party that made us free.'"[9] The American Anti-Slavery Society disbanded in March 1870, feeling there was no longer any reason for its existence. President Grant, in a message to Congress, called the amendment "a measure of grander importance than any other one act of the kind from the foundation of our free Government to the present time."[10] Finally, the amendment infuriated Democrats, which in and of itself seemed ample justification to many for its inclusion in the Constitution.

Ratification of the amendment engendered a good deal of relief as well. The nation might finally have moved past "the Negro question," as it was called. Ohio congressman and future president James A. Garfield asserted that the amendment "confers upon the African race the care of its own destiny. It places fortunes in their own hands."[11]

Others, however, took a more circumspect view. To them, the wording of the amendment was evidence of a decreasing commitment among white Americans to ensuring equal rights for African Americans. For one thing, as Charles Sumner continued to protest, the Fifteenth contained no guarantee that black Americans could hold office. Nor were uniform standards of eligibility included, which would prevent white governments from excluding potential voters through arbitrary literacy tests, or poll taxes, or tortuously formulated property requirements. The shrinking contingent of Northern Radicals decried the "lame and halting language," or noted that the amendment was "more remarkable for what it does not than for what it does contain."[12]

Negative sentiment came from other quarters. An editor at the *New Haven News* wrote portentously, ". . . the question of the elective franchise is one that [the states] will never surrender at the dictation of congress or any other power seeking to arbitrarily wrench it from [their] constitutional grasp."[13]

But for most, both the intent and the impact could not have been clearer: the Fifteenth Amendment was to add cement to an edifice of democracy built on American virtue. Naysayers, like the New Haven editor, were reminded that any attempt by unscrupulous white legislators to end-run the Fifteenth Amendment through, say, bogus literacy tests would certainly also run afoul of the equal protection clause of the Fourteenth. And, to ensure that the Constitution was adhered to by any who would seek to contort its aims, there stood the federal judiciary and ultimately the justices of the Supreme Court.

5

A Fragile Illusion

LTHOUGH SUPPORTERS OF EQUAL RIGHTS WERE LOS-
ing influence in Congress, they had gained a vital ally in the
White House. Never had America elected a president as committed to equal rights and racial justice as Ulysses Grant, and would not
do so again for at least another century.

Grant announced his intentions the day he took office, during his
inaugural parade on March 4, 1869. The former general had assembled
an immense military contingent—eight divisions—to march along the
parade route. Unmistakable, even in the swarm of uniforms, were "the
Lincoln Zouaves (colored), of Baltimore, mustered forty-eight strong," in
"blue flannel with yellow trimmings, and white legging, after the style of
the French uniform," and "the Henry Winter Davis Guards of Baltimore,
(colored), numbering between fifty to sixty men, arrived next in line with
the Zouaves."[1] Not even Lincoln had ever appeared at a state function in
front of black troops.

After four years of war, Grant had no illusions about the South. He viewed the Klan as an opposing military force—especially under Bedford Forrest—and therefore one that could only be defeated by military means. The Fourteenth and Fifteenth Amendments, both of which he favored, would be only hollow verbiage without some tangible means to back them up. And so he threw his support behind three proposed laws, one in 1870 and two in 1871, to give the Fourteenth Amendment, and the Fifteenth once it was ratified, some heft. With the president's endorsement, a mere majority, not two-thirds, was all that would be needed to make them law. If states' rights advocates saw the Fourteenth and Fifteenth Amendments as taking aim at the Tenth, these three laws, which would be called "Enforcement" or "Force" acts, fired shots right at its heart.

The first, signed into law on May 31, 1870, after the Fifteenth Amendment had been ratified, made little secret of its intent, being called "An Act to enforce the Right of Citizens of the United States to vote in the several States of this Union, and for other purposes." The first section, introduced in the House by John Bingham, contained the very sort of wording that he and Sumner had been unable to incorporate into the Fifteenth Amendment.

All citizens of the United States who are or shall be otherwise qualified by law to vote at any election by the people in any State, Territory, district, county, city, parish, township, school district, municipality, or other territorial sub-division, shall be entitled and allowed to vote at all such elections, without distinction of race, color, or previous condition of servitude; any constitution, law, custom, usage, or regulation of any State or Territory, or by or under its authority, to the contrary notwithstanding.[2]

The most important difference between the law and the amendment was that former said "shall be entitled and allowed to vote," where the amendment read "shall not be denied." The distinction, as it turned out, would be critical.

Other sections of the law, which came to be known as the "First Ku Klux Klan Act," forbade discrimination in voter registration, made it a criminal offense to deny a person either the right to vote or the right to register, specified fines and prison terms for offenders, authorized military force to keep order at polling places, and outlawed "threats of depriving such person of employment or occupation, or of ejecting such person from rented house, lands, or other property, or by threats of refusing to renew leases or contracts for labor, or by threats of violence to himself or family." It stipulated all persons, not just citizens, should be treated equally before the law, and attacked election fraud, here with particular emphasis on Northern Democrats, who were stealing elections in New York City. By extending federal enforcement to the North, Republicans were proposing a national system of election supervision.[3]

But white supremacist terror was the law's main focus. Section 6 read,

> If two or more persons shall band or conspire together, or go in disguise upon the public highway, or upon the premises of another, with intent to violate any provision of this act, or to injure, oppress, threaten, or intimidate any citizen with intent to prevent or hinder his free exercise and enjoyment of any right or privilege granted or secured to him by the Constitution or laws of the United States, or because of his having exercised the same, such persons shall be held guilty of a felony, and, on conviction thereof, shall be fined or imprisoned, or both, at the discretion of the court—the fine not to exceed five thousand dollars, and the imprisonment not to exceed ten years—and shall, moreover, be thereafter ineligible to, and disabled from holding, any office or place of honor, profit, or trust created by the Constitution or laws of the United States.

As with the Fourteenth Amendment, jurisdiction was removed to federal court.

The second section of the Fifteenth Amendment had read, "The Congress shall have the power to enforce this article by appropriate legislation," and now, only three months after its adoption, Congress had done so. The law also seemed to fall squarely under the Fourteenth Amendment's guarantee of "equal protection of the laws," which had, almost all Americans believed, been inserted in the Constitution to provide the very guarantees the new law codified.

This was just the sort of potent weapon the federal government needed to ensure the equal rights that had been promised to freedmen, and Grant intended to use it. To make certain the government had the necessary tools, in June 1870 Congress established a new cabinet-level office, which was called, provocatively to Southerners, "the Department of Justice."[4] To head the department, Grant made an odd choice.

Amos Akerman had been born in New Hampshire and attended Dartmouth College, but moved to Georgia after graduation. Although he opposed secession, he had served in the Confederate army, and had long believed the prosecution of civil rights violations should be left to the states. But he also had a deep sense of fairness. Once the war ended, he became an outspoken proponent of freedmen's rights and switched to the Republican Party. Like the president, Akerman despised the Klan and everything it stood for. He had personally been menaced by white supremacists in his home state after he announced his new party affiliation. Grant, unlike with some of his other appointments, could not have made a better choice.

Actual prosecutions were limited in 1870, less than four dozen, although by year's end 271 cases were on the docket, waiting to be brought to trial.[5] The following year, Akerman would acquire two additional tools with which to work. On February 28, 1871, President Grant signed the second Enforcement Act, which stiffened some of the penalties specified in the first act but, more significantly, mandated federal supervision of congressional elections "from registration through the counting of ballots" in any municipality of more than 20,000 people, if two residents requested it.[6]

But more was needed, especially in South Carolina, large sections of which appeared to be descending into anarchy. Grant was inundated with pleas for help. On January 17, 1871, Robert Scott, the state's Republican governor, requested increased federal commitment. "The outrages in Spartanburg and Union Counties in this state have become so numerous, and such a reign of terror exists, that but few Republicans dare sleep in their houses at night. A number of people have been whipped and murdered, and I see no remedy other than the stationing of U.S. troops in those counties."[7] Private citizens were writing to the president as well. Mrs. S. E. Lane of Chesterfield District implored,

> I write to ask your help, your protection for us . . . Sir, we are in terror from Ku-Klux threats and outrages. There is neither law nor justice in our midst. Our nearest neighbor, a prominent Republican, now lies dead, murdered by a disguised Ruffian Band, which attacked his house at midnight a few nights since. His wife also was murdered. She was buried yesterday, and a daughter is lying dangerously ill from a shot wound.[8]

The atrocities were horrific, barbaric, and sickeningly commonplace. Most of the time, the perpetrators simply disappeared back into the night. In a case that actually did result in arrests and even convictions, "a night raid was made on the home of a black Republican by the name of Amzi Rainey. Klansmen fired upon Rainey and his family while his wife was holding a young child in her arms. They shot his older daughter in the head after they attempted to rape her. Rainey was saved from death only by promising he would never again vote the Republican ticket."[9]

On March 23, 1871, Grant sent a message to both houses of Congress.

> A condition of affairs now exists in some of the States of the Union rendering life and property insecure, and the carrying of the mails and the collections of the revenue dangerous. The proof that such a condition of affairs exists in some localities is now before the Senate. That the power to correct these evils is beyond the control of the State authorities I do not doubt; that the power of the Executive of the United States, acting within the limits of existing laws, is sufficient for present emergencies

is not clear. Therefore I urgently recommend such legislation as in the judgment of Congress shall effectually secure life, liberty, and property, and the enforcement of law in all parts of the United States.[10]

To accomplish this goal, Grant asked for increased authority, including the right to suspend habeas corpus.

Democrats from the North as well as the South accused Grant of asking for dictatorial powers, and many Republicans were leery of what seemed an extreme step, but the prospect of wholesale slaughter across the South if nothing was done overrode their concerns. On April 20, 1871, Ulysses Grant signed a law that gave him the powers he had sought.

Although he sent additional troops to South Carolina, hoping to avoid what would amount to martial law, "Grant did not invoke his powers under the Ku Klux Act, and federal soldiers had no authority to undertake independent action; they were intended as escorts for state or federal officials who might fear resistance in the performance of their duties."[11]

Through the summer and early fall, federal authorities attempted to find a peaceful solution—they sponsored conferences, conceded to a number of white demands, and kept the army, as much as possible, in the background. Grant dispatched Akerman to South Carolina to see for himself. The attorney general wrote later in a letter to a friend that it was his opinion

that nothing is more idle than to attempt to conciliate by kindness that portion of the southern people who are still malcontent. They take all kindness on the part of the Government as evidence of timidity, and hence are emboldened to lawlessness by it. It appears impossible for the Government to win their affection. But it can command their respect by the exercise of its powers.[12]

Soon thereafter, Ulysses Grant suspended habeas corpus in nine South Carolina counties, the first time that had ever been done in peacetime. Federal enforcement and prosecutions drastically increased, and while in many cases convictions were hard to come by, there were enough of them that most considered the Klan to have been at least neutered. "At the beginning of 1872, federal officers felt they were on the verge of destroying the Klan. They were also heartened by the sharp curtailment of violence that had resulted from their efforts." In South Carolina, the impact had been acute. "Federal prosecutions had so demoralized members of the Ku Klux Klan there that its leaders issued orders to stop all Klan activity."[13]

With the sharp reduction in intimidation and violence—although it was by no means eliminated—black voting increased and so did the number of African Americans elected to important offices. In the 1872 elections, more than 320 federal and state legislators were voted into office, the highest number ever, forty more than in the 1870 elections, and a number not to be matched for well more than a century.[14] During that two-year period, ten African Americans were elected to the House, and one, Hiram Revels of Mississippi, appointed to the Senate.

Although these numbers would soon plummet, what is most vital to glean from this episode was that both sides had no doubt that voting by African Americans was the linchpin of their success. Guarantee the black vote and Reconstruction had a chance to succeed, perhaps even leading to racial tolerance; eliminate it and Redeemers—militant whites determined to return the South to prewar rule—would reign, with white supremacy the basis of any Southern political system. As such, the suppression of the Klan in no way implied that attempts by Redeemers to deny black Americans their right to vote were at an end. Quite the reverse. Redeemers saw themselves fighting an extension of the war they had temporarily lost on the battlefield, with their values, their futures, and what they saw as an honorable way of life at stake.

To continue their struggle, not only would violence and intimidation continue, but Southern whites would also shift to new tactics, fraud and duplicity, exploiting the very ambiguities of the Fifteenth Amendment about which John Bingham and his allies had warned. Against this second wave of voter suppression, military force would have no effect. This battlefield would be the courtroom.

6

Any Way You Slice It

The *Slaughter-House Cases*

T HE FIRST TEST OF FOURTEENTH AMENDMENT GUAR-
antees was brought to the Supreme Court not on *behalf* of black
Americans, but rather *against* black Americans. The plaintiffs
were a group of white New Orleans butchers who regularly dumped foul,
untreated animal waste into the almost impossibly polluted Mississippi
River, just upriver from the pipes that supplied the city's drinking water.
The defendants were, in effect, the men of color who were members of the
Louisiana state legislature and New Orleans city government.

Even at a time when public sanitation in the United States could be
slapdash, post–Civil War New Orleans might well have been the filthiest
and most disease-ridden city in the nation. It had been so for decades.
The problem was largely man-made, and butchers, almost all of whom
came from Gascony, in southwest France, were among the most prominent culprits. Ignoring public outcry, they persisted in sweeping the
bones, organs, body parts, dung, and urine of cows, sheep, and pigs into

the river, such that occasionally bits of these products would flow out of water taps. Periodic epidemics of cholera and yellow fever were the result. In 1859, a city physician spoke of "gutters sweltered with the blood and drainings of slaughter-pens," and that "every highway that chanced to be unpaved was broadcast with the rakings of gutters and the refuse filth of private yards and stables."[1] When Union forces took the city in 1862, General Benjamin Butler complained that "the streets were reeking with putrefying filth."[2]

In addition to being agents of misery, the Gascon butchers—notoriously independent, clannish, and hard-edged—had also conspired to keep the price of meat high. For as far back as anyone could remember, New Orleans residents had pleaded with the governor and state and city legislators to *do something*.

Finally, in 1869, they did. Louisiana passed a law that required all butchers to slaughter, gut, and carve up animals in a single facility—downriver from the water mains—and under the supervision of trained inspectors. This central slaughterhouse would be run by a private corporation licensed by the state. Butchers would pay a small fee for every animal they acquired, but would no longer be required to either purchase or lease facilities of their own. Other cities, such as Boston and New York, had enacted similar laws and watched the rate of disease fall.

Although the butchers complained loudly that they were being denied the right to practice their trade as they wished, this law ordinarily would have evoked cheering from city residents. But it did not. That was, at least in part, because the legislature that passed the bill and the governor who signed it were Republicans, and, even worse, a goodly number of those legislators were not white. Of the sixty-five Republicans in the 101-member Louisiana House of Representatives, thirty-five were black. In the state senate, seven African Americans, again all Republican, took their seats with twenty-nine whites.

Democratic newspapers assailed the new law, accusing Republicans of setting up the central slaughterhouse not to protect the health of the citizenry, but to make money through corruption and graft.[3] They also complained that the new facility would be available to anyone—which meant black butchers could use it as well.

With the encouragement of the same white supremacists who had been complaining about them for decades, the butchers sued. If they got nowhere in state court, they would appeal in federal court. There, however, they would need to find some way in which the new law violated their constitutional rights, and so they would claim that forcing them into a different place of business amounted to "involuntary servitude" in violation of the Thirteenth Amendment, and that the Fourteenth Amendment protected their "privileges and immunities" of citizenship, in this case the right to conduct business how and where they wished.

Although the butchers' appeal would seem to rest only on how the language in the two amendments was interpreted, this case would actually become a chess match between two masterful adversaries, with language only the game pieces. Each knew his opponent well, and each loathed the other. One was an unapologetic white supremacist who had resigned a seat on the Supreme Court to become one of the leaders of the Confederacy; the other was a sitting justice who had been so opposed to slavery that he had left his native Kentucky in 1850 to move to free Iowa.

Appearing for the butchers was John Archibald Campbell, who had joined the Supreme Court in 1853, after Chief Justice Roger B. Taney— author of the *Dred Scott* decision—and the other justices requested President Franklin Pierce appoint him. Campbell had been a legal prodigy, admitted to the bar in his native Georgia at age eighteen, so young that a special act of the state legislature had been required to allow him to practice. He left the Court in 1861, after his then home state of Alabama rejected the Union, and was appointed assistant secretary of war by Confederate president Jefferson Davis. After Lincoln's assassination, Campbell had been arrested and held in jail for six months as a potential conspirator.

His opponent, Samuel Freeman Miller, was a no-nonsense, plain-speaking champion of equal rights. He had been born into a slave-holding family in Kentucky in 1816, but grew to detest slavery and those who practiced it. When he fled the South, he settled in Keokuk, a Mississippi River port and a major shipping location for the same cattle, sheep, and hogs that in the 1860s would end up in New Orleans slaughterhouses.

Miller was more familiar with cholera than anyone on the federal bench—before entering the law, he had been a doctor who had specialized in its treatment. That most physicians treated the disease as if it were still the Middle Ages, employing bleedings and purgatives, had infuriated him. Miller was convinced that cholera was transmitted from unclean water, instead of "indigestible vegetables" or "filthy and intemperate habits of the urban poor," but few would listen to him.[4] He finally abandoned medicine because he could no longer bear to watch so much needless suffering and death.

Almost immediately after entering the law, Miller had gained a reputation for brilliance. He supported Abraham Lincoln in the 1860 presidential election, and the new president rewarded him in 1862 with a nomination to the Supreme Court. Miller was committed to racial equality and the goals of Reconstruction, and he harbored a particular dislike for a man he believed had dishonored the very court of which he was now a member. He wrote to a friend that he "had never seen nor heard of any action of Judge Campbell's since the rebellion that was aimed at healing the breach he had contributed so much to make," and that Campbell was then merely "a discontented and embittered old man."[5] Campbell himself bore that out. "We have Africans in place all about us," he wrote to a friend. "As jurors, post office clerks, custom house officers, and day by day they barter away their obligations and privileges . . . corruption is the rule."[6]

Miller, therefore, would hear the arguments in the *Slaughter-House Cases* with a personal and scientific interest in proper sanitation, a desire to support the biracial government of Louisiana, and a deep distaste for John Campbell. While none of these were supposed to affect Miller's judgment, Campbell knew he had to find a way to turn those prejudices to his advantage.

In fact, John Campbell was a more complex figure than Miller gave him credit for. In his early career, and during his eight years on the Court, Campbell had been known as a master of compromise. Although he was in favor of slavery and believed in the superiority of the white race, he had advocated eventual emancipation and had even freed his own slaves before taking his seat on the Court. After the election of Abraham Lincoln, Campbell had tried to persuade the new president to negotiate on Southern secession. Lincoln refused, insisting that secession was against the law and no accommodation was possible. It was only then that Campbell returned home to take a position in the Confederate government. Even his imprisonment had been as a result of an effort to persuade Lincoln to soften his stance toward the defeated South.

But either his months in an army prison or what he saw as the injustice of Reconstruction had hardened him, and as the elevation of African Americans spread through Southern society, Campbell's every energy had come to be devoted to the return of white government.

Before he could face off against his former colleagues on the Supreme Court, however, Campbell needed to lose in the state court to establish grounds for appeal. He did not expect that to be difficult, since most of the judges were Republican and they drank New Orleans water. He asserted that the Slaughter-House law had been passed as a result of bribery and vote-buying in the state legislature, which fit neatly into his theory that newly seated black legislators were either too naïve or too craven to govern honestly. As such, the law could be voided on account of fraud. He also insisted it had not been signed within the legal time limit. Finally, and most importantly, Campbell declared that the law established an illegal monopoly, which subjected those forced to do business with it—white butchers—to unfair and unconstitutional restrictions on their business.

The first two grounds, largely smoke screens, were easily swept aside by lawyers for the state. While bribery and vote-buying had more than likely been involved, Campbell had been unable to provide specifics, and no judge was going to overturn such an important law because of a couple of days' delay in its being signed. As to the charge of illegal monopoly, the Louisiana Supreme Court ruled the law fell within the state's police power and should thus be allowed to stand.

The loss gave Campbell the opportunity to end up precisely where he wanted to. At the Supreme Court, he would plead to his former colleagues that the Slaughter-House law should be overturned on Thirteenth and Fourteenth Amendment grounds. He was sufficiently savvy to recognize that with public health as a key feature of the case, he would almost certainly be up against Samuel Miller.

Knowing how much Miller wanted to rule against him, Campbell set a trap. When the proposed Fourteenth Amendment was being debated in the House of Representatives, John Bingham had made it clear that "privileges and immunities of citizenship" was meant to apply federal citizenship rights to the states. Bingham, of course, had been referring to the rights of newly freed slaves, who were guaranteed United States and state citizenship in the first sentence of the amendment.

But the "privileges and immunities" clause did not mention race, only "citizens," and so Campbell insisted that it covered white citizens as well as black. Louisiana therefore had no right to herd butchers into a common facility and force them to pay fees to ply their trade. Unless, of course, state citizenship was different than national citizenship, with different "privileges and immunities." In that case, state governments could do things the federal government could not. Although Campbell carefully avoided saying so, if there were in fact two classes of citizenship, then states could pass other laws that fit their own definition. That he had drafted an argument exalting the power of the national government at the expense of states' rights could not have been lost on the man who had resigned his seat on the Court, joined the Confederacy, and gone to prison in defense of states' rights. But Campbell was not to be deterred by such niceties.

In compromising his principles, Campbell had created an extremely clever argument. The Court could either support him and use the Fourteenth Amendment to protect a group of white, racist butchers who were poisoning New Orleans's drinking water, or they could rule against him and limit the amendment's reach by narrowing when its guarantees could be applied, especially for people of color. Although he almost certainly did not inform his clients, his personal agenda of undermining Reconstruction would be much better served if he lost the case.

Which he did.

On April 14, 1873, by a 5–4 vote, the Court ruled that New Orleans had the right to require the butchers to relocate their business to a central location run by a corporation licensed for the task. "It is not true," Miller wrote for the majority, "that [this arrangement] deprives the butchers of the right to exercise their trade, or imposes upon them any restriction incompatible with its successful pursuit."[7] (Miller also quickly dismissed the notion that requiring the butchers to relocate was "involuntary servitude," as defined by the Thirteenth Amendment.)

Miller made a point of lecturing Campbell on the meaning of the post–Civil War amendments.

> An examination of the history of the causes which led to the adoption of those amendments and of the amendments themselves demonstrates that the main purpose of all … was the freedom of the African race, the security and perpetuation of that freedom, and their protection from the oppressions of the white men who had formerly held them in slavery.

The Fourteenth Amendment, then, had not been enacted to shield white butchers from a state law meant to protect the health of its citizens.

But in his eagerness to destroy Campbell's argument, Miller fell into his trap. There was a "balance between State and Federal power," Miller wrote, and those in the federal government "believed that the existence of the State with powers for domestic and local government, including the regulation of civil rights the rights of person and of property was essential." So there was indeed a difference between citizenship in the United States and citizenship of a state, which meant that "privileges and immunities" might mean different things to each.

So, in overruling Campbell, Miller prevented the "privileges and immunities" clause of Fourteenth Amendment from being used against state laws, which was exactly what Campbell had hoped he would do. Other rights that might be considered "privileges" of citizenship—like voting—could now be left almost solely to the whim of states. As a result of Miller's blunder, the man on the Court most determined to protect black Americans turned what should have been the strongest guarantee in the Fourteenth Amendment into the weakest. And he did so using language and reasoning that would be adopted by white supremacists and Redeemers in the coming years.

Three justices wrote dissents—Swayne, Bradley, and Field—the latter of which was joined by the other two as well as Chief Justice Salmon P. Chase. Field's dissent was consistent with a lifelong commitment to laissez-faire capitalism, and he read the Fourteenth Amendment as protecting businesses, an interpretation that in the coming years would dominate American jurisprudence. To Field and his fellow dissenters, there was only one class of citizen and the butchers had been denied the privileges and immunities of that citizenship, meaning they should have been free to dump anything in the fetid Mississippi that they pleased.

As a result of the Fourteenth Amendment, Field wrote, "A citizen of a State is now only a citizen of the United States residing in that State." As a result, "the fundamental rights, privileges, and immunities which belong to him as a free man and a free citizen, now belong to him as a citizen of the United States, and are not dependent upon his citizenship of any State." Although

> the exercise of these rights and privileges . . . are always more or less affected by the condition and the local institutions of the State, or city, or town where he resides . . . in no other way can they be affected by the action of the State, or by the residence of the citizen therein. They do not derive their existence from its legislation, and cannot be destroyed by its power.

If [the Fourteenth Amendment restrictions] only refer, as held by the majority of the court in their opinion, to such privileges and im-munities as were before its adoption specially designated in the Con-stitution or necessarily implied as belonging to citizens of the United States, it was a vain and idle enactment, which accomplished nothing and most unnecessarily excited Congress and the people on its passage. With privileges and immunities thus designated or implied no State could ever have interfered by its laws, and no new constitutional pro-vision was required to inhibit such interference. The supremacy of the Constitution and the laws of the United States always controlled any State legislation of that character.

Field, whose racial attitudes could hardly be described as enlight-ened, was not above a bit of hypocrisy to buttress his argument.

[The Fourteenth] amendment was intended to give practical effect to the declaration of 1776 of inalienable rights, rights which are the gift of the Creator, which the law does not confer, but only recognizes . . . The question presented is, therefore, one of the gravest importance not merely to the parties here, but to the whole country. It is nothing less than the question whether the recent amendments to the Federal Con-stitution protect the citizens of the United States against the depri-vation of their common rights by State legislation. In my judgment, the fourteenth amendment does afford such protection, and was so in-tended by the Congress which framed and the States which adopted it.

And so, where Miller had used the language of Redeemers, Field was using the language and reasoning of the Radical Republicans. That reading of the Fourteenth Amendment could be used to secure the voting rights of African Americans—as could the Fifteenth—but only if Field and those who thought like him applied the same principles to equal rights that they were prepared to do for businesses.

Time would prove they were not.[8]

Equality by Law

The Civil Rights Act of 1875

I N 1874, WHAT REPUBLICANS HAD FEARED FOR A DECADE
finally transpired—Democrats won control of the House. Although
Ulysses Grant remained personally popular, an unbroken series of
scandals and a crushing economic downturn did his party in. When the
new Congress was sworn in on March 4, 1875, the House of Representatives would shift from a 199 to 88 Republican majority to a 182 to 102
edge for the Democrats, much of that margin emanating from the South.
Since only a third of the Senate is up for reelection every two years, Republicans would keep control, but a 52–19 majority shrank to 42–28.[1] At
the next round of senatorial elections in November 1876, the Republican majority might easily disappear. With President Grant's second term
coming to an end as well, for the first time since before the Civil War, a
Democrat would be favored to win the presidency.

Results were just as bad for Republicans at the state level. Despite
three Reconstruction amendments, numerous acts of Congress, advocacy
by Ulysses Grant, and an occupying military force, the combination of

white terror and widespread voter fraud had reduced the number of se-cessionist states that would remain under Republican control to four—Mississippi, Florida, Louisiana, and South Carolina.

With the nation still feeling aftershocks of economic collapse from the Panic of 1873, a waning commitment to securing equal rights for freedmen shriveled up. Keeping the army as an occupying force in the South was a huge drain on the nation's fragile finances, and many thought that, by now, freedmen should be able to fend for themselves. In addition, most whites continued to think of people of color as members of an inferior race, perhaps a different species altogether. Democrats had played into these feelings, run-ning on an anti-Reconstruction platform in both the North and the South.

After the November 1874 disaster, the dwindling contingent of Rad-icals had only four months to pass any further equal rights legislation. Constitutional amendments were out of the question. They had been desperate to expand equal rights to everyday activities, such as eating in restaurants, going to the theater, or taking their families to public parks. Now it seemed an impossible task. Most of those Republicans who had survived had no intention of risking their tenuous hold on national office by supporting a law that would be unpopular with their constituents.

Charles Sumner had been at it since 1870, when he proposed a bill in which the federal government would specifically guarantee "equal rights in railroads, steamboats, public conveyances, hotels, licensed the-aters, houses of public entertainment, common schools and institutions of learning authorized by law, church institutions, and cemetery associations incorporated by national or State authority; also in jury duties, national and state."[2] The notion of enforced integration in schools, churches, and cemeteries made most Republicans blanch. Sumner got nowhere.

Each year, Sumner had reintroduced his proposal, convinced that the Senate could not help but "crown and complete the great work of Reconstruction," but each year his party rejected it.[3] Then in March 1874, after a lifetime of trying to gain equality and justice for Americans of color, both slave and free, Charles Sumner died, his equal rights proposal seemingly dying with him.

But after the November 1874 elections, a strange thing happened. Championed by another Massachusetts congressman, Benjamin Butler—who had lost his own seat to a Democrat—Sumner's bill began to attract supporters. Many of them were Republicans, especially in the House, who had not backed Sumner in the past for fear of losing their seats, but had now lost them anyway. Working tirelessly and overcoming a Democratic filibuster that reduced senators to "whiling away the hours by tearing newspapers to shreds [as] stale cigar smoke choked the air, and members sprawled on the unswept carpet," Butler got Sumner's bill passed by both houses of Congress, although the schools, churches, and cemeteries provisions had to be dropped.[4] On March 1, 1875, three days before the new Congress would take office, President Grant signed it into law.

"An act to protect all citizens in the civil and legal rights," which became known as the Civil Rights Act of 1875, was an expansion of enforced equality that was explosive in scope. Section 1 read,

> All persons within the jurisdiction of the United States shall be entitled to the full and equal enjoyment of the accommodations, advantages, facilities, and privileges of inns, public conveyances on land or water, theaters, and other places of public amusement; subject only to the conditions and limitations established by law, and applicable alike to citizens of every race and color, regardless of any previous condition of servitude.[5]

The law made violators liable for up to a $500 fine for each offense, payable to the person wronged, and, if convicted in criminal court, subject to a fine of between $500 and $1,000 and up to one year in jail. Section 3 gave federal rather than state courts jurisdiction over suits arising from the law and specifically granted federal officials powers of arrest over state officials who were in violation. Section 4 took aim at jury service and guaranteed that "no citizen possessing all other qualifications which are or may be prescribed by law shall be disqualified for service as grand or petit juror in court in the United States, or of any State, on account of race, color or previous condition of servitude."

Passage of the Civil Rights Act evoked passionate response, although the direction of those passions was quite different depending on who one asked. Black Americans rejoiced and moved immediately to exercise their new freedoms. Hoteliers, theater managers, restaurateurs, tavern owners, and railroad agents were suddenly swamped by requests for first-class tickets, dress circle theater seats, front tables, or a beer at the bar. Most whites, however, were equally determined to continue to exclude African Americans from public accommodations whenever they so chose. Across the Potomac from the nation's capital, the two principal hotels in Alexandria, Virginia, closed rather than be forced to rent rooms to people of color. (Both subsequently reopened when their owners realized that refusing blacks would not land them in any legal difficulty.) In Memphis, four African Americans demanded to be seated in the dress circle at a local theater. When the management grudgingly acceded, most of the white patrons walked out. In Richmond, African Americans demanded service in restaurants, a tavern, and a barbershop, but in each case were refused.

Sentiment in the North was equally mixed. *The New York Times*, which had praised passage of the Fourteenth Amendment in 1868 as "settling the matter of suffrage in the Southern States beyond the power of the rebels to change it, even if they had control of the government," had a change of heart. "It has put us back in the art of governing men more than two hundred years," an editorial growled, "startling proof how far and fast we are wandering from the principles of 1787, once so loudly extolled and so fondly cherished."[6]

Not every newspaper felt the need to be so outraged. The *Chicago Daily Tribune* quietly, and correctly as it turned out, predicted the law would have little real impact. "At present, its effect will be mainly political. It will be used on the one side to retain the hold of the Republican party on the negroes of the South; on the other, to excite new opposition to the Republican party among the whites." The writer added, "After the provision for enforced mixed schools had been eliminated from the bill, it became a comparatively insignificant measure."

Each newspaper accurately predicted where the fate of the law would be decided. The *Times*, with Confederacy-era sarcasm, said, "The Supreme Court, in instances such as this, is the last hope of all who attach any value to that somewhat despised instrument, the Constitution of the United States." The *Daily Tribune* agreed that the constitutionality of the bill would be settled in the Supreme Court and foresaw, again correctly, that the first challenges to enforcement would come from the North.[7]

While not applicable to voting regulations, the Civil Rights Act of 1875 gave white America an image of what genuine racial equality would look like; how, if black Americans were allowed to vote freely, they might be forced into close association with a race of people almost all thought inferior and bestial, and many doubted were human at all, at least in the same fashion as whites. And whites made their feelings clear, including many who had once favored black suffrage. Most white businessmen—and voting registrars—simply ignored the law, and those denying black Americans their new rights of citizenship enjoyed the almost total support of police, politicians, and the courts. African Americans found themselves rarely successful in expanding their access to mainstream American life. A law on the books, they had learned, meant little if those to whom it was meant to apply refused to obey it and authorities then refused to enforce it.

African Americans turned to the federal courts. Any number of lawsuits were initiated in the hope that at least some judges would be unwilling to ignore a law whose provisions were so specific. In this, they were again mistaken. While in some rare instances the suits were successful, the vast majority were not. Some federal judges avoided the issue entirely, citing "an impending decision by the Supreme Court," even though the justices had not yet agreed to hear an appeal of the law.

Nor would they for five years. Then they would take an additional three years to issue a ruling. But during that time, the Court would not be idle. In a series of decisions, it would lay the groundwork for taking back from black people almost every right of citizenship that had been promised to them by the nation that had enslaved them.

The Uncertainty of Language

United States v. Reese

THAT THE RIGHT TO VOTE MIGHT NOT BE WHAT IT seemed began to come clear in April 1876, when the Supreme Court issued its first ruling that bore directly on the voting rights of African Americans.

In January 1873, William Garner, described by the Court as a "citizen of the United States of African descent," went to the tax collector in Lexington, Kentucky, to pay his poll tax of $1.50. Garner was employed, literate, and without a criminal record, and therefore could not be disqualified to vote in the state on any legal grounds. But the tax collector refused to take his money. Without a receipt for payment, Garner would be denied access to the ballot box in any election that year.

Tax collectors in Kentucky had come to regularly employ such a tactic to keep black men off the voting rolls. Garner next went to the office of the local election inspectors, Hiram Reese and Matthew Foushee, both white, and demanded a ballot for an upcoming municipal election.

Reese and Foushee refused, because, they said, Garner had failed to pay his poll tax. But Garner had come prepared and presented the two with an affidavit that he had attempted to pay the tax but had been turned away. The inspectors refused to accept the document.

That refusal just happened to be a specific violation of the Enforcement Act of 1870, which required all persons and officers in the electoral process "to give citizens of the United States the same and equal opportunity to . . . become qualified to vote without distinction of race, color, or previous condition of servitude." If an election official refused to allow any citizen to perform an "action required for voting," the citizen could present an affidavit that would qualify him.[1] Anyone convicted at trial—in federal, not state court—of denying equal access to the ballot box would be required to pay the person he wronged $500, and be liable for a jail term of up to one year.[2] Garner filed a complaint with federal officials asking those penalties be applied to both Reese and Foushee.

Garner's appearance at the tax collector's and election offices, as it turned out, had been part of a plan by Kentucky Republicans to ensure that black citizens were not turned away from the polls by white election officials. The local United States Attorney, G. C. Wharton, who had previously taken enormous risks by ignoring death threats and prosecuting Kuklux members, had set the plan in motion. He had been assured of federal support by the new attorney general, George Williams.

After their refusal to register Matthew Garner, Wharton obtained a three-count indictment against Reese and Foushee from a grand jury in Louisville, meaning the two would be forced to travel there in order to stand trial. The first and third counts referred specifically to Garner, but the second referred to the general practice of refusing black registrants without a receipt from the clerk, whether or not the applicant had attempted to pay the tax.

Reese and Foushee's lawyers were forced to resort to some creative hall-of-mirrors reasoning for their defense. "They claimed that Garner's mere offer to pay the tax was insufficient to discharge him from the statutory requirement of actually paying it . . . therefore the defendants lawfully refused to allow Garner to vote because of his failure to meet the statutory requirements for voting."[3] As such, their refusal to register Garner did not fall under the Enforcement Act, and therefore should not be in federal court.

United States v. Reese, as the case came to be known, became as much a political fight as a legal one. Democrats growled that Reese and Foushee were being persecuted, "dragged all the way to Louisville at great expense to themselves and to the government to stand trial before strangers rather than their neighbors."[4] Republicans countered that those "neighbors" would be all too happy to acquit two men who had blatantly broken the law in the name of white rule.

The government countered by assigning two special prosecutors, one of whom was a close friend of Wharton's and who would later make a name for himself as an associate justice of the Supreme Court—John Marshall Harlan. Harlan had run for governor of Kentucky as a Republican and, although he lost, amassed more votes than any Republican ever had.

The trial, in United States Circuit Court, soon focused on just how much power the federal government had to define election standards for state and local governments. That, in turn, became a question of language—just what, exactly, did the Fourteenth and Fifteenth Amendments say? The circuit judges could not agree on specifics, so the case was referred to the Supreme Court.

Although the roster of associate justices on the Court was the same as for the *Slaughter-House Cases*, there had been a significant change at the top. The universally respected Chief Justice Salmon P. Chase had died in May 1873 and been replaced by Morrison R. Waite, a man who was viewed quite differently. In fact, never had a chief justice reached the Court as a lower choice of the president who nominated him, or with less impressive credentials.

With Chase gone, Ulysses Grant came under pressure to appoint a replacement of equal stature and reputation. Some thought Grant would nominate one of the other justices—most of whom wanted the job— while others felt that he would ask a prominent lawyer to take the job, while still others insisted it would be a member of Congress.

But Grant dithered. Summer gave way to fall, but still the president refused to name a successor. With every passing week, the nation became more impatient. Democrats accused Grant of not caring enough about the most important court in the nation, while Republicans declared that he was taking his time so he could choose the best, most honorable, most qualified man available.

Instead, he chose one of his closest friends. In early November, Grant nominated Senator Roscoe Conkling of New York, a consummate political infighter, and also perhaps the most feared and powerful politician in the nation. Before submitting Conkling's name to the Senate, Grant wrote to him on November 8, 1873, to offer him the job. "When the Chief Justiceship became vacant, I immediately looked with anxiety to some one whose appointment would be recognized as entirely fitting and acceptable to the country at large. My own preference went to you at once."[5] This after waiting six months.

Roscoe Conkling was many things, but a fool was not one of them. Moving to the Supreme Court, even as chief justice, would diminish his vast power in government. He declined the appointment, a move many thought was fortunate for both the Court and the nation.

With Conkling unwilling to serve, Grant cast about for a replacement. On December 1, he again "stunned the nation" by nominating his attorney general, George Williams, who was almost immediately attacked as a "legal mediocrity" and "a weak if not corrupt politician."[6]

Democratic newspapers were fierce in their criticism—*The Brooklyn Daily Eagle* described Williams as "knowing little of all law and less than that little of the law requisite for the Government cases"—but a surprising number of the Republican newspapers were highly critical as well. *The Evansville Courier* observed, "Judicial positions in the United States at the present time seem to be going begging, and legal talent and judicial ability is a lamentably scarce commodity...Williams is, without doubt, an obscure lawyer...recognizable only as one of the White House flunkeys, and is about to reap the reward of the faithful servant in that connection."[7]

Republican senators showed their displeasure by sitting on their hands; they refused to vote and instead sent the nomination to the Judiciary Committee for "consideration." After weeks, an embarrassed George Williams asked the president to withdraw his name. He later justified his critics' assessment by being forced to resign as attorney general when his wife was accused of taking bribes so that Williams would drop a pending prosecution.

Grant then chose seventy-three-year-old Caleb Cushing, a man of high repute for intelligence, who had served as attorney general under Franklin Pierce. His sympathies were not totally clear, however. He would not have gone to war, even to keep the Union together, and certainly not to free slaves. He also had a reputation as a man who would "place political opportunity before principle."[8] But Cushing did not provoke strong opposition. Just when it appeared that President Grant had finally found a nominee that would be successfully confirmed, however, an "anonymous source" reported that in 1861, Cushing had sent a very friendly letter to Jefferson Davis, president of the Confederate States of America, accepting the split in the Union as "accomplished fact." Grant then found the letter itself and immediately withdrew Cushing's nomination.

Grant decided that his next nominee would have no trouble being confirmed, because he would choose someone no one in Washington had heard of. He found his man in Toledo, Ohio. George Williams observed that the new nominee was "supposed to be sufficiently obscure to meet the requirements of the occasion . . . at the time of his appointment had never held a federal office, had never argued a case in the Supreme Court, and was comparatively unknown in Washington."[9]

This was Morrison R. Waite. A successful lawyer who had occasionally appeared at the fringes of politics—the one time he ran for office, he lost—he was so surprised when he received the telegram informing him of his nomination that he had to confirm its veracity. To those few who had heard of him, Waite was unimpressive. Lincoln's secretary of the navy, Gideon Welles, remarked of Waite that "It is a wonder that Grant did not pick up some old acquaintance, who was a stage driver or bartender, for the place."[10] *The Nation* added, "Mr. Waite stands in the front rank of second rank lawyers."[11] Perhaps because Congress was now too fatigued to object, Waite was unanimously confirmed and took his seat on March 4, 1874.

He was not greeted warmly by his fellow justices. Not only had they been passed over for the seat Waite now held, but most of them regarded their new boss as an undeserving plodder. The only one of his colleagues who extended Waite any courtesy was Joseph Bradley, who invited the new chief justice and his wife to dinner their first night in the nation's capital. It was to be a friendship of enormous consequence for the nation.

Bradley, who had been on the Court since 1870, was everything Waite was not. He was considered one of the most technically proficient legal scholars ever to occupy a seat on the high bench, yet where Waite was affable and social, Bradley was introverted and described himself as "cold and stoical; willing to do favors without caring for the objects of them, and willing to receive them without making very intemperate demonstrations of gratitude."[12] Other than mathematics and chess, he had almost no outside interests. A dour, meticulous man with a love of mathematics and an obsession with order, detail, and punctuality, Bradley had "an extreme interest in control over his environment" and was "unconcerned with people, social life, or material rewards. His views tended to be rigid and at times narrow."[13]

But it would be difficult to describe Bradley better than he described himself. He recounted to one of his few friends, Cortland Parker, the rigorous routine of rising, eating, working, and going to bed at precisely the same time every day.

My habits are these: having sat up till 12 or thereabouts, I don't rise till 7. I then drink a glass of camomile water—dress, etc. and at 7 1/2 go into my study across the hall, and put on a pot of coffee (which is saved for me the day before) on the gas, and when hot—fill a large cup having cream and sugar in it—and drink it. Whilst drinking my coffee, an egg is boiling in the same gas jet—which I next dispose of. At 8, I am ready to go to work. At 9, I go down to family breakfast, and eat just one heaping tablespoon of mush (oatmeal, wheaten grits, or fine hominy) with cream and sugar, and return to my study. At 11 1/2 get into the coupe or carriage and go to the court which sits from 12 to 4. Return by 4 1/2 and lounge or take a walk, and dine at 6, generally light, on mutton, poultry, etc. I often take lunch at court about 2—of 6 broiled oysters, or a bowl of milk with a cracker or two. After dinner I return to my study, and generally work or read till midnight often topping it off with a glass of whiskey and water.[14]

Just weeks after Morrison Waite took his seat, Bradley turned that logic, thoroughness, and attention to detail to the language of the Fifteenth Amendment, the very question that would lie at the core of *United States v. Reese.*

In those days, each Supreme Court justice also "rode circuit," spending part of the year as a judge in United States Circuit Court in a specific part of the nation. Bradley's assigned territory included Louisiana, and there he sat in on an explosive case stemming from what would become known as the Colfax Massacre.

On Easter Sunday, April 13, 1873, upwards of 150 heavily armed white men, most on horseback, some dragging a four-pound cannon, converged on the courthouse of Colfax, seat of Grant Parish, in central Louisiana. In and around the courthouse were approximately 150 black defenders, also armed, but with antiquated, barely functioning shotguns, awaiting the invasion behind hastily constructed barricades. The confrontation had been precipitated by a disputed gubernatorial election in which both the Republican, a carpetbagger, and the Democrat, a former Confederate officer, had been declared the winner. The issue was decided in the Republican-controlled courts with a predictable outcome.

After the white men besieged the courthouse, whether they offered terms of surrender was never totally clear. Once the shooting started, however, it became apparent that the outgunned African American defenders had no chance. In short order, they gave up. After their weapons had been confiscated, the white invaders proceeded to slaughter their captives. As many as one hundred black men were shot, stabbed, or burned to death in the courthouse. Afterward, the whites claimed the blacks had fired on them after the surrender, killing a Captain Hadnot, but that seemed unlikely since the bullet that killed Hadnot had entered at an angle that could only have come from friendly fire.

Aware that Louisiana, even under a Republican governor, might not respond energetically to the killings, the federal government moved to charge members of the band with conspiracy under the very same Enforcement Act of 1870 that was used in *Reese*. In this case, the charges came under a part of the law that applied criminal penalties to activities that could be seen as interfering with the exercise of a person's constitutional rights. Ninety-eight of the white invaders were charged with banding together with the intent of depriving the black men of their First Amendment right of free assembly. Only three men were convicted, and they appealed in circuit court, where Justice Bradley had decided to participate.

The three convicted murderers had based their appeal on the wording of the Fourteenth Amendment, which said no *state* could deprive any person of life, liberty, or property without due process of law, or deny any person equal protection of the laws. That meant, they claimed, that the amendment did not apply to the behavior of ordinary citizens, and that the Enforcement Act—which applied to individuals and not states—exceeded the federal government's authority. Controlling the behavior of individuals—prosecuting "ordinary crimes"—was solely the responsibility of state governments.

Justice Bradley's response would alter the course of American history.

There were occasions, Bradley wrote, in which the federal government could control the behavior of private citizens, but some very specific conditions had to be met. The only time the federal government could pass "positive laws" to protect individual rights was if that right did not exist before the Constitution defined it. The notion of "new rights" versus "old rights" was as confusing to most lawyers as to everyone else, so to illustrate his point, Bradley gave some examples.

One was the Fifteenth Amendment.

"The Fifteenth Amendment confers *no right to vote*," Bradley wrote.

"That is the exclusive prerogative of the states. It does confer a right not to be excluded from voting by reason of race, color or previous condition of servitude, and this is all the right that Congress can enforce."[15]

Bradley's pivot was precisely what Bingham and Sumner had feared, and totally changed both the amendment's meaning and its potential as a tool for the federal government to protect black voters. Under Bradley's definition, if an African American was threatened, beaten, and his house burned to the ground in order to terrorize him into not voting, and the state refused to prosecute the offenders, the federal government could do nothing, unless the victim could prove that the actions were motivated only by race. He had therefore transferred the burden of proof from the state, to demonstrate it had not discriminated, to the individual whose right to vote had been denied, to demonstrate it had. That task was difficult enough, but it also had the potential, which was realized, to become virtually impossible depending on the standard of proof the Court would require.

In this one opinion, Joseph Bradley had strangled the equal rights guarantees of not one but two constitutional amendments. He also freed the three murderers, leaving the government to appeal to the Supreme Court, where they would again argue the case before, among others, Justice Bradley. That case, *United States v. Cruikshank*, would be decided the same day as *United States v. Reese*. If Bradley's reasoning held up in Supreme Court, it would establish a precedent that all lower courts would be required to follow.

Which was precisely what occurred on March 27, 1876. Although Morrison Waite would write both opinions, each came from the cold, measured mind of Joseph Bradley.

In *Cruikshank*, Waite wrote, "The fourteenth amendment prohibits a State from depriving any person of life, liberty, or property, without due process of law; but this adds nothing to the rights of one citizen as against another." Waite added that the First Amendment right of assembly "was not intended to limit the powers of the State governments in respect to their own citizens, but to operate upon the National Government alone." As a result, "for their protection in its enjoyment ... the people must look to the States. The power for that purpose was originally placed there, and it has never been surrendered to the United States."[16] So, despite what the drafters of the amendment had intended and what those ratifying the amendment thought they were agreeing to, the Bill of Rights applied to the federal government only, not the states.

In *Reese*, Waite lifted Bradley's language almost verbatim. "The Fifteenth Amendment to the Constitution does not confer the right of suffrage, but it invests citizens of the United States with the right of exemption from discrimination in the exercise of the elective franchise on account of their race, color, or previous condition of servitude, and empowers Congress to enforce that right by 'appropriate legislation.'"[17] From there, the question became what Congress may or may not do to enforce the amendment. "The power of Congress to legislate at all upon the subject of voting at state elections rests upon this amendment, and can be exercised by providing a punishment only when the wrongful refusal to receive the vote of a qualified elector at such elections is because of his race, color, or previous condition of servitude." And because the third and fourth sections of the Enforcement Act of 1870 were not "confined in their operation to unlawful discrimination on account of race, color, or previous condition of servitude," they were "beyond the limit of the Fifteenth Amendment and unauthorized."

And so the rule of "state action" passed into the jurisprudence. Neither decision was criticized at the time, since it seemed that the language was straightforward enough and matched the wording of the amendment. But dig a bit deeper and the notion becomes a good deal fuzzier. What, for example, constitutes the "state"? According to Bradley and Waite, it was a sort of disembodied entity, a product, words of a statute printed in law books. For if they expanded that definition to include people, such as the legislators or the governor who had approved such a law, how could not they also include those acting in the name of the state to administer it, like Reese and Foushee? But if they had accepted Reese and Foushee as state actors, they, as individuals, could not deny any person equal protection of the laws or due process of the law without running afoul of the Fourteenth Amendment. In other words, regardless of the statute they were administering, state actors would be forbidden to transgress the amendment's guarantees. All of which would have made the Enforcement Act of 1870 constitutional after all.

To take the notion even further, does "state action" include "nonaction," meaning if a state or any state actor refuses to protect its citizens, regardless of their color, are they then denying "persons" their Fourteenth and perhaps Fifteenth Amendment guarantees? In *Cruikshank*, did Louisiana's refusal to act against the murderers grant the federal government the right to do so as a civil rights violation? There was nothing in either the amendments or the statutes to prevent the Court from choosing these interpretations rather than the more restrictive ones they did.

And so, while Waite and especially Bradley seemed simply to be applying cold, hard logic in *Reese* and *Cruikshank*, they were actually taking a subjective stance that by coincidence fell on the side of that era's racial attitudes, and their own. In doing so, they enabled not only the intimidation and violence by which African Americans had been denied their rights, but also the contrivance and fraud that white supremacists had begun to turn to in order to achieve the same ends by less obvious and offensive means.

There were those who questioned the decisions, but their voices were not heard. In 1879, a Department of Justice attorney stationed in South Carolina wrote,

> I have been forced by the unfortunate condition here, to give to *Reese et al* and *Cruickshank et al* my severest study. I made last spring a careful abstract with notes of these and all kindred cases and came to the conclusion then, which is much stronger now, that with the single exception of a few sections, relating to the election of federal officers, the federal election laws are a delusion and farce . . . [If white vigilantes] . . . break up meetings by violence, there is no remedy, unless it can be proved to have been done on account of race, etc., which can't be proved . . . With colored men crowding my office, it is hard to make them understand my utter helplessness.[18]

9

Rutherfraud Ascends,
but Not Equal Rights

T O THE SURPRISE OF BOTH HIS SUPPORTERS AND HIS
detractors, Ulysses Grant decided not to run for a third term
in 1876. In Grant's place, Republicans nominated Rutherford
B. Hayes, a former Union army general who after the war became a congressman and then a "reform" governor of Ohio. Democrats chose a reformer of their own, Governor Samuel Tilden of New York, who had
successfully attacked the almost impossibly corrupt Tammany Hall political machine run by William Magear "Boss" Tweed.

Hayes ran as all Republicans had, as a friend to black Americans. He
felt he had little choice. Without the black vote in the South, he appeared
to have no chance of being elected. But while Hayes was pledging to
maintain the social advances of Reconstruction, Tilden aimed his appeal
at "white Southerners who sought to recapture the control of their state
governments from Republican carpetbaggers and from newly free African Americans."[1] If Tilden were elected, white Southerners knew, he
would surely withdraw the army from the South.

When the ballots were counted, Tilden had won the popular vote easily and could solidly claim 184 electoral votes, one short of the number needed for election. Hayes could claim only 165. Twenty electoral votes had yet to be assigned, nineteen of which were in Florida, Louisiana, and South Carolina, three of the four secessionist states still under Republican control. Still, Tilden was generally assumed to have won each of the three, since, in what originally seemed a surprise but should not have been, he had won every other state in the South. (Hayes had won in the Midwest and West, and so the contested electoral vote in Oregon was almost certain to be his.)

But soon reports began to drift in that throughout the South, black voters had been intimidated, brutalized, or denied the right to vote. Fraud had been everywhere, with ballot boxes stuffed with nonexistent Democratic votes, and Republican votes destroyed. Although the violence was not new, this was the first presidential election in which fraud seemed to have been the dominant tactic among white supremacist Democrats. Still, no matter how he achieved it, if even one of these disputed electoral votes went to Tilden—and just by the count, he certainly seemed entitled to some of them—he would be the new president.

Almost every newspaper in America reported Tilden as the winner. *The New York Times*, however, which on the day before the election had proclaimed "Republican Success Certain," ran a different headline the day after the election: "Result Still Uncertain."[2] During the Civil War, the *Times'* managing editor, John C. Reid, had been held as a prisoner at the infamous Andersonville prison, and he despised Democrats. On election night, Reid convinced local Republican leaders to contest the election even though Tilden seemed to have won.[3] The New Yorkers telegraphed fellow Republicans, telling them to dispute the results in any Southern state where Tilden's victory might be overturned. Official challenges were filed in Louisiana, Florida, and South Carolina.

The next day, the *Times* reported, "The Battle Won. Governor Hayes Elected—The Republicans Carry Twenty-one States, Casting 185 Electoral Votes."[4] To get to 185, the *Times* had awarded all three states' electors to Hayes. The article claimed to be based on canvasses, although the *Times* was vague on just who had done the canvassing.

Canvassing boards were indeed appointed in each state by the sitting Republican governments, although not until after the *Times* ran its piece. Staffed largely by party hacks—former Attorney General George Williams served on the Florida board—it came as no surprise when each state confirmed what the *Times* had reported and declared Hayes the winner.

Democrats were furious. The party that was all too happy to win as a result of fraud felt differently about losing because of it. Very real threats of armed revolt spread throughout Washington. Militias were raised in the countryside and calls for secession were heard for the first time since the war. A shot was fired at Hayes's home in Ohio while the candidate was having dinner inside.

Nothing in the Constitution or federal law discussed what to do in such a situation, but both sides knew they had to do something. Eventually, they decided to appoint a fifteen-man Electoral Commission—five senators, five representatives, and five Supreme Court justices. Fourteen would be members of the two parties, divided equally, and the fifteenth would be someone both sides agreed would judge the issue on its merits only. Almost certainly, this meant that one man would choose the next president of the United States. Anyone who had previously voiced even a whisper of preference for the Democrats or the Republicans would be unacceptable to the other party. With both sides almost ready to go to war, many doubted that such a man even existed.

But incredibly, that man *did* seem to exist. Even better, he was available. He was Associate Justice David Davis. A Lincoln appointee, he was so trusted as an independent that it was said, "No one, perhaps not even Davis himself, knew which presidential candidate he preferred."[5]

After Davis had been named, however, Democrats decided that they were not all *that* comfortable with the Republican-appointed justice, so they thought to shift the odds a bit. Before the commission could meet, the Democratic-controlled state legislature in Illinois offered Davis a vacant seat in the United States Senate. Republican newspapers denounced this transparent attempt to butter up the swing vote. Both sides assumed Davis would decline the seat and remain on the Court, but that the honor of being named senator just might help tip his vote toward Tilden.

But then, confounding everyone, Davis accepted. He resigned his seat on the Court to be senator from Illinois. He never said why, but he clearly did not want the responsibility of selecting a president by himself.

Since four of the justices were already on the commission, one of the remaining four would be forced to take Davis's place. Each was closely associated with one of the political parties. For reasons never made public, Joseph Bradley was the man chosen. Democrats denounced the choice as a fix, but after the Davis fiasco, their credibility was strained. Bradley, who did not share Davis's hesitancy, accepted the appointment and thus became the only man in American history empowered to choose a president essentially on his own.

Bradley, ever careful and meticulous, and proud of both his objectivity and his intellect, drew up a detailed written opinion for each man. But Joseph Bradley was one of those people who, after careful consideration of the facts, always seemed to come down on the side of a question that matched the beliefs he held going in. And so it was here. Bradley chose Hayes.

Democrats' fury was renewed. Some once more threatened rebellion. Rumors circulated that an army of 100,000 men was prepared to march on the capital to prevent "Rutherfraud" or "His Fraudulency" from being sworn in. In the House of Representatives, Democrats began a filibuster to prevent Hayes's inauguration.

What happened next has been a subject of debate among historians ever since. The most widely accepted version is the simplest and the most likely. "Reasonable men in both parties struck a bargain at Wormley's Hotel. There, in the traditional smoke-filled room, emissaries of Hayes agreed to abandon the Republican state governments in Louisiana and South Carolina while southern Democrats agreed to abandon the filibuster and thus trade off the presidency in exchange for the end of Reconstruction."[6] The "Compromise of 1877," as it came to be known, made Rutherford B. Hayes the nineteenth president of the United States. As one of his first orders of business, the man who had run for president promising to defend the civil rights of black Americans ordered federal troops withdrawn from the South. Without the army to enforce fair voting, the intimidation, murder, and fraud that had come to characterize Southern elections could proceed undeterred.

When the soldiers marched out of the South, they took Reconstruction with them.

A Slight Case of Murder

The Strange Journey of *Strauder v. West Virginia*

O N FRIDAY, APRIL 19, 1872, BOTH NEWSPAPERS IN Wheeling, West Virginia, featured stories describing the same lurid event. The headline in the *Daily Intelligencer* read, "Horrible Murder. A Colored Woman Tomahawked by Her Husband. He Brains Her with a Hatchet. The Murderer Escapes." Not to be outdone, the competing *Daily Register* wrote, "A Deliberate and Brutal Murder. A Negro Kills His Wife with a Hatchet. A Sickening Sight. Escape of the Murderer. Inquest and Testimony."[1]

The circumstances of the crime were reported to be straightforward. Taylor Strauder, a local carpenter who appeared to be a hardworking and otherwise law-abiding citizen, had, without provocation, savagely murdered the woman he had married only months before. The heinous act had been witnessed by nine-year-old Fanny Green, Anna Strauder's daughter by a previous marriage. "Taylor Strauder killed my mother with a hatchet," she told the coroner's jury. "He struck her two times on the head with it; my mother was sitting on the rocking chair; Taylor Strauder was sitting on the lounge just back of her, and I was lying on the lounge; he asked mother where his shoes were, she said they were where he had left them last night, and he picked up the hatchet and struck her." Then, according to the girl, Strauder had fled. Sheriff's deputies testified the fugitive was nowhere to be found.

It was not long before details of another motive began to leak out. Strauder, acquaintances said, was an extremely jealous man who had made the mistake of marrying a woman who was energetically unfaithful. He had been out drinking the night of the murder and was taunted by a companion who had heard stories of Anna's proclivities. When Strauder arrived home, already in a foul mood, he heard the back door of the cottage in which he lived slam shut as he was entering through the front. He later claimed to have glimpsed a white man hurrying from the house. Once inside, he accused his wife of entertaining other men, and the two fought nearly all night. Early the following morning, the fight resumed. Finally, rather than continue to deny her husband's accusations, she allegedly turned to him from her rocking chair and said, "What are you going to do about it?" Moments later, the hatchet fell across Anna Strauder's temple.

A careful search of the area was unsuccessful in revealing Strauder's whereabouts, so a reward of $200 was posted for his capture. Wheeling, the seat of Ohio County, is set on a narrow spit of land wedged between Pennsylvania and Ohio, so the manhunt was conducted in all three states. Strauder was described as "a very light mulatto: about 32 years of age: about 5 feet and 10 inches in stature and stoutly built. He has a rather spare face, with high cheek bones, and wore when last seen here a scattering beard on his chin."[2] Less than one week later, he was apprehended in Pittsburgh, although whether he had been caught or had given himself up remained unclear. He was returned to Wheeling, jailed, assigned a lawyer, and left for what everyone expected to be a brief wait until the judicial system dispensed with him.

But what neither Taylor Strauder nor any of the law enforcement personnel, lawyers, judges, or jurors who would be involved in this case could have known was that the murder of Anna Strauder would not only set in motion an incredible three-decade odyssey for the accused, but also set the scene for what has been called one of the most important voting rights decisions in American history.

*   *   *

Taylor Strauder proved to be a cooperative and affable prisoner, popular with both the guards and the other inmates. He made no trouble, did not issue hollow protests of innocence, was devoid of self-pity, and seemed resigned to meeting "the Great Judge," as he phrased it. As further word of Anna Strauder's infidelities made the rounds, Ohio County authorities decided not to rush to bring her killer to trial, but to let him remain in jail rather than hang. But West Virginia had a law stipulating that anyone accused of a crime who, after indictment, remained in prison without trial for three sessions of the circuit court would go free. The sessions commenced in May and October, so it was not until the third of these, the May 1873 term, that Strauder was actually brought before a judge. The lawyer originally assigned to defend him had died in a gas lamp explosion, so the firm of Davenport and Dovener became the new defense counsel.

George Davenport was a veteran and highly respected trial lawyer, but he assigned his junior partner, Blackburn B. Dovener, thirty-one years old, to plead the case. Dovener had just recently been admitted to the bar, and this would be his first experience in state circuit court. He was a staunch Republican who had left his native Virginia to fight for the Union. Dovener had entered the army as a private, raised a company of soldiers while still a teenager, and during the conflict had been promoted to captain. After his discharge, he had briefly captained a riverboat before turning to the law.

Perhaps because he wanted to impress in his first court case, Dovener attacked the Strauder case as if he were charging the Confederate lines at Chancellorsville. He immediately made a motion to remove the trial to federal court. In March 1873, West Virginia had passed a law that stated, "All white male persons who are twenty-one years of age and who are citizens of this State shall be liable to serve as jurors, except as herein provided," the exceptions being state officials. Dovener argued that restricting the jury to whites violated the equal protection clause of the Fourteenth Amendment. His motion to remove the case was denied.

On May 9, 1873, Taylor Strauder was found guilty of first-degree murder and sentenced to be hanged. Local newspapers, aware that the case was by then familiar to their readers, were forced to create an even more bloodthirsty version of the crime, little of which bore any relation to the truth, but which made calls for Strauder's speedy execution that much more insistent.

Within three months after their marriage, he attempted to force her into the cellar of their house that he might cut her throat with a razor. Because of his bad treatment of her, she had determined to leave him and apply for a divorce. He is reported to have said, "If you can't live with me you shall never marry any one else. I will kill you first." The night before the murder, Strauder went home about 11 o'clock. Finding a child of his wife's, by her first husband, in the bed, he threw it out on the floor, and a quarrel ensued, whether about the child or on account of his accusing her of infidelity will never be known; at any rate they quarreled, and on the morning of Thursday, April 18, 1872, when they arose from their bed, he asking her some question in regard to his shoes and, receiving an answer that seems to have soured him, he seized a hatchet, and with the pole or head of it, struck her once on the temple and once behind the left ear. The little daughter of the woman, awakened by the noise, saw the terrible deed. She attempted to scream, but Strauder threatened to kill her too if she made any outcry. The poor little thing frightened half to death was compelled by him to lie down on her couch and cover up her head in the bedclothes, thus giving him a chance to escape. After a while, it must have seemed to her an age, she uncovered her head and found her stepfather gone. Jumping out of bed, she ran to her mother, whom she saw leaning over the arms of a rocking chair speechless and the crimson tide flowing from her wounded head, and said, "Mamma, hold up your head; then, maybe, it won't hurt you." She was only seven years old, and could not realize that her mother was dead. Strauder, in the meantime, fled.[3]

Two weeks later, Dovener was back in court, submitting motions to gain Strauder a new trial. Although he maintained the Fourteenth Amendment argument, he and Davenport had added other exceptions, one of which was a claim that one of the jurors was not a United States citizen and another that one of the jurors had expressed an opinion on Strauder's guilt. The motions were denied and Strauder was given an August 29, 1873, date for his execution. Dovener, to the outrage of many in the community, once again announced his intention to appeal.

During the delay, Strauder remained fodder for local news, and the tone of the reporting began to change. While awaiting his fate, he was reported to have undergone a spiritual conversion. In July, "the pastor of the 5th Street African Methodist Church and several of the members of that congregation visited the jail on Sunday evening and administered the rite of baptism ... Afterwards they engaged in devotional services ... Jailer Kennedy informs us that the condemned man deeply feels his position and that Strauder is misunderstood."[4]

Strauder, by then the longest tenured prisoner in the Ohio County jail, had also come to be on such good terms with his jailers and local deputies that they openly advocated that the man who had cleaved in his wife's skull with a hatchet be allowed to live. Two weeks before his execution date, Dovener succeeded in getting a stay pending his motions for a new trial. The state supreme court would make the ruling, but not until January 1874. On August 29, a newspaper ran a small item about the execution under the heading, "Not today."[5]

As it turned out, not in January 1874 either. With Taylor Strauder now seemingly a permanent tenant of the county jail, the state supreme court adjourned the matter until July. Then, in what was a surprise to all parties, none more so than Taylor Strauder, the court agreed with his lawyers, and on July 21 sent the case back to circuit court for retrial. They did so not on constitutional grounds, but rather due to a procedural error by the prosecutors in filing the charges.[6] In September, Strauder's attorneys moved to have him released as three court terms had passed. When that was denied, the case went once more to a grand jury, which returned a second indictment in October. On November 5, 1874, Strauder was once again convicted of first-degree murder and sentenced to hang, and just as quickly Blackburn Dovener was back in court, petitioning for a new trial.

It remains unclear why Dovener—and Davenport, who had by this time become active in the case—displayed such tenacity for an ax murderer who had not denied that he had committed the crime of which he was accused and had been tried for it and convicted twice. At this stage, there was no indication they were intending a constitutional test—their appeals were based almost entirely on procedural challenges—nor were they being paid to drag the process out. It may have been simply that these two lawyers believed fervently in the canons of their profession and that every possibility of saving their client must be exhausted before they gave up.

In January 1875, their petition was denied, and Strauder was yet again given a date of execution, this time March 26. He took the news placidly, as always, and was the object of great sympathy from jail personnel with whom he had by then been associated for almost three years. But sympathy was tempered with uncertainty. As late as early March, one newspaper reported that bets were being taken on whether or not the sentence would be carried out.[7] Sure enough, the very next week, a state supreme court judge granted a stay of execution, pending a decision on appeals by the defendant.

From there, the appeals went back and forth for almost two years, never resolving, never prompting a new trial, a West Virginia version of *Bleak House*'s *Jarndyce v. Jarndyce*. All the while, Taylor Strauder remained in the Ohio County jail, not free, but not especially restrained

either. Three days before Christmas 1876, the Ohio County commissioners made their annual inspection of the jail, accompanied by reporters. As
they opened the door, "Immediately a colored man came out of one of the
cells to the left and approached the barred door. The turnkey handed him
a key, which he took and proceeded to lock up in their cells the prisoners
who were sauntering idly about taking their regular afternoon exercise.
The prisoners all safely in their cells, the colored man returned to the
door and handed back the key."

"The colored man," the reporter observed, "was no other than Taylor
Strauder, the noted wife murderer, [who] appeared to be well acquainted
with the party, and a great favorite as well, as he shook hands cordially all
around and conversed freely with them."

Time, apparently, had also softened the community's outrage.

> Poor Strauder! He has been a prisoner for nearly five years, and yet his
> fate is as uncertain as upon the dreadful day when he committed the
> bloody deed for which he is held to answer . . . During his incarceration
> he has earned the confidence and esteem of the officers of the prison,
> and is a valuable assistant to the turnkey in the discharge of his various
> duties, he has always behaved himself in an exemplary manner, and is
> treated by his fellow prisoners with the utmost respect.[8]

He had also taught himself to read and write and mentioned that he
intended to write a book about his experience as a prisoner.

By June 1877, with no movement in the case, some began to argue
for Strauder to be granted clemency, but none was forthcoming. Finally,
in November, the state supreme court denied each of the myriad motions
that Davenport and Dovener had made, including one that asked the
trial be removed to federal court due to discrimination in jury selection.
Finally, the question that would become the basis for the constitutional
challenge was put into focus. The court wrote, "A prisoner is not entitled
to have a case removed into the U.S. Circuit Court for trial upon his
petition supported by affidavit setting forth that he is a colored man, and

that such prejudices exist in the State against his race that he cannot get justice in the State Courts, and that also by a law of the State only white men can get upon the jury."[9] The court instructed the case be returned to circuit court for reimposition of sentence. George Davenport immediately filed notice that he would apply to remove the case to the United States Supreme Court on Fourteenth Amendment grounds.

Four months later, the Court had not decided whether to take the case, and the circuit court had dallied in imposing a new sentence. Sentiment against hanging Strauder had grown in the community, so even if he was condemned, "a strong effort will be made to have the Governor commute his sentence."[10] Before that could happen, however, on April 15, 1878, Morrison Waite announced that the Supreme Court would hear the appeal. Ten days later, Taylor Strauder, now a local celebrity, marked his sixth anniversary as a prisoner in the county jail, the longest any inmate had ever been incarcerated in that facility. He even petitioned the county for $150 to help defray the cost of Davenport and Dovener's upcoming trip to Washington, but the county commissioners turned him down, albeit with some reluctance.

Strauder v. West Virginia was not heard until October 1879, but it was billed as one of the most important cases regarding African American civil rights ever heard by the Supreme Court. To add to the drama, United States Attorney General Charles Devens, a former Union army general who had served with Grant, had joined the Strauder team to prosecute the appeal, and Senator John Brown Gordon of Georgia, a former Confederate general who had served with Lee, would aid the state attorney general in defending it.

The decision would not be handed down for some months, but in the interim it was reported in January 1880 that "Taylor Strauder has improved the leisure of his confinement in jail in writing another book."[11] No record of any such writings exist.

On March 1, 1880, the Court finally rendered its verdict. By a 7–2 vote, the justices ruled that Strauder's conviction would be overturned because he had been deprived of equal protection of the laws as guaranteed to him under the Fourteenth Amendment.

William Strong wrote the opinion. Born in Connecticut and raised in Pennsylvania, Strong was an abolitionist Democrat who had switched to the Republican Party in 1858 to support the candidacy of Abraham Lincoln. He served on the Pennsylvania Supreme Court after the war, and when Edwin Stanton died four days after being confirmed to the Court in December 1869, he was appointed by Ulysses Grant to take his place. Strong prided himself on being a man of principle—he would resign in perfect health in December 1880 to set an example for other justices who remained on the Court even though faculties were diminished. Strong lived until 1895.

Despite his abolitionist credentials, Strong's record left his commitment to equal rights suspect. In 1872, in *Blyew v. United States*, he took a narrow view of the Civil Rights Act of 1866 to free two white men who had been convicted in Kentucky of murdering a black family with an ax. One of the victims, a woman in her eighties, was blind. Kentucky had a law that did not allow blacks to testify against whites, but the principal witness against the killers was the seventeen-year-old son of the murdered family who identified them on his deathbed, and said that one of the men had said "he intended to go on killing niggers."[12]

As a result, the trial took place in federal court, since the Civil Rights Act of 1866 stipulated

that the district courts of the United States, within their respective districts, shall have, exclusively of the courts of the several States, cognizance of all crimes and offences committed against the provisions of this act, and also, concurrently with the circuit courts of the United States, of all causes, civil and criminal, affecting persons who are denied or cannot enforce in the courts or judicial tribunals of the State or locality where they may be any of the rights secured to them by . . . this act.

Those rights included "to make and enforce contracts, to sue, be parties, and *give evidence*, to inherit, purchase, lease, sell, hold, and convey real and personal property, and to full and equal benefit of all laws and proceedings for the security of person and property, as is enjoyed by white citizens."[13] The specific purpose of the act, about which there was no misunderstanding, was to protect newly freed slaves from what might be oppressive state laws or discriminatory application. The Blyew murder case would have seemed just the sort of discriminatory behavior for which the law had been passed.

Justice Strong, however, did not agree. He chose to interpret the phrase "affecting persons who are denied or cannot enforce in the courts or judicial tribunals of the State or locality" to preclude *victims* of crimes and apply only to those *accused* of crimes. "Obviously the only parties to such a cause are the government and the persons indicted," he wrote. "They alone can be reached by any judgment that may be pronounced." With this interpretation, Strong was able to then say that obviously discriminatory state legislation did not come under the purview of a law enacted precisely to deal with discriminatory state legislation. Blyew and the other murderer went free.

In his *Strauder* opinion, Strong opened with an important distinction.

> It is to be observed that the first of these questions is not whether a colored man, when an indictment has been preferred against him, has a right to a grand or a petit jury composed in whole or in part of persons of his own race or color, but it is whether, in the composition or selection of juror by whom he is to be indicted or tried, all persons of his race or color may be excluded by law solely because of their race or color, so that by no possibility can any colored man sit upon the jury.[14]

Citing the *Slaughter-House Cases*, he also was careful to point out for what reason the Fourteenth Amendment was adopted.

This is one of a series of constitutional provisions having a common purpose—namely, securing to a race recently emancipated, a race that, through many generations, had been held in slavery, all the civil rights that the superior race enjoy . . . At the time when they were incorporated into the Constitution, it required little knowledge of human nature to anticipate that those who had long been regarded as an inferior and subject race would, when suddenly raised to the rank of citizenship, be looked upon with jealousy and positive dislike, and that State laws might be enacted or enforced to perpetuate the distinctions that had before existed, discriminations against them had been habitual.

Strong then gave his view on white America's obligations. "The colored race, as a race, was abject and ignorant, and in that condition [slavery] was unfitted to command the respect of those who had superior intelligence. Their training had left them mere children, and, as such, they needed the protection which a wise government extend to those who are unable to protect themselves."

From here, Strong could have gone in either direction—that the West Virginia statute was in violation of the Fourteenth Amendment, or that it was reasonable given black jurors' inability to make the judgments necessary to arrive at a fair verdict. He chose the first.

The very fact that colored people are singled out and expressly denied by a statute all right to participate in the administration of the law as jurors because of their color, though they are citizens and may be in other respects fully qualified, is practically a brand upon them affixed by the law, an assertion of their inferiority, and a stimulant to that race prejudice which is an impediment to securing to individuals of the race that equal justice which the law aims to secure to all others.

Taylor Strauder's conviction was therefore overturned. Justices Field and Clifford dissented on the grounds that the Fourteenth Amendment's protections applied only to "civil rights," not "political rights," to which, according to Field and Clifford, jury composition belonged. Political rights, Field insisted, were the province of state governments alone. Whether or not there was an objective dividing point in the hazy distinction between civil and political rights would be pivotal in the coming decades.

★ ★ ★

Now that Strauder was again back on their hands, West Virginia officials were left with the question of what to do with him. Fanny Green, the only prosecution witness who could testify directly to the crime, was now seventeen and was certain to be attacked ferociously by Blackburn Dovener if she were called as witness. Dovener had protested from the first that the girl had been coached, and he was almost certainly correct.

Even if the state did opt for a retrial, the case had to clear hurdles in federal circuit court, where Dovener petitioned to have Strauder released on a writ of habeas corpus, or at least freed on bail while Ohio County officials decided whether to retry him. That process dragged on for a year, until finally, on April 30, 1881, Judge J. J. Jackson ordered Strauder freed. But even that did not end the matter. As he walked out of the courtroom, he was once again arrested. West Virginia had decided to try him again after all.

Strauder's reaction was hardly one of surprise. As he stepped off the train with his captor,

> looking very well . . . dressed neatly and tastefully," he said, "Yes sir, I am here again, and under arrest, but this don't amount to anything. There wasn't any use in arresting me no how, as I intended to come right here as soon as ever I got free. Did it surprise me any? Not a bit. I 'spected it all the time. I knew of the intention of the parties here shortly after they made the move. Do I feel uneasy? Not a bit. The trou-

ble has all been gone over once, and I don't think I should have to use the same gauntlet again. I feel sure that I shall be free in a few days.[15]

And so he was. Three days later, he was taken before a justice of the peace and discharged.

The following year, Strauder got married again, this time to Minnie Johnson, a woman, possibly white, he had met while he was in jail. Minnie Johnson died three years later—of natural causes—while Strauder seems to have been away, on the job as a riverboat carpenter. Taylor Strauder then slipped from public view.

For Blackburn Dovener, it was the reverse. Regardless of where one stood on the particulars of the case, *Strauder v. West Virginia* was a legal triumph. Dovener became one of his state's most sought-after attorneys. Just two years after he secured Strauder's final release, Dovener was elected to the West Virginia state legislature, and in 1894 to Congress, representing West Virginia's First District, where he would serve for six terms.

But Dovener was not yet through with Taylor Strauder. In April 1898, with Dovener now a respected national figure, his erstwhile client was back in the news.

> Taylor Strauder, known as Andrew E. Strauder, shot and probably fatally wounded Ida Houston, his white sister-in-law, tonight. She in turn shot him in the forehead, neck and shoulder, and he may die. Strauder was separated from his wife, Katherine Strauder, a few months ago, she refusing to live with him when she heard he had murdered his first wife in Wheeling. He demanded admittance to her home, at 5 Arthur Street tonight, was refused and then forced the door in. He fired two shots at Mrs. Strauder, neither taking effect and the Houston woman then rushed to a trunk and secured a revolver. Just as she was about to fire, Strauder fired three times at her, one bullet entering the abdomen. The wounded woman emptied her revolver at Strauder, three shots taking effect. The life of the woman is almost despaired of, and physicians fear Strauder's wounds will end in death.[16]

The article also noted that Strauder, who had actually been married three times, was an extremely jealous man who suspected his wife of infidelity.

Word of Strauder's arrest and imminent death rekindled interest in his earlier trials. Dovener, by now reluctant for the public to be reminded that, because of his efforts, a murderer had gone free, granted an exclusive interview to the *Wheeling Daily Intelligencer*, in which he attempted to put the best possible face on the affair. He concluded, "As a result of this long fight against the discrimination on colored men, the legislature of our state amended the jury law by striking out the word 'white,' and it, as amended, remains the law today."[17]

In a final irony, Strauder did not die of his wounds, nor did Ida Houston. He was arrested, tried, convicted of attempted murder, and sentenced to prison. It was only then that Taylor Strauder disappeared permanently into history. Already in his sixties, he most likely died in jail, but there is no record of when or where it occurred, or where Strauder's final remains are interred.

After twelve years in Congress, Blackburn Dovener was defeated for renomination in 1906. He lived for eight more years until his death at age seventy-two, and was buried in Arlington National Cemetery.

Tightening the Knot

Virginia v. Rives

Strauder v. West Virginia WAS NOT THE SUPREME COURT'S last word on equal rights, however. Not two hours later, it established a far less expansive standard in a case every bit as odd as that of the West Virginia ax murderer.

It all started when a white teenager yelled "school-butter."

Although the term sounds silly today, it seems that in the 1870s it was a most extreme insult. "To any who have known the conditions existing in backwoods schools it is unnecessary to explain this phrase," a Kentucky man wrote.

What it originally meant, if indeed it meant anything, the writer has never been able to learn, nor to obtain a reasonable explanation. But from rural Pennsylvania to Arkansas, and even in parts of Indiana and Michigan, it was known as the most humiliating insult, and one certain to provoke swift revenge. All rules against fighting stood aside in favor of a pursuit of the person who called the word to the school.[1]

In mid-November 1877, Aaron Shelton's younger brother, likely about sixteen, yelled "school-butter" as he was passing an African American school in Patrick County, Virginia. Patrick County was in the eastern part of the state, on the border of North Carolina; along with Henry County, immediately to the east, it was named in honor of the famous Virginia patriot and orator, who also happened to be one of the state's most fervent defenders of slavery.[2]

What happened next was not totally clear. The younger Shelton complained to his brother that some of the students at the school, including eighteen-year-old Lee Reynolds, had given him a "ducking," which usually meant pushing him under water, although this incident might have involved simply pouring water on his head. Lee Reynolds's brother Burwell, who was nineteen, was also said to have been a participant.

About two weeks later, on November 27, Aaron Shelton, who was twenty-two and "of extraordinary physical development," was passing the school to fetch a load of logs for his uncle's sawmill. He yelled "school-butter," without provoking a response. Later that day, however, during recess, in which the teacher had "left his school in charge of one of the grown and advanced scholars," another of Aaron Shelton's brothers, this one only thirteen, yelled "school-butter" at the those playing outside. They chased him and he ran to where his brother was loading his wagon.

That provoked a confrontation in which Aaron Shelton told the black children that he would yell "school-butter" whenever he wanted, and that if anyone objected, "he would shoot their heart-strings out." If the teacher interrupted, he would shoot him as well. One of the black children was the Reynolds brothers' younger sister, to whom Shelton used "abusive language." That evening, "Shelton and the Reynolds boys had a dispute about some logs Shelton's uncle had cut and left in the road."

The stage was then set for the final confrontation between Aaron Shelton and the Reynolds brothers. It took place on November 29, 1877, when Shelton was hauling a wagon up the road to pick up the load of logs. Lee and Burwell Reynolds were leading their father's team of horses in the opposite direction on the same road. A quarrel ensued. According to one of Shelton's younger brothers, Green, who was a witness to the events, the confrontation quickly escalated, and Lee Reynolds took a shot at Shelton with the rifle he always carried. The shot missed. Shelton, wielding a heavy stick, then charged Lee Reynolds and knocked him to the ground. "At that time, Burwell Reynolds ran up and stabbed Shelton in the back with a large butcher knife." Aaron Shelton died on the spot.

Lee Reynolds was arrested at the scene. His brother fled the county but was soon caught. Each claimed that Green Shelton's version of the events was a lie: no gun was ever fired; Aaron Shelton started the fight by charging at Lee with a length of lumber; the knife had been Shelton's; he died after being stabbed in the struggle he began; Burwell Reynolds had merely tried to separate the two, as Shelton was much stronger than Lee.

Not surprisingly, which version residents of Patrick County believed was determined almost solely by race. Since the grand jury that was to decide whether or not to bring criminal charges was all white, both brothers were indicted for first-degree murder, the most serious offense possible. For Lee Reynolds in particular, the charge was extreme because he had not personally had a hand in Aaron Shelton's killing.

The Reynoldses' lawyers were white, and, like Blackburn Dovener, were war veterans. This time, however, the two men—Colonel William Martin and Captain A. M. Lybrock—had fought for the Confederacy. Martin, in his sixties, had a long record of public service, and "as a lawyer, orator, and statesman, he was regarded as the peer of any man in Virginia."[3] He had lost a brother in the war. Although they had fought to protect slavery, they would defend the Reynolds brothers with as much energy as Blackburn Dovener had exhibited with Taylor Strauder.

Their first problem was in jury selection. Virginia law stated, "All male citizens twenty-one years of age, and not over sixty, who are entitled to vote and hold office, under the constitution and laws of this state, shall be liable to serve as jurors." In practice, however, a trial judge—and all the judges in Patrick County were white—picked a pool of potential jurors as he wished, and then placed their names in a box from which the actual trial jurors were selected. For this trial, as for just about every trial in Virginia, the judge chose a jury pool that was also exclusively white. Martin and Lybrock petitioned the judge to include men of color, since the verdict of an all-white jury was almost certain to be unfavorable to the defendants. The judge refused, replying that he had chosen the jury pool according to law. That no black men were included—or were ever included in Patrick County—was not an issue for the court.

Martin and Lybrock then asked that the trial be moved to federal court on constitutional grounds. The judge refused. Lee and Burwell Reynolds chose to be tried separately and each was found guilty, Burwell of first-degree murder, Lee of second. On technical grounds, Martin and Lybrock managed to get a new trial for each. Their motion to have the retrial moved to federal court was denied.

Lee was again found guilty and sentenced to eighteen years in prison. Martin and Lybrock, however, succeeded in obtaining a hung jury for Burwell on the grounds that first-degree murder, which required Burwell to have decided in advance to kill Shelton, had not been proven. That Burwell would be convicted of second-degree murder, like his brother, there was no doubt. At that point, Martin and Lybrock filed a motion with United States District Court Judge Alexander Rives to have both cases heard in federal court.

They could not have made a better choice.

Bright, quirky, and fearless, Rives had spent his entire adult life following his own dictates with little or no concern for the opinions or even the loathing of friends, family, neighbors, or peers. Both his mother—a Cabell—and his father were members of the "First Families of Virginia," with a long tradition of gracious living, deference to authority, and slave owning. From an early age, Rives not only demonstrated a dislike of all three, but made it quite clear that he would live his life as he pleased. He put them on notice just after his twentieth birthday, when, rather than taking a bride from Virginia gentry, he chose a minister's daughter, two years his senior, and an immigrant besides. The two would remain married until her death in 1861 and would have ten children. (Rives took a new wife the very next year.)

After Hamden-Sydney College, in which he enrolled in 1821 at age fifteen, Rives studied law at the University of Virginia. Upon graduation, he accepted a professorship at a small Virginia college, resigned it soon afterward, and returned to Charlottesville to start a law practice. For a time, he handled mostly real estate transactions, but in the 1830s he became involved in local politics as a Whig. There, he continued to speak his mind and make enemies, including engaging in a feud with Governor Thomas Gilmer because of Rives's harsh views on slave-owning. The two did not speak for years.

In 1845, Rives leapt into the public eye under extremely peculiar but quite revealing circumstances.

When officials at the University of Virginia had attempted to crack down on a series of pranks by a group of students who called themselves "Calathumpians," disturbances had erupted that escalated into full-blown riots. The Calathumpians had formed the year before, and was composed of "exemplary students bent on 'fun, frolic, and childish folly.'"[4] With alcohol as a contributing agent, the students soon began to engage in behavior that their elders did not deem childish folly at all. When three Calathumpians were suspended in February 1845 for "raising a scene of disorder at one of the college hotels"—dormitories—the others in the group put on masks and "made an attack with sticks and stones on the home of the chairman."

A truce was arranged and held for about six weeks. In April, Calathumpians surrounded the home of an unpopular professor, raised a din with horns and drums, and soon afterward began pounding on his windows, terrifying his wife. They had only dispersed when the professor appeared with a rifle and promised to shoot anyone who refused to leave. The Calathumpians retreated but were soon laying siege to the homes of university officials across the campus. Windows were broken, and even the famed university rotunda, designed by Thomas Jefferson, was pitted with damage from stones.

University officials began to consider calling in the militia, something they very much did not want to do. They considered the campus almost a separate state, quite superior to the town that surrounded it. But before they were forced to make the fateful decision, a savior appeared.

> A member of the Charlottesville bar, Alexander Rives, an able but eccentric man, without invitation from anyone, hurried up from town, and through his influence, the students announced that a meeting of their body would be held at four o'clock that afternoon. In the meanwhile, they promised . . . that they would refrain from all disturbances . . . At four o'clock, about seventy students assembled, and after an address by Rives, who had held no communication with the Faculty or the executive committee, they formally pledged themselves to commit no further breach of the peace.[5]

And so, the Calathumpian revolt ended.

Although he obviously held appeal for students, Rives continued to infuriate just about everyone else. His family was incensed that he opposed secession, which he had done even as a young man. In 1832, when he was only twenty-six, he had written to James Madison, who was then eighty-one, and asked if secession would be legal under the Constitution, as many Virginians—and most of the Rives and Cabell families—believed it was. "The opinions of the chief architect of our political systems should not be misconstrued or perverted to sinister purposes," he wrote to Madison. He signed the letter, "A Friend of Union and State Rights."[6] Madison replied that he did not believe a state may "at will" renounce its agreement to remain in the Union. "A rightful secession requires the consent of the others, or an abuse of the compact absolving the seceding party from the obligation imposed by it."[7]

In the decade before war broke out, Rives again turned to politics and served in the Virginia state legislature. He left government when Virginia left the Union. Rives remained in Charlottesville during the conflict, never masking his belief that Virginia's secession was illegal. It is likely that only his personal reputation saved him from violence at the hands of secessionists. After the defeat of the Confederacy, he was appointed to the state's highest court and then, in 1870, decided to run for Congress as a Republican. He lost, but was appointed by President Grant as a federal district court judge. And there he had continued to serve when the Reynolds brothers' motion arrived on his desk.

Rives loathed abuses of power, and in the conviction of Lee Reynolds and the near-conviction of Burwell Reynolds, that is precisely what he saw. Rives declared the trial judge's refusal to include African Americans in the jury pool a violation of the United States Constitution, in denying them a trial by a jury of their peers. Although he did not put it in those terms, Rives had clearly ignored precedent and used Fourteenth Amendment guarantees to apply the Bill of Rights to the states.

He also decided that simply ordering the trial moved to federal court in Danville, where he sat, would not be enough. So he sent federal marshals to take the brothers into custody and hold them in safety until they could be tried in federal court by a jury that included men of color.

This legal kidnapping of the defendants "created no small stir amongst the bar," newspapers reported. "Its substantial effect is to strip the State courts of their jurisdiction in cases where a negro is tried unless a black jury is empanelled to try him, and looks as if the honorable Judge sought either to force the judges of the State courts to put negroes on their juries or to take the cases from them."[8]

Rives was unperturbed. "In my own court," he said in an interview, "I have always ordered mixed juries, and have not discovered that any harm resulted from it; on the contrary, the lawyers seem to prefer them."[9]

But "a small stir amongst the bar" was soon replaced by huge storm of protest. Judge Rives was called a usurper and worse. Rives's "capture" of the Reynolds brothers was called "a flagrant and unconstitutional encroachment upon the exclusive and unquestionable authority of the State."[10] When the Virginia legislature was criticized by a Philadelphia newspaper for announcing that it intended to "look into" the situation, a Virginia newspaper responded that the author was "a man who either regards all the people of the United States as slaves, or else regards the southern people as slaves."[11] White Southerners were quite fond of accusing Northerners of treating them like "slaves," seeming to forget that it was the South, not the North, in which human slavery had been important enough to fight a war over.

Some critics used reason, trying to demonstrate that all-white juries were more fair.

> The absurdity of the decision, that a verdict of a white jury against a negro is not good, is scarcely worth while discussing. Judge Rives, in fact, instead of placing the two races on a civil equality, does exactly the reverse, and decides that the whites and negroes have different rights and different privileges—that a white man must have a white jury to try him, a negro a colored jury.[12]

Other articles claimed black criminals *begged* to be tried by a white jury.[13]

While reaction in the South was predictable, feelings in the North were often just as extreme. An editor in *The Brooklyn Daily Eagle* wrote that the issue was "whether a colored man, on trial for a criminal offense which is clearly within the exclusive jurisdiction of a State court, has a right to demand a jury composed in whole or in part of men of his own color." He then added, "If such a right exists in Virginia, it also exists in New York."[14]

Eventually, the Virginia legislature did take up the matter, and in January 1879 drafted an official twelve-point proclamation denouncing Rives and calling his action "unwarranted by the Constitution" and "destructive of the rights of the people of each State to protect life, liberty, and property in their own way, by their own courts and officers," which "ought at once be remedied by proper judicial action." The governor was "instructed to direct the Attorney-General to institute proceedings in the name of this Commonwealth before the Supreme Court of the United States."[15]

Rives responded in character. Instead of backing down, he issued arrest warrants for five Virginia county judges who had publicly refused to seat black jurors, the judge in the Reynolds case not among them. Then he locked them up. And he did not intend to stop there. "That the Judge is not dismayed by the adverse criticism on his conduct, not only in the State, but throughout the country, is certain. He has determined to carry on the war against the offending State Courts everywhere, and will demand the indictment of other Judges, who, as he claims, have violated the law."[16]

The judges petitioned to the Supreme Court to be released on a writ of habeas corpus. *Ex parte Virginia*, the judges' petition, which had been joined by the Commonwealth, would be reported out immediately with *Virginia v. Rives*, the Reynolds brothers' appeal.

In the first case, whether Judge Rives had acted properly in removing the Reynolds brothers to federal jurisdiction depended on whether their Fourteenth Amendment rights had been violated, which led directly to Virginia's law governing the selection of potential jurors. In *Strauder*, West Virginia law had restricted jurors to white men; Virginia law did not. Still, for practical purposes the effect was same, since, as Alexander Rives had made plain, Virginia trial judges simply refused to consider African Americans for jury service, although most had not made a point of saying so. Virginia claimed judges were merely adhering to its laws, which made no mention of race and were therefore nondiscriminatory. Would the Court take into consideration that—whatever Virginia law might have said or not said—it was clearly being administered in a discriminatory fashion, as Rives had insisted?

The decision, handed down immediately after *Strauder* on March 1, 1880, was unanimous. As in *Strauder*, it was written by Justice Strong.

As was common in cases involving discrimination against African Americans, the justice began with lofty rhetoric: "The plain object of these [enforcement] statutes, as of the Constitution which authorized them, was to place the colored race, in respect of civil rights, upon a level with whites. They made the rights and responsibilities, civil and criminal, of the two races exactly the same."

Then, however, Strong pointed out "that [neither] the Constitution or laws of Virginia denied to [the defendants] any civil right, or stood in the way of their enforcing the equal protection of the laws. The law made no discrimination against them because of their color, nor any discrimination at all … It does not exclude colored citizens."[17] The state, therefore, was blameless.

As for the trial judge who "confined his selection to white persons, and refused to select any persons of the colored race, solely because of their color," Strong restated that the Fourteenth Amendment "was intended for [African Americans'] protection against *State action*, and against *that alone.*" And so, "any action [that] was not the state, but a person," such as the trial judge, "was not covered under the Fourteenth Amendment." And so, Judge Rives's actions were deemed improper and the Reynolds brothers were ordered returned to state custody.

Rives fared better in *Ex parte Virginia*. For the majority opinion in a 7–2 decision, Justice Strong, again citing a published intention to discriminate, refused to grant the writ of habeas corpus to the five jailed judges. Rives then announced his attention to make each of them stand trial.

In April 1880, Rives held trials for two of the five jailed county judges in federal court, but, in an irony, mixed-race juries acquitted them both. Rives declined to pursue the matter further and freed the other three. In June, Burwell Reynolds went on trial in Danville, the very city in which Alexander Rives sat as a federal judge. Perhaps because of the previous incarceration of his colleagues, the trial judge included black men in the jury pool, and four of them were chosen to sit on the jury. That is perhaps why, although Burwell Reynolds was convicted, it was only of manslaughter, a lesser charge than murder. He was sentenced to five years' imprisonment, much lighter than the eighteen years Lee had originally received. Lee Reynolds did even better. The prosecution declined to prosecute him before a mixed-race jury, and he went free.[18]

Soon, however, jury selection in Virginia reverted to its pre-Rives state. Judges continued to insist that black jurors were not required, even in cases in which a black person was plaintiff or defendant, an opinion sustained by the Virginia Supreme Court of Appeals. As such, local judges were free, as before, to avoid placing black men in the jury pool wherever possible.

* * *

The impact of the Court's rulings on March 1, 1880, was immense, but to appreciate the impact, the three cases must be taken together and not viewed as separate events. While *Strauder* is widely cited, many analyses fail to blend in *Rives*. As such, *Strauder* can easily be seen as a victory for equal rights.[19] But *Rives* disemboweled *Strauder*—it was a discrimination handbook. It assured white Southerners that as long as they did not *announce* their intent to discriminate by putting references specific to race in their laws or their constitutions, they were free to treat American citizens of color pretty much as they pleased in jury selection, voter registration, or anything else. These were lessons that white Southern Democrats learned all too well, and black Americans paid with their freedom and their lives. One can gussy up the analysis by referring to "state action," "original intent," "political rights vs. civil rights," or any other jargon, but at its core, this was law with a wink and a nod. If anyone is looking for a case that defines the Court's view of equal rights, it is *Rives*, not *Strauder*.

The following year in *Neal v. Delaware*, the Court refined the principle. There, a black man accused of raping a white woman petitioned to have his case removed to federal court since the grand jury that indicted him and the petit jury that would hear his case would be exclusively white. The state constitution, which predated ratification of the Fourteenth and Fifteenth Amendments, had restricted voter registration to free white males over the age of twenty-one. But with the amendments in effect, Delaware courts "held that the restriction to a 'white' citizen is without effect." Delaware, however, did not change the law and not a single black man had since been called to sit on a Delaware jury.[20]

Although the case would ordinarily have seemed to fall under the *Rives* rule, Delaware, unlike Virginia in the *Rives* case, made no attempt to refute Neal's claim. In fact, the chief justice of the Delaware Supreme Court had stated precisely the opposite. "That none but white men were selected is in nowise remarkable in view of the fact—too notorious to be ignored—that the great body of black men residing in this State are utterly unqualified by want of intelligence, experience, or moral integrity to sit on juries." As such, Strong's opinion in *Rives*, that the mere assertion of discrimination—regardless of overwhelming support by the facts—"fell short of showing that any civil right was denied, or that there had been any discrimination against the defendants because of their color or race," did not apply.

Justice Harlan, speaking for a 7–2 majority, ruled for the plaintiff on the grounds that he had provided ample evidence of discrimination.

> The showing thus made, including, as it did, the fact ... that no colored citizen had ever been summoned as a juror in the courts of the State ... presented a *prima facie* case of denial, by the officers charged with the selection of grand and petit jurors, of that equality of protection which has been secured by the Constitution and laws of the United States. It was, we think, under all the circumstances, a violent presumption which the State court indulged, that such uniform exclusion of that race from juries, during a period of many years, was solely because, in the judgment of those officers, fairly exercised, the black race in Delaware were utterly disqualified, by want of intelligence, experience, or moral integrity, to sit on juries.

Justices Field and Waite dissented. After noting, "It is obvious that the mere fact that no persons of the colored race were selected as jurors is not evidence that such persons were excluded on account of their race or color," Field posited, "It would seem, when the law has been obeyed, as in this case, that something more than the mere absence of colored persons from the panels should be shown before they can be set aside." Then he concluded, "And the fact that colored persons had never, since the act of Congress of May 1, 1875, been selected as jurors may be attributed to other causes than those of race and color."[21] It would have been interesting if Justice Field had enumerated just what those possible other causes were.

Strangling the Constitution

The *Civil Rights Cases*

C HALLENGES TO THE CIVIL RIGHTS ACT OF 1875 reached the Supreme Court in 1880, just after the *Strauder* and *Rives* decisions had been handed down, but Morrison Waite refused to schedule a hearing for another three years. Finally, on March 29, 1883, the justices heard arguments on the five appeals, which would be decided together and called the *Civil Rights Cases*.

As the *Chicago Daily Tribune* had predicted, none of the five cases came from the Deep South. One originated in California, where "a colored person [was refused] a seat in the dress circle of Maguire's theatre in San Francisco," and a second in New York City, where "a person, whose color was not stated, [was denied] the full enjoyment of the accommodations of the theatre known as the Grand Opera House."[1] The remaining three cases originated in Missouri, Kansas, and Tennessee.

Waite had given no reason for the delay beyond vague pronouncements of procedural problems, but by the time the cases were heard, the nation's rejection of Reconstruction was near complete. Horatio Seymour, who had narrowly lost the popular vote to Ulysses Grant in 1868, wrote that while he would not "impeach the patriotism" of those who had implemented the Reconstruction programs, "in their eagerness to extend the jurisdiction of the General Government, they went too far, and exposed the country to unforeseen dangers."[2] Seymour was not alone. Even most Republicans had concluded that a good deal of the program had been a mistake. Much of the party had turned against African Americans, and Republican candidates were openly courting white votes in the South. C. Vann Woodward wrote, "The wing of the Republican party that raised the loudest outcry against Hayes's policy of deserting the Negro promptly abandoned him and threw support to . . . any white independent organization available."[3]

And so, when the Court was finally ready to rule on the constitutionality of the Civil Rights Act of 1875, no one expected it to be much of a contest. And as a matter of law it was not—the vote was 8–1. But as to larger questions, those of what America should stand for, whether or not honor was as important a national value as power, the *Civil Rights Cases* were quite a contest indeed. The main combatants were two of the justices, the seemingly ubiquitous Joseph Bradley (representing the eight) and the former Kentucky slaveholder, John Marshall Harlan (the one).

★   ★   ★

Harlan had come to the Court to replace David Davis. At first look, Harlan seemed exactly what those who accused Hayes of selling out black America would have expected. In addition to being raised in a family of slaveholders, he had opposed the Emancipation Proclamation, had spoken out passionately against the three postwar amendments, and, at age twenty-one, had joined the anti-immigrant, anti-black, anti-Catholic, semi-secret society called the "Know Nothings," whose motto was "Put none but Americans on Guard." As Harlan wrote later, "On the evening of my initiation, an oath was administered to me which bound me to vote only for native Americans, and, in effect, only for Protestants."[4] Harlan, at six foot two and 240 pounds, with a shock of red hair and a deep, booming delivery, was soon giving speeches all over Kentucky in support of the party's nativist, bigoted agenda.

But Harlan, like Abraham Lincoln, was that rare man who was not afraid how he might look if he abandoned views he had held since childhood when he realized those views were wrong.

Harlan's conversion began because he opposed secession. He campaigned tirelessly to keep Kentucky loyal—and Kentucky, although a slave state, remained in the Union—and when war did break out, he raised an infantry regiment to fight for the North. He was commissioned into the Union army as a colonel and distinguished himself in battle. Fighting arm in arm with German immigrants and Catholics, Harlan emerged from the war with his Know-Nothing sentiments abandoned.

His views on slavery, however, were unchanged and based on a strong commitment to rights of property holders to not have what they owned taken from them. He opposed the Thirteenth Amendment on the grounds that it was "a flagrant invasion of the right of self government."[5] He also believed the amendment broke a promise made to the slaveholders of Kentucky who had chosen to remain in the Union, and violated property rights guaranteed by the Constitution. His opinion of the Fourteenth and Fifteenth Amendments was no better, and after the war he joined the Conservative Party. At that point, if forced to choose between the major parties, he would certainly have become a Democrat.

With the presidential nomination of Ulysses Grant, however, Harlan's views changed once more. He had known Grant during the war and respected his toughness and commitment to the United States. Although the Democrats, who dominated Kentucky politics, were urging Harlan to join them and perhaps even to run for office, Harlan instead aligned himself with Grant and the Republicans.

Kentucky Republicans, thrilled to have attracted such a prominent convert, nominated Harlan for governor in 1871. The only chance he had to win in a heavily Democratic state was to attract a heavy turnout among African Americans—those who could still vote—and so, as in his soldiering days, he found himself getting to know people against whom he had previously been prejudiced. Again showing his capacity for personal growth, Harlan totally changed his perspective on issues of equal rights.

"I rejoice," announced the man who had opposed the Thirteenth Amendment late in the campaign, "that [slavery] is gone; I rejoice that the Sun of American Liberty does not this day shine upon a single human slave upon this continent; I rejoice that these human beings are now in possession of freedom, and that that freedom is secured to them in the fundamental law of the land, beyond the control of any state." Then he added, noting his attitudes of the past, "Let it be said that I am right rather than consistent."[6]

Harlan lost the election, but he amassed more votes than any other Republican in Kentucky's history. He was nominated again four years later. In this election, the Civil Rights Act of 1875 was a major issue. Of that law, Harlan said, "Under the law of Kentucky, any one of the colored men within the sound of my voice has the same right that any white man possesses to ride in one of your cars from here to the city of Louisville."[7] Harlan lost once more, by an even narrower margin, and was instrumental in gaining the presidential nomination for Rutherford B. Hayes the following year. On October 16, 1877, the president nominated him to be associate justice of the Supreme Court. On Thanksgiving Day 1877, Harlan learned by telegram that he had been confirmed.

In early 1878, John Marshall Harlan came to Washington and joined Joseph Bradley on the Supreme Court.

★ ★ ★

The key question in the *Civil Rights Cases* was once again how much or how little the Fourteenth Amendment guaranteed every person in America fair and equal treatment under the law. Were the officials who refused to enforce the Civil Rights Act—and, by extension, who denied qualified African Americans the right to vote—"states" or, as the Court seemed to have ruled in *Reese*, ordinary people? The difference here was that in *Reese*, the registrars were not seen as in violation of guaranteed rights because they had simply followed the law—or so they said—and refused to register a person who had not paid his poll tax; in the five *Civil Rights Cases*, state employees had refused to respond to complaints that private individuals were violating a federal law.

An additional factor was the question of whether the Fourteenth Amendment took precedence over the Tenth. Ordinarily, a law that was passed later—the Fourteenth—would take precedence over an earlier law—the Tenth. In fact, in arguing his case, Solicitor General Samuel F. Phillips claimed that very thing: that the Fourteenth Amendment's insistence on "equal protection of the laws" overrode the Tenth by defining new areas "delegated to the United States." Equality, then, as defined in the Fourteenth Amendment, was appropriate to be ensured by Congress.

But the Waite Court had in the past seemed to disagree. It had ruled, for example, that the Bill of Rights guarantees did not apply to the states, and that the states alone could decide whether or not such fundamental liberties as freedom of speech, freedom of the press, free exercise of religion, or freedom of peaceable assembly would apply within their borders. Attorneys for the defendants in the *Civil Rights Cases* played to that stance, accusing Phillips of trying to broaden the Fourteenth Amendment to achieve social goals that neither Congress nor the Constitution had intended. But of course, the drafters of the Fourteenth Amendment had made it plain that they meant to do precisely that.

With the law so imprecise, the justices could find support in any interpretation of the Constitution they chose. Through Justice Bradley, they chose to support white supremacy.

★ ★ ★

Bradley kept the definition of "ordinary people" broad. He wrote that the Fourteenth Amendment did "not invest Congress with power to legislate upon subjects which are within the domain of State legislation, but to provide modes of relief against State legislation, or State action."[8] Bradley was, in essence, choosing broad construction for the Tenth Amendment and strict construction for the Fourteenth. In addition, although the defendants in these five cases were all private business owners, Bradley made a point of not making an exception for state employees. In fact, he added, "Individual invasion of individual rights is not the subject matter of the amendment." And so, according to this definition, "subjects which are within the domain of State legislation" would include, say, voting registrars. And since the Civil Rights Act of 1875 was an unconstitutional incursion on the rights of states not justified by the Fourteenth Amendment, Bradley continued, it was unconstitutional and must be struck down.

The decision and the legal reasoning surprised no one. The Court had been creating precedent for this decision for years. But then Bradley did something unexpected. Seemingly unable to restrain himself, he added commentary on the entire effort to obtain equal rights for black Americans. He began by dismissing the notion of extending the Thirteenth Amendment, which prohibited slavery, to apply to the type of discrimination alleged in these cases as "badges of servitude." "It would be running the slavery argument into the ground," he wrote, "to make it apply to every act of discrimination which a person may see fit to make as to the guests he will entertain, or as to the people he will take into his coach or cab or car, or admit to his concert or theatre, or deal with in other matters of intercourse or business."[9]

He was not done. From there, Bradley asserted,

When a man has emerged from slavery, and, by the aid of beneficent legislation, has shaken off the inseparable concomitants of that state, there must be some stage in the progress of his elevation when he takes the rank of a mere citizen and ceases to be the special favorite of the laws, and when his rights as a citizen or a man are to be protected in the ordinary modes by which other men's rights are protected.

That a justice of the United States Supreme Court could make such a statement in the face of literally thousands of incidents of beatings, murder, rape, and intimidation of African Americans by whites; despite the reign of terror waged by the Ku Klux Klan and other violent Redeemer groups; despite the most obvious ploys to deny the vote instituted by whites against blacks; despite vagrancy laws, rigged juries, and rampant violation of contract rights—is simply astonishing.

This, however, seemed the Court's point all along. The justices who concurred with Bradley had all but announced that they, as well as the white population they represented, wanted to be out of the business of protecting a class of Americans whom they held to be of no value. As Oliver Wendell Holmes would later write,

> The very considerations which judges most rarely mention and always with an apology, are the secret root from which the law draws all the juices of life. I mean, of course, considerations of what is expedient to the community concerned. Every important principle which is developed by litigation is in fact and at bottom the result of more or less definitely understood views of public policy.[10]

But then there was the one. At the same inkstand at which Chief Justice Roger B. Taney had written the infamous *Dred Scott* opinion, John Marshall Harlan, the former slave owner from Kentucky, wrote what was to become one of the most praised opinions in the history of the Supreme Court.

"I cannot resist the conclusion that the substance and spirit of the recent amendments of the Constitution have been sacrificed by a subtle and ingenious verbal criticism," Harlan began. Then he quoted Edmund Plowden, an English legal theorist, who in 1574 wrote, "It is not the words of the law, but the internal sense of it that makes the law; the letter of the law is the body; the sense and reason of the law is the soul."[11] There are those, of course, who insist that the law must be soulless in order to be fair; that souls can be subject to the feelings, even the whims, of those who claim to be acting at their behest. But Joseph Bradley was the epitome of the soulless legal practitioner; it would difficult to categorize his opinion in the *Civil Rights Cases*, or even in *Cruikshank*, as "fair."

Harlan also chided his colleagues for ignoring what those who en-acted the amendments had intended to achieve.

> Constitutional provisions, adopted in the interest of liberty and for the purpose of securing, through national legislation, if need be, rights in-hering in a state of freedom and belonging to American citizenship have been so construed as to defeat the ends the people desired to ac-complish, which they attempted to accomplish, and which they sup-posed they had accomplished by changes in their fundamental law . . . The court has departed from the familiar rule requiring . . . that full effect be given to the intent with which they were adopted.

But he saved his harshest words for Bradley's words about African Americans being "special favorites of the laws."

> What the nation, through congress, has sought to accomplish in ref-erence to that race is, what had already been done in every state in the Union for the white race, to secure and protect rights belonging to them as freemen and citizens; nothing more. The one underlying purpose of congressional legislation has been to enable the black race to take the rank of mere citizens. The difficulty has been to compel a recognition of their legal right to take that rank, and to secure the enjoyment of privileges belonging, under the law, to them as a component part of the people for whose welfare and happiness government is ordained.

Harlan closed with this famous passage:

> Today it is the colored race which is denied by corporations and in-dividuals . . . rights fundamental in their freedom and citizenship. At some future time, it may be that some other race will fall under the ban of race discrimination. If the constitutional amendments be enforced according to the intent with which . . . they were adopted, there cannot be, in this republic, any class of human beings in practical subjection

to another class ... The supreme law of the land has decreed that no authority shall be exercised in this country upon the basis of discrimination ... against freemen and citizens because of their race, color, or previous condition of servitude.[12]

History may have praised Justice Harlan, but most of white America did not. Harlan's ideals were as unwelcome in the North as in the South. *The New York Times*, pleased to find its prediction that the Court would overturn the law accurate, wrote in an editorial that "the whole matter is now remanded to State authority in which it rightfully belongs."[13] The writer added, "it is doubtful if social privileges can be successfully dealt with by legislation of any kind." He pointed out, however, all too correctly that "the decision is unlikely to have any considerable practical impact, for the reason that the act of 1875 has never been enforced. The general practice of railroads, hotels and theatres has remained unchanged and has depended mainly on the prevailing sentiment of the communities in which they are located."
The Brooklyn Daily Eagle agreed.

There was a time when this decision would have created some excitement, but that time passed years ago ... The Negro gained nothing by the passage of the Civil Rights act, and he will lose nothing by having it declared a dead letter. The decision simply gives him notification ... that his advancement from a position of mere dependency on his white neighbor was to be brought about, not by fulminations of politicians but by self-respect, patience, hard work and general good behavior on his own part.

The editor also observed, "The decision is interesting as another proof that the Supreme Court continues to be ... true to the spirit and structure of our Government ... There, if nowhere else ... loyalty to the fundamental law of the land has found a home."[14]
Southern newspapers were gleeful. *The Atlanta Constitution* pro-

claimed in a headline, "A Radical Relic Rubbed Out. Special Rights for None but Equal Rights for All. A Triumph of Law and Sense Which Strengthens the Decree That the Republicans Must Go."[15]

Not every white newspaper praised the decision. The *Hartford Courant* wrote sadly, "We regret that the judicial authority of the land has felt a duty . . . to wipe out of existence a law that for nearly ten years has worked no harm to anybody, and has been a testimony on the part of the American people of their sincerity in demanding equal rights for all men."[16] Of course, most of white America had done no such thing.

Black newspapers were unanimous in their outrage at the decision. The *Boston Hub* charged that the Court had deliberately cast the power of the judiciary against equal rights. The *Louisville Bulletin* exclaimed, "Our government is a farce, and a snare, and the sooner it is overthrown and an empire established upon its ruins the better." *The New York Globe* denounced Bradley as reaffirming the "infamous decision of infamous Chief Justice Taney [in *Dred Scott*] that 'a black man has no rights that a white is bound to respect.'"[17]

One of the most interesting reactions came from William Strong, who had retired from the Court to reenter private practice. He wrote to Justice Harlan, "At first I was inclined to agree with the Court but since reading your opinion, I am in great doubt. It may be that you are right. The opinion of the Court, as you said, is too narrow—sticks to the letter, while you aim to bring out the Spirit of the Constitution."[18]

Although the *Civil Rights Cases* decision did not bear directly on voting, it enabled, even encouraged white America to keep itself separate from the nation's black citizens; said that it was acceptable for them to shun those whom most whites thought members of an inferior race; raised, in fact, the distinct possibility that as far as the United States Supreme Court was concerned, they might well be members of an inferior race. Why then should they be allowed to vote?

The Curious Incident of the Chinese Laundry and Equal Protection

O N JANUARY 24, 1848, A CARPENTER NAMED JAMES Marshall discovered metallic flakes near the American Fork River in north-central California while supervising the construction of a sawmill for John Sutter, a Swiss-born businessman who wanted to create the beginnings of a new city inland from the Pacific Coast. The flakes were gold. Neither Marshall nor Sutter registered a claim, both for secrecy's sake—Sutter feared his plans for the settlement would be upended—and because, at the time, California was owned by Mexico. Just one week later, however, the Treaty of Guadalupe Hidalgo transferred control of the Southwest, including the land around Sutter's mill, to the United States.

Everyone who had been working at or near the site, at the base of the Sierra Nevada Mountains about 130 miles northeast of San Francisco, was aware of Marshall's find, and couldn't care less whether a new city was built or not. Most of the crew quit to prospect for gold, unconcerned that the bulk of the land belonged to the man they had supposedly been working for. Sutter tried to kick them out without making a fuss, and his former workmen did their best not to publicize their activities to avoid being overrun themselves. But gold is not a secret easily kept, and by May 1848, word began to leak out. It was not until the following year, however, that the full-blown Gold Rush began.[1]

Upwards of 80,000 would-be millionaires descended on California. San Francisco's population exploded, growing from about 800 people in 1848 to 25,000 just two years later. Ninety percent of those 80,000 prospectors came by way of the eastern United States, either overland or by steamship, but many others came from across the Pacific, almost all of them from China. Most arriving Chinese intended to stay at "Gold Mountain" only long enough to allow them to return home rich to a country whose economy was near collapse and in which famine was widespread. At first, the hardworking Chinese were, if not welcomed, at least accepted by the other miners. But as gold became scarcer and Chinese became more plentiful—there would be 24,000 within three years—a strong backlash developed.

In 1850, California instituted a prohibitive twenty-dollar-per-month tax on foreign miners. Although the tax was repealed the following year, it was replaced in 1852 by a four-dollar-per-month tax, which was still more money than a man barely able to feed himself while working sixteen-hour days could afford to pay. Most immigrant whites could avoid the levy simply by not broadcasting their origins, but Chinese miners did not have the same option. (Mexicans, another target group, were also forced to pay or abandon their claims.)

With the tax in place and violence against those who continued to work their claims becoming commonplace, Chinese miners reluctantly gave up the hunt for gold and entered more prosaic lines of work. Some hired themselves out as workers in mining camps, where they were paid next to nothing and subjected to constant verbal and physical abuse. Others became farm laborers, while still others settled in cities—mostly booming San Francisco—and sought to open their own businesses. Most occupations were closed off, but one obvious opportunity was in laundering. Most of the men who arrived in California to hunt for gold came alone. Mining was dirty, dusty work, but washing grimy, mud-caked clothes was considered a "woman's job." Some of the more successful single men shipped dirty clothes to Hong Kong and waited months for their return. For the rest, since local Spanish and Native American women charged too high a price, Chinese men filled the void. Within a few years, the Chinese came to dominate the laundry business in San Francisco.

Among the less entrepreneurial Chinese, railroad construction siphoned off large numbers of laborers in the 1860s, but that opportunity eventually came to an end. Still, with the West growing quickly, there was a constant need for cheap labor, and the Chinese could be worked hard and paid little. In 1868, China and the United States signed the Burlingame Treaty, the first agreement between the Qing Dynasty and a Western power that was considered to be "equal."[2] China was granted most-favored-nation trade status, immigration and economic cooperation were encouraged, and, significantly, subjects of each nation—which included American missionaries—were guaranteed full protection of the law while living or working in the other.

But whites in the West quickly soured on the deal and became determined to halt what they saw as a deluge of pollution by an inferior race. While laborers were key targets—they were widely viewed as depressing wages for white workers—Chinese women, assumed to be prostitutes, also aroused particular antipathy.

Eventually, nativists put sufficient pressure on their congressional delegations that in 1875 Congress passed the Page Act, the first law in American history that restricted the entry of specific "undesirable" elements. Horace Page, a California Republican, had introduced the bill to "end the danger of cheap Chinese labor and immoral Chinese women." It stipulated that "the immigration of any subject of China, Japan, or any Oriental country, to the United States" must be "free and voluntary," nor could any immigrant from those countries have "entered into a contract or agreement for a term of service within the United States, for lewd and immoral purposes." It was "the duty of the consul-general or consul of the United States residing at the port from which it is proposed to convey such subjects" to make the determination, which he was free to do according to whatever standards he chose. In case the American foreign officer was too lenient, an additional inspection would be held when the boat docked at a domestic port.[3] Since it was difficult on the gangplank of a ship to determine what a person might eventually do for a living or what a woman's morals were, most were turned back simply for being Chinese.

While the Page Act was enacted to stanch the flow of new immigrants, the California state legislators took aim at those already in the United States. They enacted a series of laws intended to deny Chinese immigrants, almost none of whom were citizens, either employment or housing. For example, one law, an 1870 San Francisco ordinance called "the Sanitary Act," stipulated that all housing must have 500 cubic feet of air for each occupant. The law was enforced only in Chinatown, where immigrants, most of whom were working for impossibly low wages, lived in equally cramped conditions. Conviction meant either a fine or jail for both the building's owner and the tenants. Since almost no one could afford the fine, which could run to as much as $500 for the landlord, droves of Chinese were sent to what soon became horribly overcrowded local jails.

But although few Chinese could speak English, they had nonetheless acquired a keen understanding of how to negotiate the American legal system. Each time California or San Francisco passed a discriminatory law, Chinese businessmen hired white lawyers to bring suit in either state or federal court. And they generally won. One of the cases, in 1879, involved a city ordinance that ordered all male prisoners to have their hair cut to one inch from their scalps. This was an extraordinary humiliation of Chinese prisoners, since the "queue," the long braid worn down their backs, was required in their society as a sign of respect to the Qing emperor. And since failure to wear the queue meant death, any man with his hair shorn could not return to China. (That preventing an immigrant from returning home was an odd way to shrink the Chinese population did not seem to have occurred to the city fathers.) When a laborer named Ah Kow was jailed under the Sanitary Law and then had his hair shorn, his lawyers contested both his imprisonment and what had become known as the "Pigtail Law."

When the statute was upheld in state court, the decision was appealed to federal court, where Justice Field was sitting on circuit. Field was hardly a friend of the Chinese. In a run for the California state senate in 1851, he had sought to reassure white residents. "I have always regarded the immigration of the Chinese in large numbers into our state as a serious evil," he wrote, "and likely to cause great injury to the morals of our people as well as their industrial interests."[4] Those sentiments were not just for public consumption. As he observed to a friend three decades later, "You know I belong to the class who repudiate the doctrine that this country was made for the people of all races. On the contrary, I think it is for our race—the Caucasian race."[5]

Nonetheless, in *Ah Kow v. Nunan*, Field voided the conviction and declared the California law unconstitutional. While such a decision was already highly unusual—to say nothing of being incendiary to the white population—Field's reasoning was more so. Calling the law "spiteful and hateful," Field wrote:

> The equality of protection thus assured to every one whilst within the United States, from whatever country he may have come, or of whatever race or color he may be, implies not only that the courts of the country shall be open to him on the same terms as to all others for the security of his person or property, the prevention or redress of wrongs and the enforcement of contracts; but that no charges or burdens shall be laid upon him which are not equally borne by others, and that in the administration of criminal justice he shall suffer for his offenses no greater or different punishment.[6]

Never before had the Fourteenth Amendment guarantee of "equal protection of the law" been used to void a state or federal statute. Equally significant was Field's assertion that the Sanitary Law was "special legislation imposing a degrading and cruel punishment upon a class of persons who are entitled, alike with all other persons within the jurisdiction of the United States, to the equal protection of the laws." In other words, because the language of the amendment specifically said "any person" and not "any citizen," its protections were not reserved for the native born.[7]

But Field's opinion was pushing against a very strong tide. Three years later, in 1882, Congress passed and President Chester Arthur signed the Chinese Exclusion Act, which denied entry into the United States to Chinese laborers, the first immigration law passed in the United States that restricted immigration of a specific national or ethnic group. The Page Act had, in theory, only prohibited laborers brought to the United States against their will, although in practice application had been much broader. The Chinese Exclusion Act, which was also applied far more broadly than its wording, would, despite the fact that the Burlingame Treaty was still on the books, halt virtually all Chinese immigration for almost a century.[8]

As with the Page Act, local laws against the Chinese proceeded in parallel to national efforts. In 1880, the San Francisco Board of Supervisors passed an ordinance that required all laundries operating within the city limits not constructed of brick or stone to obtain a special operating license. This, they claimed, was because of the extreme fire hazard created by laundries housed in wooden buildings. At the time, there were 320 laundries in San Francisco, all but ten wood framed. Ninety percent of all the city's buildings were, in fact, of wood construction.

While, like the Sanitary Law and similar ordinances, the laundry law was evenhanded on its face, three-quarters of the city's laundries were Chinese-owned. After the law took effect, 280 license applications were submitted. Eighty were granted—all to white owners; 200 were denied—all but one for Chinese.[9] Not one Chinese laundry owner was granted a license.

One of those denied was the proprietor of the Yick Wo laundry. The proprietor's name is uncertain—it may have been Lee Yick—but he had apparently come to the United States in 1861 and had been operating his business for twenty-two years. Like most Chinese immigrants, he had never become a United States citizen. Although the Yick Wo laundry had passed inspections by both the fire wardens and the health department, the proprietor was ordered to close his business down. When he refused, Sheriff Peter Hopkins arrested him. Not bothering to certify the actual identity of the man he had brought to the station, Hopkins had the man booked as Yick Wo.

When "Yick Wo" refused to pay the mandated ten-dollar fine, he was sent to jail for ten days. Hopkins had arrested 150 other Chinese laundry owners who refused to close their shops, and almost all of them were sent to jail as well.

But the Chinese Laundrymen's Guild, the Tung Hing Tong, had become a powerful force in the city. To contest the arrests, they hired Hall McAllister, the best lawyer in San Francisco—and the highest paid. McAllister was "said to have made more money out of his profession than any lawyer in America."[10]

McAllister was born in Savannah, Georgia, in 1826, a son of that state's leading lawyer. He went to Yale, graduating in 1846, but soon after he returned home to practice, tales of riches just waiting to be picked up off the ground proved too much to resist. In February 1849, Hall McAllister, his brother Ward, and a cousin, Samuel Ward, left Georgia and almost four months later, they reached San Francisco. But none of the three had come to California to practice law. Nor did they intend to pan for gold. Rather, they would make their fortunes from the miners, not from the mines. They had hauled a stock of dry goods across America and set up two tents in a vacant lot to ply a merchant's trade. Instead of mounting some mundane sign on the tents, they decided to be whimsical. The father of the brothers, Matthew Hall McAllister, had given the trio his old tin shingle, so outside one of the tents was hung M. HALL MCAL-LISTER, ATTORNEY AT LAW.[11]

They did a brisk business, their customers either amused or confused by the sign at the entrance. But one day, a group of sailors showed up and insisted on speaking with the lawyer. Hall McAllister was reluctant to move from a venture he was certain would make him rich to one he saw as a dead-end business, representing men with little money who often felt only a passing obligation to pay.

But the sailors persisted. Their captain, it seemed, had refused to pay them for the voyage from New York—he said they had signed on for a round trip and they would get paid when the ship returned to New York. The sailors insisted the captain had promised to pay them half in San Francisco and owed them $1,000. McAllister, motivated by caprice as much as anything else, took the case.

In court, the captain presented the contract signed by each member of the crew, and sure enough, it appeared that the seamen had agreed to forgo payment until the ship returned to New York. But McAllister noticed something odd when he held the pages up to the light. Some of the original writing seemed to have been carefully erased and different text inserted in its place. He pointed out this palimpsest to the judge and won the case.

The sailors paid him half, $500, and suddenly dry goods had lost their allure. In a boomtown like San Francisco, there were always a multitude of swindles, frauds, misappropriations of funds, and violations of contract to create a steady stream of clients more than willing to pay hefty fees to a wunderkind attorney—McAllister was still only twenty-three years old. He was soon buried in an avalanche of legal work, and in his first full year as an attorney, he reportedly earned $150,000.[12]

The next year, McAllister's father realized that the gold in California was not just what could be dug out of the earth. He decided to join his two eldest sons and journeyed to California with other members of the clan, including another son, Cutler. They opened a law firm, McAllister & Sons, and did a thriving business. Three years later, President Franklin Pierce nominated Matthew Hall McAllister to be a federal circuit court judge. After he was confirmed, he regularly heard cases in which his son was one of the lawyers, which did nothing to hurt Hall McAllister's record of victories at trial. The elder McAllister appointed Cutler as clerk of the court, and the family triumvirate was complete.[13]

That a Hall McAllister would accept a case from the Tung Hing Tong infuriated city officials—and many of its citizens—but there was little they could do about it. They filed a more-than-one-hundred-page brief—to McAllister's thirteen—trying to overwhelm state court judges with reasons why the laundry law was fair. And indeed, the California Supreme Court sided with the city. Soon afterward, a parallel case, *re Wo Lee*, was taken directly to federal court. In rendering his decision, Judge Lorenzo Sawyer lacerated the city, accusing the board of supervisors of selectively using a vaguely written law to "drive the Chinese laundrymen out of business." He wrote further, citing, as had Field, the Fourteenth Amendment, "That it [means] prohibition to the Chinese, it seems to us must be apparent to every citizen of San Francisco who has been here long enough to be familiar with the cause of an active and aggressive branch of public opinion and of public notorious events. Can a court be blind to what must be necessarily known to every intelligent person in the State?"[14] But Sawyer could go no further. He reluctantly ruled that the federal district court lacked the authority to overturn the California Supreme Court's ruling in *Yick Wo*. He did, however, urge that the case be appealed to the United States Supreme Court, which he hoped would grant a speedy review.

Which it promptly did. In January 1886, the two cases were combined and heard in Washington as *Yick Wo v. Hopkins*. *Yick Wo* was not the first case that the Court had heard regarding discriminatory laws against Chinese laundrymen in California, and while the previous results would not have been encouraging to most attorneys, Hall McAllister did not need more than the narrowest of openings.

One year earlier, in January 1885, the Court had delivered an opinion in *Barbier v. Connolly*, a case in which, using Stephen Field's *Ah Kow* opinion as precedent, the equal protection clause had been used to challenge a San Francisco ordinance prohibiting laundries from operating between ten o'clock at night and six in the morning. The law had been enacted, according to the board of supervisors, because of night washing, drying, and especially ironing, which was said to be a fire hazard and "endangered the public health and the public safety, prejudiced the wellbeing and comfort of the community, and depreciated the value of property in their neighborhood." Since Chinese launderers were the only ones who worked through the night, they were the only ones arrested and prosecuted for violating the ordinance. They claimed that the ordinance was enacted solely to target them for prosecution, but the Court, in a unanimous opinion authored by Field himself, disagreed.

Field concluded,

> The 14th Amendment does not interfere with the police power of a state to prescribe regulations to promote the health, safety, peace, morals, education, good order, and general welfare of its people ... The fact that a special burden is placed upon a certain class does not render it class legislation or deny the equal protection of the law, as special burdens are often necessary for the general welfare ... What regulations are necessary in the exercise of the police power, and to what business, trade, or occupation they shall apply, is a question for the legislative branch of the government to determine, and every presumption is to be indulged in favor of the validity of such a statute.[15]

The same could have been said about the Sanitary Law, of course, short hair being much less likely to be a conduit to disease than long hair, particularly under prison conditions, but Field never explained why this case differed from *Ah Kow*. Still, his opinion in *Barbier* is much more consistent with his overall view.

Two months later, in *Soon Hing v. Crowley*, the Court once again unanimously ruled, again through Justice Field, that the night work prohibition was a legitimate exercise of police power, but further that the Court was in no position to rule on the motives of those who enacted the law, even in the face of public statements that it had been directed against the Chinese.

Noting that "the principal objection of the petitioner to the ordinance in question is founded upon the supposed hostile motives of the supervisors in passing it," Field wrote:

> There is nothing, however, in the language of the ordinance or in the record of its enactment which in any respect tends to sustain this allegation. And the rule is general, with reference to the enactments of all legislative bodies, that the courts cannot inquire into the motives of the legislators in passing them except as they may be disclosed on the face of the acts or inferable from their operation, considered with reference to the condition of the country and existing legislation. The motives of the legislators, considered as to the purposes they had in view, will always be presumed to be to accomplish that which follows as the natural and reasonable effect of their enactments. Their motives, considered as the moral inducements for their votes, will vary with the different members of the legislative body. The diverse character of such motives and the impossibility of penetrating into the hearts of men and ascertaining the truth preclude all such inquiries as impracticable and futile. And in the present case, even if the motives of the supervisors were as alleged, the ordinance would not be thereby changed from a legitimate police regulation *unless in its enforcement it is made to operate only against the class mentioned*, and of this there is no pretense.[16]

It was in that final sentence that McAllister perceived his opportunity. Although bringing an action that charged selective enforcement of the law was hardly new, using equal protection as the lever had no precedent in Supreme Court jurisprudence. In *Ah Kow*, Field had ruled against a statute that had been enacted with obvious prejudice, "spiteful and hateful," not one that had merely been enforced as such. But the selectivity in granting permits left little to the imagination—"It's not rocket science," Justice Anthony Kennedy observed later, "to figure out that something was drastically wrong."

So McAllister and his co-counsel based their appeal on the claim that Yick Wo and the other Chinese launderers had been denied Fourteenth Amendment guarantees, both of "due process" and, again using Justice Field's *Ah Kow* opinion as precedent, "equal protection of the laws."

His brief read,

> Your petitioner and more than one hundred and fifty of his countrymen have been arrested upon the charge of carrying on business without having such special consent, while those who are not subjects of China, and who are conducting eighty odd laundries under similar conditions, are left unmolested and free to enjoy the enhanced trade and profits arising from this hurtful and unfair discrimination. The business of your petitioner, and of those of his countrymen similarly situated, is greatly impaired, and in many cases practically ruined, by this system of oppression to one kind of men and favoritism to all others.[17]

The Court rendered its verdict on May 10, 1886. As in *Barbier* and *Soon Hing*, the decision was unanimous, but this time for the plaintiff rather than the defendant. Justice Stanley Matthews wrote the opinion. To start, Matthews categorically denied precedent for the previous cases, which "involved simply a prohibition to carry on the washing and ironing of clothes in public laundries and washhouses . . . from ten o'clock at night until six o'clock in the morning of the following day." Those, he said, involved an ordinance that applied to all launderers equally—even though only the Chinese worked through the night—and fell under the government's legitimate right to legislate for the safety and well-being of its citizenry.

This case, Matthews wrote, was different. The ordinance in question gave arbitrary power to the supervisors to decide who could remain in business and who could not, all without applying known standards or giving explanation. Although Yick Wo and his co-petitioners "complied with every requisite deemed by the law or by the public officers charged with its administration necessary for the protection of neighboring property from fire or as a precaution against injury to the public health," they were ordered to close their businesses.

> No reason whatever, except the will of the supervisors, is assigned why they should not be permitted to carry on, in the accustomed manner, their harmless and useful occupation, on which they depend for a livelihood. And while this consent of the supervisors is withheld from them and from two hundred others who have also petitioned, all of whom happen to be Chinese subjects, eighty others, not Chinese subjects, are permitted to carry on the same business under similar conditions. The fact of this discrimination is admitted. No reason for it is shown, and the conclusion cannot be resisted that no reason for it exists except hostility to the race and nationality to which the petitioners belong, and which, in the eye of the law, is not justified.

As such, the California law was applied "with an evil eye and an unequal hand." That Yick Wo and his co-petitioners were not citizens did not matter. "The Fourteenth Amendment to the Constitution is not confined to the protection of citizens. It says: 'Nor shall any state deprive any person of life, liberty, or property, without due process of law; nor deny to any person within its jurisdiction the equal protection of the laws.'" The judgments of the lower courts were therefore reversed and Yick Wo, Wo Lee, and the other launderers were set free, where they promptly sank into obscurity.[18] For Hall McAllister, however, the victory in Washington was the capstone to a brilliant career and cemented his place as one of San Francisco's most prominent citizens.[19]

Yick Wo v. Hopkins has long been considered one of the nation's most important civil rights rulings, cited more than 150 times in subsequent Supreme Court opinions in cases ranging from apportionment to jury selection to loitering. But occasionally questions have also been raised as to why justices who had not seen fit to apply Fourteenth Amendment guarantees to African Americans in a string of civil and voting rights cases suddenly became sympathetic to Chinese laundrymen. The answer may be found in another unanimous decision the Court handed down the same day.

Santa Clara County v. Southern Pacific Railroad Company was a relatively banal tax case involving a new California constitution that altered the way in which property was valued. One provision denied to railroads certain deductions that were available to individuals. When the railroads refused to pay their vastly increased tax bills, state and local governments brought suit. What set the case apart were the grounds on which the railroads justified their actions.

Their brief attested,

> That the provisions of the Constitution and laws of California in respect to the assessment for *taxation of the property of railway corporations* operating railroads in more than one county, *are in violation of the Fourteenth Amendment* of the Constitution insofar as they require the assessment of their property at its full money value without making deduction, as in the case of railroads operated in one county and of other corporations and of natural persons, for the value of the mortgages covering the property assessed, thus imposing upon the defendant *unequal burdens, and to that extent denying to it the equal protection of the laws.*[20]

Although Justice Harlan, writing for the Court, agreed with the railroad that California had overstepped its taxing power, he did not address the Fourteenth Amendment issues in his opinion. But in the case syllabus, which appeared in the court record above Harlan's opinion, the reporter included a statement made by Chief Justice Waite regarding that issue.

> One of the points made and discussed at length in the brief of counsel for defendants in error was that "corporations are persons within the mean-

ing of the Fourteenth Amendment to the Constitution of the United States." Before argument, Mr. Chief Justice Waite said: The court does not wish to hear argument on the question whether the provision in the Fourteenth Amendment to the Constitution, which forbids a State to deny to any person within its jurisdiction the equal protection of the laws, applies to these corporations. We are all of the opinion that it does.[21]

While there is no direct evidence as to whether *Yick Wo* was decided in the laundrymen's favor because the Court viewed them as constitutionally wronged individuals, or because the justices were protecting constitutionally wronged businesses, it would not be unreasonable to assume that the second explanation is the more likely. Regardless of what motivated the unanimous Court to rule as it did, unfair application of a facially fair law seemed to provide a tool that attorneys for African American plaintiffs could use to press for voting rights in a Redeemed South.[22]

14

Mississippi Leads the South

W
HILE THE COURT'S DECISION IN THE *Civil Rights Cases* did not directly impact voting rights, it did serve to accelerate a de facto process that had begun virtually the day the Civil War ended and had stalled but by no means ended during Radical Reconstruction. "Almost immediately, whites began to map out a new master-servant relationship, one they hoped would look as much as possible like the old—excepting little other than its element of actual human ownership."[1] When Justice Bradley announced both that private individuals were immune from the postwar constitutional amendments and that African Americans could not seek redress in federal courts, except in cases where state governments officially announced their intentions to discriminate, he helped usher in a period of de jure racial discrimination that would last almost a century and was in many ways as odious as slavery itself.

With the Supreme Court, if not overtly an ally, certainly not an enemy, white Southerners could begin to consider moving from the second stage of voter suppression—fraud and contrivance—to the third—disfranchising black Americans with the law. Contrivance, after all, can be an uncertain currency, and some that were employed in the Redeemed South were ludicrous. Southern officials had been forced to openly defend tissue ballots, ballot boxes with false bottoms, and ballot box stuffing. South Carolina had introduced a device called the "eight-box ballot," each box designated for a specific candidate or party. A voter was required to match the ballot to the box or his vote would be invalidated. The manner in which the ballot and the ballot box were labeled rendered it virtually impossible for someone not literate to cast a valid vote. Whites unable to read were given assistance by poll workers, whereas blacks were left to try to decipher the system on their own. Despite the obvious intent of disfranchising African Americans, the eight-box ballot law comported with the Court's previous rulings.

So egregious were these practices that in 1890, Thomas Brackett Reed of Maine, the sitting speaker of the United States House of Representatives—and a Republican—published an article in the *North American Review* attacking white Southern Democrats. One of his targets was the eight-box law, and he cited an 1888 speech by John P. Richardson III, governor of South Carolina, who had extolled the practice. "We have now the rule of a minority of four hundred thousand [whites] over a majority of six hundred thousand [blacks]," Richardson had said. "No army at Austerlitz or Waterloo or Gettysburg could ever be wielded like that mass of six hundred thousand people. The only thing which stands to-day between us and their rule is a flimsy statute—the Eight-Box Law—which depends for its effectiveness upon the unity of the white people."[2]

"No form of government can be based on systematic injustice; least of all a republic," Reed complained. "All governments partake of the imperfections of human nature and fall far short not only of the ideals dreamed of by good men, but even of the intentions of ordinary men. Nevertheless, if perfection be unattainable, it is still the duty of every nation to live up to the principles of simple justice, and at least follow the lights it can clearly see."[3] While Republicans had not always been paragons of "simple justice," they certainly seemed so by comparison.

To prove it, Reed needed to look no further than the words of Southern whites themselves. Of ballot box stuffing, for example, he had any number of examples to choose from.

> Where else on earth would you get such a declaration as came from John P. Finley, of Greenville, Miss., for twelve years treasurer of his county—a declaration made in the presence of his fellow-citizens— that he did not consider ballot-box stuffing a crime, but a necessity; that in a case of race supremacy a man who stuffed a ballot box would not forfeit either his social or business standing; and that ballot-box stuffing, so far as he knew, was looked upon by the best element in the South as a choice between necessary evils?

Reed offered another example. "You would search far before you would find the parallel of what Watt K. Johnson said. 'I would stuff a ballot-box,' said he, 'if required to do it, to put a good Republican in office, as I would a Democrat, as my object is to have a good honest government.' 'Good honest government' by ballot-box stuffing!"[4]

But not all Southern Democrats were so sanguine about the wisdom of perpetuating fraud. In Mississippi, Judge J. J. Chrisman told his fellow Democrats,

> Sir, it is no secret that there has not been a full vote and a fair count in Mississippi since 1875—that we have been preserving the ascendency of the white people by revolutionary methods. In plain words, we have been stuffing the ballot boxes, committing perjury, and here and there in the state carrying the elections by fraud and violence until the whole machinery for elections was about to rot down. The public conscience revolted . . . it required no Solomon to see that the ballot-box-stuffer cannot always be relied on to elect the best man to office.[5]

However much revulsion Southerners claimed to feel, there was no arguing with results. In Mississippi, for example, the entire congressional delegation and virtually the entire state government were white and Democrat, even though blacks outnumbered whites in the state's population by 742,559 to 544,851. Still, despite terror, fraud, and what seemed to be an exercise in futility, black Americans continued, even at risk to their lives, to attempt to vote. For a permanent solution that would be immune to the vagaries of Congress and even the Supreme Court, white Democrats would need to use the law to disfranchise a group of American citizens that the Constitution now said could not be denied the vote on account of race. Since, with *Strauder* on the books, no discrimination could be prescribed by statute, Democrats sought "a means of disenfranchisement which, on its face, would be noncoercive and nonviolent."[6] Savvy Mississippi Democrats realized that the most effective way to achieve that end would be by copying the very stratagem Radical Republicans had employed twenty years before—if the Reconstruction South had been forced to adopt new constitutions to guarantee blacks the vote, the Redeemer South would do the same to take it away. And so a move began in Mississippi to convene a constitutional convention "principally with a view to changing suffrage qualifications."[7]

At first, it seemed that those who favored such an approach could simply tap into the lingering resentment engendered by the constitution that had been forced on Mississippi in 1868. Judge Solomon S. Calhoon, a convention proponent, observed that "the effrontery of such a collection of irresponsible men undertaking to frame organic law, aroused intense indignation and scorn, which extended beyond the makers to the work and persisted against that constitution as long as it existed."[8]

But Mississippians soon realized that drafting a new constitution was not going to be the simple, straightforward operation they assumed it would be. While whites were virtually unanimous in their desire to disfranchise African Americans, there were any number of other contentious issues that constitutional debates would inevitably dredge up. Mississippi had an economic class divide in which small farmers deeply resented the power of large landowners and the centralization of wealth. They wanted any new constitution to mandate that judges be elected rather than appointed, that corporations be taxed at the same rate as small farmers, that legislation favoring moneyed interests be drastically restricted, and that the legislature be structured to more reflect what they saw as popular will. Even denying black Mississippians the vote turned out to be more difficult to achieve than first thought—poor and illiterate white men might easily be swept away as well, which would erode the power of state officials with large numbers of such voters in their districts. One of Mississippi's United States senators, Edward C. Walthall, called a convention "an unnecessary, expensive, and dangerous experiment" which would "restrict the elective franchise by imposing on it conditions which would strike down tens of thousands best white Democrats in Mississippi."[9] James Z. George, Walthall's colleague in the Senate, was in favor, stating that it would "enable us to maintain a home government under the control of the white people of the state."[10]

Because of this uncertainty, "Several ineffectual efforts were made between 1876 and 1890 to have a Constitutional Convention called; these efforts failed because a majority of the white people seemed firmly convinced that a convention would be powerless to so far disfranchise the negroes as to give the white people a majority of the electors of the state."[11]

But with the United States Supreme Court showing a willingness to tacitly support white supremacy, momentum began to build. A resolution calling for a convention passed in the state house of representatives in 1886, but failed in the senate. In 1888, the resolution passed in both houses, but was vetoed by Governor Robert Lowry. During this period, Mississippi Democrats had to content themselves with the traditional means of denying black citizens the vote—fraud and terror.

Some Democrats viewed the inaction with growing alarm. On January 1, 1888, W. L. Nugent, president of the Mississippi Bar Association, warned,

[Negroes] cannot, in their present state of enlightenment be allowed to administer the affairs of the State. Their majority must not be allowed, encouraged or stimulated to assert itself to the injury of both races ... The ignoring of [Negroes'] plain constitutional and statutory rights, though necessitated by our present surroundings, must ultimate in greater evils than we now seek to avoid, unless some remedy be ascertained and supplied; society cannot long bear the strain of a continued disregard of suffrage rights, even though required for its preservation ... The difficult and almost impossible task ahead of us is, to secure to the white people the control of public affairs with full consent of the negro; to bring the colored voters, by just methods, to a thorough recognition of existing conditions, and of their complete incompetency; and to devise some plan by which, consistent with absolute right, continued and continuing good government may be secured, to ourselves and our children.[12]

While few disagreed with Nugent's assessment, fear that a new constitution would be drafted at the expense of some white voters as well as black continued to dominate the process.

As 1888 drew to a close, however, those fears became moot. In the presidential election of that November, Republican Benjamin Harrison succeeded in defeating incumbent Grover Cleveland, although Harrison received fewer popular votes and Cleveland won every electoral vote from Delaware to Texas. But Cleveland, a native New Yorker, lost his home state and its thirty-six electoral votes when his anti-corruption message stoked the ire of Tammany Hall politicians, for whom corruption was something of a religion. Without New York, and no power base in the Midwest and West, Cleveland was finished.

With his base of strength in the former Confederacy, Grover Cleveland had hardly been a friend to African Americans. He "seemed indifferent to upholding Reconstruction-era laws in the South. Between 1886 and 1888, the Cleveland Administration brought only 24 such cases into federal court, and during Cleveland's entire four-year term, the Justice Department secured only two convictions under the Enforcement Acts."[13]

Harrison, on the other hand, realized all too well that Republicans had no hope of ever winning a Southern state without a hefty number of black voters, and Republicans needed to find a way not only to get African Americans to the ballot box, but also to make sure that their votes were counted. Harrison had promised during his campaign to ensure fair elections in the South, a commitment that appealed to northern Republicans for political reasons, not because they had any desire to expend government resources to achieve racial justice.

In 1889, with Harrison's blessing, Henry Cabot Lodge of Massachusetts announced his intention to introduce a federal elections bill in the House, a measure that would provide, for national elections, oversight of voter registration, access to the ballot, and supervision of vote counting in any congressional district where one hundred people requested it. A federal election supervisor would be appointed in each judicial circuit and granted sweeping powers, which included investigating anyone who attempted to deny the vote to a qualified person and, if appropriate, recommending prosecution to the Justice Department.

Lodge attempted to downplay the notion that the supervisors would usurp state prerogatives.

> These officers have no power whatever to interfere with local officers or existing methods. Their only duty is to protect the honest voter, secure evidence to punish wrong-doers, and make public every fact in connection with the election. The State systems, whether they provide for the secret and official ballot or otherwise, are all carefully protected under this law against any interference from United States officers.[14]

Southerners were not persuaded. To them, the Lodge bill was nothing less than the resurrection of the same Reconstruction initiatives that Democrats had spent two decades trying to get rid of. They called it a "force bill," an extremely pejorative epithet in the post-Reconstruction South.

Faced with the prospect of the federal government taking control of its elections, Mississippi Democrats' reluctance to call a constitutional convention evaporated. Incendiary issues such as distribution of power in the legislature, rights of small farmers, and election of judges became unimportant, subordinated to the "all absorbing suffrage question," the "leading matter" that a constitutional convention would address.[15]

A Mississippi editorial read,

> It is frankly admitted that the great question before [the convention] is a political one—how to frame the laws so as to keep the control of the State with the whites for all time to come, how to prevent it from ever falling again into the hands of negroes and carpet baggers as it did in 1868 ... Mississippi is safe today under white rule, nor can we see any danger ahead to white supremacy; but it has been deemed wise to take the proper precautions now, and to frame a constitution that will render negro supremacy impossible. This is the great and important question which has been discussed in advance, which promises to be the leading matter before the convention.[16]

In November 1889, Mississippi elected pro-convention Robert Stone as governor, replacing Robert Lowry. Stone took office in January 1890, and the following month the state legislature passed a resolution authorizing a constitutional convention to meet in August of that year, which Governor Stone signed. In March 1890, Henry Cabot Lodge introduced his bill in the House of Representatives, and another Massachusetts Republican, George Frisbie Hoar, introduced a similar bill in the Senate.

Delegates would be chosen for the Mississippi convention by county, which meant that populist issues would weigh on the process. But the fights would only be intraparty, among Democrats. Although a movement began in the Republican Party, particularly among black voters, to elect as many delegates to the convention as possible, Democrats, by the usual means, made certain that virtually none would be elected. The usual means included murder—Marsh Cook, a white Republican, was ambushed and killed on a country road while campaigning to be a delegate. As a result, of the 135 delegates chosen, only two were Republicans, both from Bolivar County, in the heart of the black belt, where 3,222 whites lived among 26,737 blacks.[17] One of these was the convention's only black delegate, Isaiah Montgomery, who had risen from slavery, owned by Jefferson Davis's brother, to become perhaps the wealthiest black landowner in the state. Montgomery was on record as willing to acquiesce to disfranchisement.

On July 2, 1890, the Lodge bill passed the House by six votes. Although prospects in the Senate were unclear, with a Democratic filibuster in the wind, when the Mississippi constitutional convention met the following month, the potential for federal inspectors making certain that elections were conducted according to law was on the mind of every Democrat. Ensuring that "according to law" would prevent African Americans from voting was the unquestioned single most important feature to be incorporated into the convention's product. As delegate James K. Vardaman, later to be elected both governor and United States senator, observed, "There is no use to equivocate or lie about the matter. Mississippi's constitutional convention of 1890 was held for no other purpose than to eliminate the nigger from politics ... let the world know it just as it is."[18]

On the eve of the convention, the Jackson *Daily Clarion-Ledger* ran a prescient editorial.

> If the force bill now pending in Congress, passes, it is fortunate for Mississippi that she will be able through her Constitutional Convention soon to assemble to put such restrictions on suffrage as to render it largely nugatory and deprive it of much of its power for evil. Other Southern states are not so favorably situated, but the example set by Mississippi can be followed by them if the measures adopted prove adequate to meet the evil.[19]

Although there was unanimity of purpose, the question of method continued to be thorny—no state had ever attempted to end-run the Fifteenth Amendment before, and the delegates in Jackson felt the eyes of the South, if not the entire nation, on their every move. Even whether or not poor whites should be stricken from the rolls was not clear—depending on the rules for apportionment, wealthier counties with a more educated and literate population might stand to gain power in state government if poor whites were denied the vote along with blacks. In some cases, however, the "white counties" needed poor whites, and some black belt counties were willing to have poor whites disfranchised as long as blacks were denied the vote as well.

Another factor, perhaps an overriding one, intruded into this hodge-podge. The second section of the Fourteenth Amendment stipulated that if citizens of a state were denied the vote on account of race, the state would be penalized by a reduction in their House of Representatives delegation, so any method of reducing or eliminating the African American vote could not seem to do so overtly. The *Natchez Daily Democrat* wrote, "Some are hoping for a new and undiscovered solution of the suffrage question, but these will be disappointed, as time and circumstances have not yet exhumed the key to any solution outside the old Democratic methods," meaning fraud and intimidation.[20]

The easiest solution seemed to be accepting the black vote—or at least some of it—but diluting it with a vast increase in the white vote. A number of schemes were floated along these lines. One was a proposal to give the wealthy additional votes, based on the amount of property they held or property taxes they paid, but that aroused too much of a furor among the populist farmers to have any serious chance of adoption. But other proposals to water down the black vote by increasing the white vote got a more enthusiastic reception. One of these was a proposal that Mississippi become the first state in the Union to officially grant the vote to women.

Enfranchising women was the subject of serious debate, which went on for weeks. Agitation for women's suffrage was nationwide by 1890, and more than a few men foresaw women casting ballots sooner rather than later. There was a question of how to limit eligibility to white women, but there seemed any number of ways to ensure that black women could be kept off the voting lists. Conservatives were aghast at the idea, however, and the *Clarion-Ledger*, the state's leading newspaper, moaned that Mississippi would be "a laughing stock of the country."[21] Eventually, but not without reluctance, the idea was abandoned, and disfranchisement was entrusted to a committee to find a solution.

Before getting to voter eligibility, the committee was forced to deal with apportionment. Power in the state legislature had resided largely with the black belt counties in the western third of the state. Representation was based on total population, but because so few black men actually voted, black belt whites exercised a disproportionate degree of control in state government. The plan that emerged would sharply curtail their influence. Although no county would see a decrease in representation, thirteen additional lower house seats were created and assigned to white counties. In addition, a number of new legislative districts were created by carving out the white sections of black counties.

At first there was furious opposition from black county delegates, but with Senator George and Judge Calhoon throwing their full weight behind reapportionment, the black belt county delegates grudgingly agreed. "Senator George himself said that the reapportionment of representation was not the plan he would approve for a 'homogeneous free people, the main body of whom are capable of self-government.' He regretted to disturb the legislative apportionment but felt that such a step was 'demanded by the fundamental necessity of the situation.'"[22]

With apportionment resolved, George and his colleagues turned to disfranchisement. They settled on a series of rules that, while making no reference to race, would disqualify almost every black Mississippi resident while admitting almost every poor, illiterate white. Provisions included a two-year residency requirement, an annual poll tax, and an elaborate test, which required an applicant to read and interpret a section of the state constitution chosen by a local official. This last qualification purported to be a test for literacy—which had previously been dismissed as it would have disqualified thousands of whites—but the committee had added a wrinkle to keep that from occurring. Whether or not an applicant had satisfied the requirement was left solely to the registrar's judgment. In theory—and, as it turned out, in practice—whites could be given the most simple clauses to read (and if necessary be helped along by agreeable poll workers) while African Americans were given serpentine, incomprehensible clauses, which had been inserted into the document for that very purpose.

In 1946, race-baiting Senator Theodore Bilbo, during his campaign for reelection, remarked, "The poll tax won't keep 'em [blacks] from voting. What keeps 'em from voting is section 244 of the constitution of 1890 that Senator George wrote. It says that a man to register must be able to read and explain the constitution when read to him ... And then Senator George wrote a constitution that damn few white men and no niggers at all can explain."[23]

Literacy tests were not new. As a University of Mississippi law professor pointed out in 1910,

> An amendment requiring that every person 'be able to read any article of the Constitution, or any section of the statutes of this state, before being admitted an elector,' was overwhelmingly adopted by Connecticut in 1854, being the first law of its kind in the United States. This step was taken as a protection against illiterate foreigners who were moving to the state in great numbers.[24]

But the new constitution was drawn up not merely to prevent any new registration by Mississippi's extensive African American population, but also to disqualify those already on the rolls. It required reregistration of every potential voter in the state, included a list of disqualifying crimes—bribery, burglary, theft, arson, obtaining money or goods under false pretenses, perjury, forgery, embezzlement, or bigamy—thought to be committed disproportionally by African Americans, and required a voter to be "of good moral character."

When African Americans were off the voting lists, they would be stricken from jury rolls as well. Finally, to ensure the new constitution's adoption, the state legislature changed a law that required the document be submitted to the voters and instead allowed a vote among the very delegates who had drawn it up to be sufficient.

George and Calhoon's efforts notwithstanding, the franchise sections of the new constitution were not universally met with relief and praise. Instead, the new requirements, particularly the "understanding" section, 244, were widely condemned. Critics groused that the clause would either be ineffective in disfranchising blacks or too effective in disfranchising whites. There was no shortage of shrill moral outrage, as by delegate L. W. Magruder, who called the plan "a fraud on its face—the serpent whose trail is on every section."[25]

But criticism dried up when white Mississippians realized how effective Senator George's clause would be—that it would reduce African Americans to political irrelevancy. By 1892, when Grover Cleveland regained the White House—he had learned his lesson from four years earlier—black voting in Mississippi was already fast becoming a memory.

And so, when the delegates ratified their new constitution on November 1, 1890, a new era in the post-Reconstruction South was born.

15

The First Test

Mills v. Green

I N SOUTH CAROLINA, FRAUD, INTIMIDATION, AND EVEN
the eight-box law were not sufficient for white supremacist Democrats. To their astonishment and disgust, African Americans
continued to vote, albeit in ever dwindling numbers. Blacks even succeeded in electing some of their number to positions in state government,
and one, George Washington Murray, to the United States House of
Representatives.

To buttress its disfranchisement efforts, in 1882, the state legislature
passed a law that required all voters to reregister by June of that year or
be forever barred from voting. The only exceptions were for men turning
twenty-one after that date or moving to South Carolina from another
state or country. Residency requirements, a poll tax—nonpayment of
which was made a criminal offense—and voting registrars who made it
as difficult as possible for men of color to register would, it was expected,
drastically cull the voting rolls. In addition, a man registered to vote in
one precinct was required to reregister if he moved to another, a provi-

sion aimed at black farm laborers, whose work was crop-oriented and seasonal.

But still, black voters were not dissuaded. "Over the last decades of the nineteenth century, black voters' persistence continued to frustrate white racists . . . Whites needed more than legislation to stop them."[1] When Mississippi's 1890 constitution did not immediately arouse ire in the federal courts, white South Carolinians came to understand that they might have been handed a blueprint for finally ridding the state of both black voters and black officeholders.

But as in Mississippi, while there may have been agreement on the need to eliminate African Americans from the voting rolls, there were deep conflicts as to just which white men should rule in their place. Here also there were deep divisions between small farmers and the financial elite. But unlike in Mississippi, where the most powerful and influential politicians had lined up against the populists, in South Carolina, populists had the inexorable force that was Benjamin R. "Pitchfork Ben" Tillman as their savior.

Even by the standards of racist Southern congressmen who got their start in the post-Reconstruction South and eventually dominated Congress—and would be instrumental in the enactment of New Deal legislation decades later—Tillman was unusual. He was known for outsized rhetoric—in addition to his comment about President Cleveland, Tillman bragged about murdering an African American to prevent him from voting, and insisted he would personally lead a lynch mob for any black man accused of raping a white woman. As a youth, Tillman had lost an eye—not in the Civil War in which he had never served, but afterward, as a result of a tumor. He never wore an eye patch, which gave him a somewhat grotesque backwoods mien, and added to the popular view of him as an unlettered, lower-class lout.

He was anything but.

Tillman's family owned considerable land, and he, in his own right, was a successful farmer before he entered politics. Nor was land the only inheritance received by Tillman from his family. An uncle, John Tillman, who is described as a man of strong intellectual qualities, left him a large library of the best English literature. Perhaps there may be a bit of the romantic in that picture of Tillman spending a good part of each day 'lying on the piazza floor reading French history and *Paradise Lost*,' but there can be no question as to his strong interest in books as well as in farming.[2]

Tillman was sufficiently savvy to downplay all that and bill himself as the champion of small farmers—men he privately viewed with contempt. When a close friend asked why he raised "so much hell" in his campaigns, Tillman replied, "Well ... if I didn't the damn fools wouldn't vote for me."[3] In office, Tillman prided himself on being a reformer, and to a great degree he was. He was an advocate for public education, of limiting the vast oligopolistic power of railroads, of revising tax and crop mortgage laws to benefit small farmers and business owners, and even of limiting work hours in cotton mills. To his supporters, it was easy to exaggerate Tillman, an elitist to his dying day, as "a man of the people."

But there was nothing exaggerated about Tillman's deep and abiding racism. "From the 1870s to the early twentieth century, it was hard to find an individual who played a role at more moments of crisis or who stood more whole-heartedly for the social and political order known as white supremacy."[4] He had first formed the Red Shirts in 1876 to fight against Republican rule, mainly through violence against black voters, and dedicated himself to returning African Americans to the bestial role he was convinced they merited. If anything, violence against black voters increased in subsequent elections, with Tillman urging on his Red Shirt followers.[5]

Tillman was elected governor in 1890, his main campaign vow to totally remove African Americans from the political process. He called for a new constitution to protect "Anglo-Saxon Supremacy," and "with that end in mind, he used Mississippi as his model for action ... Consequently, over the next two years, Tillman worked assiduously at having a similar constitution adopted in South Carolina. By December 1892, Tillman finally had enough support in the legislature to authorize a referendum on whether to call a constitutional convention."[6]

Even then, Tillman faced determined opposition from Republicans, African Americans, and, most significantly, anti-populist white Democrats. Although the Democrats did not band together with either white or black Republicans to form a Fusionist movement, they did have common cause, which resulted in, among other actions, a series of lawsuits attempting to halt the calling of a convention. In one, *ex parte Lumsden*, two white lawyers sued on behalf of two white men, one a former slave owner, and a black tailor, Lawrence Mills.

According to the 1882 voter registration law, new voters—those who recently turned twenty-one or moved to South Carolina from another state—could register only on the first Monday of each month, and only through July in order to vote in that year's fall election. "The limitation was vigorously enforced with respect to blacks and white Republicans."[7] Mills had become eligible in 1890, but on numerous occasions had been denied admittance to the registrar's office in Richland County—they had literally closed the door in his face—and so had been unable to register. The two white men had not been denied the right to vote, but had neglected to register, one because he had been out of town, and the other because he had been unaware of the law.

The lawsuit failed in state court. Soon afterward, in the November 1894 elections, Tillman's referendum on calling a convention passed by a mere 1,879 votes, a result that Republicans and many conservative Democrats denounced as fraudulent. They were almost certainly correct, since in areas of Tillman's strength, the pluralities were a good deal larger than even what had become the ballot-box-stuffed norm. In fact, a Charleston newspaper would later admit, "there is little doubt that the call to a convention was fairly defeated," and the conservative Democrat who had lost the race for governor called the election "the most fraudulent and outrageous ever held in this state."[8] By whatever means, Tillmanites had gained firm control of the state legislature and a call for a constitutional convention.

Pressing their advantage, on December 24, Tillman's legislature passed a law that scheduled an election for convention delegates for the following summer, and included restrictive rules for who would be allowed to vote for those delegates. Anyone wishing to cast a ballot for convention delegates was required to prove, in writing, that he had registered and voted in every election since becoming eligible, which for most black voters was impossible. Many poor whites would have also found providing such documentation difficult, but with Tillman's supporters in charge of most of the registration offices, this was not considered a serious impediment. The registration period itself was to be in March and only ten days long.

Republicans and conservative Democrats vowed to do what they could to block the convention. George Murray used what little influence he had to organize resistance, and also tried to help black voters register, an effort in which he largely failed as black applicants "were turned away in droves" by Tillman's registrars.[9]

After the registration closed, in an attempt to prevent the election, the two white lawyers who had lost in *Lumsden*, Henry Obear and Charles Douglas, filed a new action, this time in federal court, with Lawrence Mills, the black tailor, as the sole plaintiff. Mills, specifically citing W. Briggs Green, the registration supervisor for Richland County, claimed that he had been prevented from registering and that the restrictions themselves were discriminatory in violation of the Fourteenth Amendment, since they were clearly intended to deny black South Carolinians due process of the law. As such, the election of delegates should not be allowed to go forward, which would mean a new constitution could not be drafted. Obear and Douglas also threw in privileges and immunities, although the *Slaughter-House* precedent seemed unlikely to be broken. Oddly, they made no Fifteenth Amendment claim, although their argument would seem to have been a textbook example of denial or abridgement of the right to vote "on account of race." South Carolina argued that the law in no way denied due process since it would apply equally to blacks and whites. In addition, the state claimed the federal court had no jurisdiction, since "the matters, facts, and things alleged and complained of in the bill are matters relating to the political duties of [Green's] office."[10]

The case would normally have been heard by Judge Charles Simonton, but Simonton, a South Carolina native, had been embroiled in a fierce battle with Governor Tillman over the laws governing liquor dispensaries and deferred to his Fourth Circuit colleague, Nathan Goff.[11] (Tillman left the state house for the United States Senate in March 1895, leaving the governor's chair to a close ally, John G. Evans.) Goff, from West Virginia, heard Mills's appeal on April 19, 1895. Given that the courts had never overturned a law that did not announce itself as discriminatory—at least for African Americans—no one, especially Tillman and his supporters, was particularly worried.

But Nathan Goff broke with tradition and applied the law based on what was readily apparent even to white supremacists. (They had, after all, made no secret of their intentions.) He issued a temporary order on April 20, which he made permanent on May 8, 1895, in a blistering opinion. As to South Carolina's voting requirements in general, he wrote,

> A careful examination of the registration enactment of the state of South Carolina . . . brings me to the conclusion that if a voter who was duly qualified and entitled to register in May and June, 1882, did not, on account of absence, sickness, inadvertence, or other cause, register when the books were open in that year, he was not only prevented from voting at the general election in November, 1882, but was and has been prevented—under the law—from voting at all elections held in the state subsequent to said election in 1882. This seems almost incredible, yet I think it is correct. The statement is appalling, the outrage stupendous, the result close to the border land that divides outrage from crime. It is not necessary to discuss it further; likely the least said about it the better.[12]

As far as the convention act of 1894 was concerned, Goff said,

The one object that controlled the minds of those who formulated the enactment I have been considering was how to successfully destroy the greatest number of the ballots of the citizens of African descent, while at the same time to interfere with as few as possible of those of the white race. The fact is that, with a candor that was as frank as it was amazing, this was virtually admitted during the argument of this case. It is evident that the effect of this registration system is to fearfully impede the exercise of the right of suffrage by the colored voters of the state of South Carolina. It to a great extent, defeats their constitutional right to vote, and it seems to be its leading—I must be permitted to say, its only—object, the effect being to so legislate as to apparently respect constitutional requirements, but at the same time to stab to the death the rights and immunities guaranteed by them.[13]

Goff's opinion was the first since the ratification of the Fourteenth and Fifteenth Amendments to directly attack the transparent sleight of hand freely employed by the Redeemed South to deprive African Americans of their civil rights.

South Carolina whites were either aggrieved or outraged. One editorial read,

Up to last Thursday, both white factions were practically agreed that the Negro majority in this State should be eliminated by disfranchisement; but the question as to whether this should be accomplished with or without also disfranchising 'a single white man,' presented a formidable issue. Now that Judge Goff has practically decided that all Negroes will be entitled to vote in the approaching election, the important question is not whether a 'single white man' shall be disfranchised; but whether the white men can control the convention . . . The majority of the white people of the State only want justice.[14]

For outrage, one need look no further than Ben Tillman. "Governor Evans and Senator Tillman, upon hearing of Goff's decision, flew into an apoplectic rage and made vague threats of violent revolution."[15]

Instead, however, they appealed the ruling to circuit court, where the case, now *Green v. Mills*, would be heard in Richmond, Virginia. According to the rules then in place, Judge Goff would have been entitled to sit on the three-man panel, and even chair it. But, like Judge Simonton in the original action, he chose to recuse himself, this time in favor of Supreme Court Chief Justice Melville Fuller, who was in charge of the Fourth Circuit.

Morrison Waite had died in March 1888, and on April 30 President Cleveland nominated Melville W. Fuller to take his place. Fuller had practiced corporate law for three decades, was politically active—some said a hack—and, like his predecessor, had no judicial experience. If Waite's nomination had been met with accusations of mediocrity, Fuller, for many, did not represent a step up. He was described by a critic as the "fifth best lawyer in the city of Chicago," not meant as a compliment to either the man or the city. *The New York Times* praised Fuller's affability, his friends in both parties, the social prominence of his wife, his friendship with President Cleveland, and the number of his visits to plead cases before the Supreme Court as an attorney. Missing from the *Times* article and most other descriptions of Fuller was any praise for excellence or an incisive legal mind.[16] The *New-York Tribune* called Fuller "unknown," and said he was "practically a man without a record. His availability seems to have been the principal cause that led to his appointment."[17] Fuller seemed hardly the man to entrust with the civil rights of African Americans. He had "led legislative opposition to Lincoln's Emancipation Proclamation, had supported state constitutional provisions that rejected black suffrage and black migration, and had helped segregate Chicago schools."[18]

Although all the parties agreed that a quick ruling was vital—the convention was, after all, scheduled to meet in just a few months and delegates needed to be chosen—Fuller and his two fellow judges did not hear South Carolina's appeal until June 7, 1895. Four days later, they announced their decision. Judge Goff's ruling was set aside and the state was therefore free to proceed with the election of delegates under a set of rules that Goff had found—and events would prove—blatantly discriminatory. To justify his decision, Fuller, for the first time in such cases, employed a rationale that the Court would subsequently use to good effect to avoid enforcing the constitutional guarantees of equal rights.

Fuller wrote,

> It is well settled that a court of chancery is conversant only with matters of property and the maintenance of civil rights. The court has no jurisdiction in matters of a political nature, nor to interfere with the duties of any department of government, unless under special circumstances, and when necessary to the protection of rights of property, nor in matters merely criminal, or merely immoral which do not affect any right of property ... To assume jurisdiction to control the exercise of political powers, or to protect the purely political rights of individuals, would be to invade the domain of the other departments of government or of the courts of common law ... To interfere in the mode asked for by the complainants, would be to stop a popular election in one portion of the State, and thus arrest, as to it, the wheels of government.[19]

As for "irregularities in the conduct of an election, for receiving illegal or rejecting legal votes," Mills and other African Americans must look to the state laws that had been enacted for the purpose of denying them recourse to those very practices. On the Fifteenth Amendment, Fuller wasted almost no energy. "No discrimination on account of race, color or previous condition of servitude is charged, or pointed out as deducible on the face of the acts in question," he wrote with a healthy dollop of disingenuousness. He based this statement on his observation that Mills had suffered no injury at the hands of South Carolina because no election had taken place in which he was denied the right to vote. And while it was true that Mills "had claimed 'no threatened infringement of rights of property or civil rights,' [Fuller ignored] the fact that the very purpose of Mills's case was to ameliorate such a threat."[20] In fact, Tillman, in an interview with a Charleston newspaper, had said, "The one overpowering and essential idea which made the convention a necessity was the preservation of white supremacy by such purification of the suffrage as will save us from negro domination in future under any and all conditions."[21] It is difficult to read such a statement and not conclude that "discrimination on account of race, color or previous condition of servitude" was not present, but Fuller managed to do so.

With race discrimination and thus the Fifteenth Amendment off the table, Fuller was free to revert to what has become known as the "political question doctrine," and claim, as he did, a lack of jurisdiction. The theory is sound enough—requiring the judiciary to avoid substituting itself for either the legislative or the executive is fundamental to a system of separation of powers. In a tradition that stretches back to John Marshall in *Marbury v. Madison*, the Supreme Court has traditionally eschewed the "activist" position and declined to issue rulings that would inappropriately inject itself into the political process.

The problem is in application—just what is or is not political can come and go as practicalities demand. In contemporary society, "activist judges" have become a particular target of conservatives, yet it is difficult to imagine two cases more "political" than *Bush v. Gore* and *Citizens United*, in each of which conservative justices imposed themselves on the legislative process, to the applause of their philosophical bedfellows.

In Melville Fuller's time, the political question doctrine was used as a means of avoidance, and he was the first justice to use the political question doctrine to tap-dance around an equal rights appeal. "Where Goff was willing to act on what he knew to be true, Fuller stubbornly, and to a degree conveniently, refused to do likewise."[22]

With Fuller's ruling, the door was flung open for Tillman and Evans, and they rushed on through. Elections for delegates were held in August and, as everyone but Melville Fuller and his fellow judges might have predicted, Tillman's "Reformers" won 112 of the 160 seats. Forty-two seats went to conservative Democrats, who, whatever their differences with the Tillmanites, agreed with them on the need to disfranchise African Americans. Finally, in a state where eligible black male voters outnumbered whites by 130,000 to 100,000, only six black delegates were elected to be delegates.

The convention first met in Charleston on September 10, 1895, and continued until December 4, when, as in Mississippi, the constitution was ratified by the delegates rather than being submitted to the people. In early October, a preliminary plan was released to the public. Like the Mississippi constitution, it contained residency requirements, a poll tax, property tax, and a reading and understanding requirement. But Tillman's plan had an unusual wrinkle. Anyone who was "able to read and write any section of this Constitution, or show that he owns and pays taxes on $300 worth of property in this State" before January 1, 1898, would be registered for life. But "a separate record of all illiterate persons thus registered, sworn to by the registration officer" was to be filed with the clerk of court and in the office of secretary of state.

The record to be kept of the poor and illiterate infuriated some Democrats, who thought no white man should be on the same list as "sea island negroes." Tillman's fellow United States senator John L. M. Irby, also a convention delegate, exclaimed in an interview with the *Piedmont Headlight*, which was reprinted in newspapers across the state,

> I look upon that report as a political monstrosity, one of the most dangerous schemes ever concocted in the brain of man, and I shall fight it and vote against it if I have not another member upon the floor at my back. I do hope that The Headlight will go to work without delay and arouse the white voters of our State as to the danger that threatens both the poor and illiterate white men and also the political supremacy of the Anglo-Saxon race in our State.[23]

Irby and Tillman loathed each other, but Tillman was savvy enough to realize he couldn't afford to alienate conservative delegates, and the "poor and illiterate register" was removed. The final version required "residence in the State for two years, in the County one year, in the polling precinct in which the elector offers to vote four months, and the payment six months before any election of any poll tax then due." The property tax requirement for poor whites was eliminated, but written proof of payment of the previous year's poll tax was required.

Most significantly, the "reading and understanding" clause was made two-tiered. For one group,

> Up to January 1st, 1898, all male persons of voting age applying for registration who can read any Section in this Constitution submitted to them by the registration officer, or understand and explain it when read to them by the registration officer, shall be entitled to register and become electors. A separate record of all persons registered before January 1st, 1898, sworn to by the registration officer, shall be filed ... and such persons shall remain during life qualified electors unless disqualified by the other provisions of this Article.

It was assumed that white men, regardless of literacy or wealth, would qualify under these provisions.

For the second,

> Any person who shall apply for registration after January 1st, 1898, if otherwise qualified, shall be registered: *Provided*, That he can both read and write any Section of this Constitution submitted to him by the registration officer or can show that he owns, and has paid all taxes collectible during the previous year on property in this State assessed at three hundred dollars ($300) or more.

There was a broad list of disqualifying offenses, once again skewed to the types of offenses thought to be committed by African Americans. No one could register or vote who had been "convicted of burglary, arson, obtaining goods or money under false pretenses, perjury, forgery, robbery, bribery, adultery, bigamy, wife-beating, house-breaking, receiving stolen goods, breach of trust with fraudulent intent, fornication, sodomy, incest, assault with intent to ravish, miscegenation, larceny, or crimes against the election laws." In case too many whites were caught in that net, "the pardon of the Governor shall remove such disqualification."

The constitution also disqualified those deemed to be "idiots, insane, paupers supported at the public expense, and persons confined in any public prison."

There was an additional section of the new constitution not involving suffrage, but of great significance for the future. "Separate schools shall be provided for children of the white and colored races, and no child of either race shall ever separate be permitted to attend a school provided for children of the other race."

★ ★ ★

In September, while the newly elected South Carolina constitutional convention delegates were preparing to join in removing the state's citizens of color from the political process, Obear and Douglas had launched an appeal of the circuit court decision overturning Judge Goff's injunction. They filed their motion with the Supreme Court on September 4, 1895, one week before the convention met, but the Court did not enter the appeal until September 19. More than a month would pass before the Court formally accepted the submission on October 25, by which time the convention had formulated its draft of suffrage rules to which Senator Irby had taken such umbrage.

South Carolina's defense was simple. The state objected to the filing on the grounds that, since the election of delegates had already taken place, "there is now no actual controversy involving real and substantial rights between the parties to the record, and no subject matter upon which the judgment of this Court can operate." The Court agreed. "We are of opinion," wrote Justice Gray, "that the appeal must be dismissed upon this ground, without considering any other question appearing on the record or discussed by counsel."[24]

Gray added,

> The duty of this Court, as of every other judicial tribunal, is to decide actual controversies by a judgment which can be carried into effect, and not to give opinions upon moot questions or abstract propositions, or to declare principles or rules of law which cannot affect the matter in issue in the case before it. It necessarily follows that when, pending an appeal from the judgment of a lower court, and without any fault of the defendant, an event occurs which renders it impossible for this Court, if it should decide the case in favor of the plaintiff, to grant him any effectual relief whatever, the court will not proceed to a formal judgment, but will dismiss the appeal.

And so the merits of the case were never discussed, nor was the Court required to evaluate South Carolina's conduct with respect to the guarantees of the Fourteenth and Fifteenth Amendments.

While Gray's reasoning was sound, as was Fuller's in the circuit court appeal, he, like Fuller, chose to avoid an alternative that would have comported more with real-world events than the politically palatable alternative he chose. Where Fuller and his fellows could have—and should have—prevented a hopelessly tainted election, Gray and his colleagues should have—and could have—voided it. Instead they chose an approach well suited to Beckett, Ionesco, or Joseph Heller.

> In June, when the matter came before the Fourth Circuit, Chief Justice Fuller reversed Goff's injunction because the delegates election had not yet happened and thus had not injured Lawrence Mills. Now, subsequent to that election and subsequent to his injury, the Supreme Court

turned down his appeal, because, it held, the registration requirements were dead letters.[25]

As a result, when the new South Carolina constitution was formally ratified on December 4, 1895, African American participation in the affairs of their government was a dead letter as well.

16

Peer Review

Williams v. Mississippi

I N DECEMBER 1895, TWO DAYS AFTER CHRISTMAS, THE body of Eliza Brown was discovered under a pile of clothing in the shack in which she lived in Washington County, Mississippi. She had been strangled, and her live-in lover Henry Williams had disappeared. There had been bad blood between the two, Williams having voiced strong suspicions to friends that Eliza had been unfaithful, and so he was immediately sought as a prime suspect in the murder.

Williams was found hiding in an attic a few days later and was arrested. His statements to police were muddled. For the most part, he denied killing Eliza Brown, although at one point said he couldn't be certain whether he had done so or not, presumably because he was drunk. Williams also said that when he had arrived home on Christmas Day, he had observed another man leaving, hat in hand, although he could not identify the man, nor did any other evidence of the visitor turn up. Williams was adamant that he had not hidden the body under the clothing—Eliza Brown took in washing for a living—but he admitted freely that he was not unhappy his lover was dead, and insisted she would have felt the same way if it was him lying there instead.

The case appeared to be uncomplicated, with evidence of Williams's guilt strong if not absolute. As with Virginia's Reynolds brothers, if Henry Williams had been white, it might have been possible to plant some doubt in jurors' minds. But here again, a domestic killing by a black man did not promise to result in anything but an abbreviated trial followed by a guilty verdict and death sentence.

Which was precisely how events played out. Henry Williams was indicted by an all-white grand jury, its members drawn from local voting rolls, and then convicted, on June 16, 1896, by a similarly comprised petit jury. He was quickly sentenced to hang by a white judge.

Under most circumstances, the execution of Henry Williams on the scheduled date of July 30, 1896, would have proceeded without fuss or fanfare, and Williams would have become nothing more than a statistic in the annals of Mississippi jurisprudence. But Henry Williams was to become a good deal more than that, because his lawyer, Cornelius J. Jones Jr., intended to make his client the centerpiece of one of the most important voting rights cases brought before the United States Supreme Court since the end of the Civil War.

★ ★ ★

To say it was rare for a black lawyer to induce dread among white Mississippi politicians in the 1890s is an understatement, but that is precisely what Cornelius Jones did. Indefatigable and fearless, by the time he took up Henry Williams's case, Jones had already spent more than five years on a crusade to overthrow the 1890 Mississippi Constitution.

Jones had been born in Vicksburg, Mississippi, in 1858, the son of two slaves who registered their marriage after the city fell to Ulysses Grant in July 1863. He attended a Freedmen's Bureau school, after which he eventually enrolled at the newly commissioned Alcorn University—named for Mississippi governor James Alcorn, a Confederate general who had become a Republican—the facilities purchased for $40,000 from Oakland College, an institution for Southern white gentry that had closed at the onset of the Civil War. Alcorn's first president was Hiram Revels, the first African American to serve in the United States Senate, who resigned that seat to accept the position.

While there is no official academic record, Jones must have been a quite talented student. After he left Alcorn, he did a stint as a school-teacher in Louisiana, then returned to Mississippi to study law. There he was hired by Anselm McLaurin, considered the foremost criminal lawyer in the state. McLaurin would be elected governor, appointed as senator, and become "one of the most active, diligent, practical, and courageous members" of the 1890 convention.[1] As such, Anselm McLaurin would burnish his reputation by helping to draft the document that disfran-chised virtually every black man in Mississippi, against which Corne-lius Jones would crusade for the remainder of his life. But for whatever reason—and he never said why—in the years before the convention was called, this bastion of white society was drawn to the young black lawyer.

In 1888, as he turned thirty, Jones decided to enter politics. Black voters, once a majority in Mississippi, had receded in number but were still sufficiently represented that Jones won a seat in the state legislature. As soon as the voting provisions of the 1890 constitution went into effect, however, he was turned out of his seat. Whether due to personal animus or to seek justice for his fellow African Americans—or both—Jones was soon using the legal system to test the provisions that had denied him and his fellow black legislators their positions in government.

The first case he found was, as with Henry Williams, an ordinary murder, a workplace killing. On December 12, 1892, a black laborer named John Gibson killed the manager of the Refuge Plantation, Rob-ert Stinson, in a dispute over docked wages.[2] Gibson admitted to be-ing drunk and seeking out and confronting his victim. What was odd about the case was that while Gibson was not armed, the plant manager was—with a six-shooter and a heavy wooden staff. Facing Gibson down, the plant manager beat him with the stick until Gibson collapsed into the dirt. Gibson struggled toward the manager, who fired his revolver. But the shots missed and Gibson succeeded in reaching the other man. During the ensuing struggle, four more shots were heard and the plant manager crumpled to the ground, dead on the spot. Gibson attempted to flee but was almost immediately captured.

A verdict of self-defense, at least as far as the murder charge was concerned, could easily have been rendered, but instead, as was routine for black men in Mississippi, Gibson was quickly indicted, tried, and sentenced to hang, with every person on the bench, in the jury box, or pleading for the prosecution being white.

Cornelius Jones had not been Gibson's lawyer at trial, but took over for his appeal and succeeded in winning a new trial, purely on a technicality. At the second trial—which all concerned knew would have the same outcome as the first—Jones laid the groundwork for an eventual appeal to federal court on Fourteenth Amendment grounds, specifically that Gibson had been denied due process because he had not been judged by a jury of his peers. "His peers," of course, meant other African Americans, none of whom had served on the grand or petit juries. That, according to Jones, was due to a new method of selecting jury pools implemented in 1892, which drew jurors from voting post-1890 rolls, and they contained virtually no African Americans. The previous law, based on the 1880 state constitution, had allowed 7,000 adult African American men to be eligible for jury service in Bolivar County, where the trial would take place. Since Gibson's crime had been committed before the 1892 change took effect, Jones claimed the jury pool should have been chosen based on the earlier statute. As it was, "the great prejudice prevailing against him among the white race" ensured Gibson's conviction and denied him the constitutional protections to which he was entitled.[3]

Jones filed a motion to quash the indictment on both Fourteenth Amendment grounds and the constitutional prohibition against ex post facto laws. The motion was denied. Gibson was once more convicted and sentenced to hang.

By the time Jones filed another appeal, this one to remove the case to

federal court, he was also representing another accused murderer, Charley Smith. Jones made a similar motion at Smith's trial to have the case
removed to federal court. This motion was denied as well. Although the
case against Smith was not terribly strong—the prosecution could only
prove that he had started a brawl in which another man had been shot
and killed—he too was convicted and sentenced to be hanged. Jones appealed both Gibson's and Smith's convictions to the Mississippi Supreme
Court, where, as expected, he lost. He then announced his intention to
bring his appeal to the United States Supreme Court.

To press the action, Jones journeyed to Washington, where he
teamed with another African American attorney, Emmanuel Hewlett,
a well-connected law school graduate of Boston University. Jones took
his appeal to the public as well as to the Court, and became a frequent
speaker at churches and to civic groups. Word got around, and soon Cornelius Jones found himself the subject of numerous laudatory articles in
both the black and the white press. A talk he gave at the Vermont Avenue Baptist Church was covered by the Washington *Evening Star*, at
the time the capital's leading newspaper. The subject of the meeting, the
Star noted, "was to lay before the colored people of the city the merits of
the case of John Gibson and Charley Smith against the state of Mississippi . . . Much interest is being manifested in the case, not only by the
colored people here, but throughout the south generally, as it involves the
question of colored men serving on juries in the south."[4]

"Both of the plaintiffs are colored men," the article continued, "and
have been three times convicted by the Mississippi state courts of murder,
and the supreme court of the state has three times reversed the decision of
the lower courts." The implication that Jones had succeeded in thwarting
Mississippi was overstated, but gives a sense of the favorable reception he
had received.

From here, the *Star* observed, Jones had "carried [the case] to the
state supreme court upon the grounds that there were no colored men
on the juries which indicted and convicted the men. The supreme court
sustained the lower courts in excluding colored men from jury duty, and

upon this Judge White of the United States Supreme Court in July last granted a writ of error, and certified the case to the Supreme Court."

The newspaper excerpted Jones's speech. "There is a practice prevailing in many of the courts of the south," he was quoted as saying, "and especially the state of Mississippi, wherein negroes, in state courts, are uniformly excluded from jury service, however well qualified, and this exclusion is on account of their race and color. The exclusion is effected by state officers purposely and intentionally." Jones insisted this was a "gross violation" of the Fourteenth Amendment to the Constitution, and expressed confidence the justices would agree with him. If they did, "it will revolutionize the present system of jury service in many states of the south."

Smith was argued on December 16, 1895, and *Gibson* two days later. African American newspapers could not contain their praise for the crusading black lawyer from the cradle of white supremacy who might change history by pleading landmark cases to the highest court in the land. "Mr. Jones is a Mississippian by birth," *The Washington Bee*, a black newspaper, wrote, "and a man who enjoys the full confidence and respect of the citizens of his State, regardless of race or color. Having occupied many places of honor with great credit, we are also creditably informed that the judges of the courts of the State and members of the bar respect him for his manly bearing and knowledge of the law in the conduct of his cases."[5]

Jones, however, did not conduct *Gibson* or *Smith* well at all. The first hurdle he and Hewlett faced was to persuade the justices that the Supreme Court should even be hearing the cases. If he could not provide evidence that black potential jurors had been excluded *specifically* on racial grounds, there would be no federal jurisdiction in either case. Such demonstrations, however, had become increasingly difficult. Savvy white Southern legislators would no longer make the mistake that West Virginia had in *Strauder*; nor would a state official make a damning public statement, as had the Delaware Supreme Court chief justice in *Neal*. The only avenue that seemed open was that which had been used successfully in *Yick Wo*, that the administration of laws facially race-neutral had been obviously and blatantly discriminatory.

But Emmanuel Hewlett, who wrote the brief in *Gibson*, did not cite *Yick Wo*. Rather, he attempted to portray the case as an extension of *Strauder* and *Neal*. He stated that "there had not been for a number of years any colored man ever summoned on the grand jury of said county court; and that the colored citizens were purposely, on account of their color, excluded from jury service by the officers of the law charged with the selection of said jurors." This was a dubious strategy at best, but made worse because Jones and Hewlett presented no evidence in either case that demonstrated willful discrimination by Mississippi officials, only certified statements by the plaintiffs that the discrimination in jury selection had been present.

They also blundered in citing the *Slaughter-House Cases* as their justification for seeking Fourteenth Amendment relief. "It was designed," Hewlett wrote, "to assure the colored race the enjoyment of all of the civil rights that under the law are enjoyed by white persons, and to give that race the protection of the Federal government in that enjoyment, when it should be denied by the States." But the *Slaughter-House Cases* had done precisely the opposite by creating different "privileges and immunities" of citizenship for the nation and the states, therefore allowing Mississippi to conduct jury pool selection and voter registration—if it avoided openly and verifiably discriminating—pretty much as it pleased.

Decisions in both cases were reported out on April 16, 1896, and both were unanimous. Justice Harlan wrote in *Gibson*,

> There was either no evidence offered in support of the motion, or, if offered, it does not appear in the record, and in this case we can do nothing but affirm the action of the [Mississippi Supreme Court] in denying this motion. The affidavit appended to the motion in its terms affords no sort of evidence ... that the affiant had any personal knowledge touching any of the facts relied upon as grounds for upholding the motion.[6]

Harlan affirmed the principle that laws must be applied equally to all citizens, but since Jones and Hewlett had not sought to invoke the *Yick Wo* principle of discriminatory application, Harlan reverted to the *Rives* rule in which a state had to announce discrimination to trigger a Fourteenth Amendment violation.

> It is clear that the accused in the present case was not entitled to have the case removed into the Circuit Court of the United States unless he was denied by the constitution or laws of Mississippi some of the fundamental rights of life or liberty that were guaranteed to other citizens resident in that State. The equal protection of the laws is a right now secured to every person without regard to race, color or previous condition of servitude; and the denial of such protection by any State is forbidden by the supreme law of the land. These principles are earnestly invoked by counsel for the accused. But they do not support the application for the removal of this case from the state court in which the indictment was found, for the reason that neither the constitution of Mississippi nor the statutes of that State prescribe any rule for, or mode of procedure in, the trial of criminal cases which is not equally applicable to all citizens of the United States and to all persons within the jurisdiction of the State without regard to race, color or previous condition of servitude.

Gibson was thus denied, as was Smith in a similar ruling. Both were subsequently hanged.

The following month, Harlan would break with his colleagues and be the sole dissenting vote in *Plessy v. Ferguson*, an intense defense of equal protection of law for all citizens, in which he wrote,

> In view of the constitution, in the eye of the law, there is in this country no superior, dominant, ruling class of citizens. There is no caste here. Our constitution is color-blind, and neither knows nor tolerates classes among citizens. In respect of civil rights, all citizens are equal before the law. The humblest is the peer of the most powerful. The law regards man

as man, and takes no account of his surroundings or of his color when his civil rights as guaranteed by the supreme law of the land are involved.

(Less often quoted were the words that immediately preceded these: "The white race deems itself to be the dominant race in this country. And so it is in prestige, in achievements, in education, in wealth and in power. So, I doubt not, it will continue to be for all time if it remains true to its great heritage and holds fast to the principles of constitutional liberty.")[7]

One month after that, Henry Williams was convicted of murder and sentenced to death.

While taking up Williams's appeal, Cornelius Jones decided to run for Congress in Mississippi's third congressional district in the November 1896 election. His opponent would be a six-term incumbent, Democrat Thomas Catchings. Although he had served in the Confederate army only as a private, after his election to Congress, local newspapers had taken to referring to him as "General Catchings." Jones had little hope of besting Catchings—even if all the disfranchised black voters had been allowed to cast ballots, local election officials would have tossed them in the river—but as with the Gibson and Smith cases, Jones intended to use the contest to mount a fresh assault on the 1890 constitution.

On Election Day, Catchings received more than 80 percent of the votes. Soon afterward, Jones filed an official challenge with the House of Representatives, claiming that the Mississippi Constitution's provisions granting or denying adult males the right to vote violated the United States Constitution. Although this was essentially the same assertion that had been dismissed by the Supreme Court, Congress was a different venue, one more attuned, Jones hoped, to public opinion. As was standard in voting challenges, Jones was awarded $2,000 to press his claim, which Mississippi newspapers disparagingly insisted was his sole motivation. While Jones undoubtedly welcomed the money—it was a good deal more than he could make representing largely indigent black criminal defendants—that his motives ran deeper was disquieting for Mississippi whites.

Although his challenge was soon dismissed—and provoked little mention in the press—the white political establishment in Mississippi had taken notice. They thought enough of him to make him the subject of eviscerating articles in state newspapers. For example, in December 1896, *The Greenville Times* discussed Jones's challenge and his previous failures to successfully contest the Mississippi Constitution in the United States Supreme Court. "These experiences should have taught any head less thick than that of an African that he was wasting his time. If he had been conscientiously fighting for a principle he would no doubt have been convinced, but it is the double temptation of lucre and prestige with his race that actuates this chronic contestant."[8]

Jones tried again in 1898, this time using an ingenious ploy. Mississippi law stated that if an amendment to the state constitution was up for a vote, then it must be printed on the same ballot as that of the candidates for office or else be judged void. That year, an amendment to cede both control and the cost of maintaining levees on the Mississippi River to the federal government was to be put to a vote, but through an oversight, state officials printed a separate ballot. When Jones learned of the error—only days before the votes were to be cast—he instructed his supporters, Republicans both black and white, to show up at the polling station and file affidavits instead of ballots. The affidavits would state that the voter came to polling station to cast his vote for Cornelius Jones, but when he discovered the ballot was illegal, filed this document instead. From there, Jones would once again contest the election, claiming that under Mississippi law, all ballots for Catchings were illegal. He would again be granted $2,000 to pursue his claim.

This time, the white press was waiting for him. Aghast that white voter indifference might actually result in the election of a black man, local newspapers urged their readers to go to the polls. "There is nothing more dangerous than the apathy which follows a feeling of absolute security in politics," wrote the editor of *The Greenville Times*,

and that is a danger which is now threatens us . . . After the last congressional election in this district a contest was inaugurated by the negro Republican candidate which menaced the peace of the district and the seat of its representative much more seriously than was suspected by the general public. It is quite possible—probable, even, that a similar attempt may be made in the present election. There is also a possibility that Democratic members may be arbitrarily unseated on whatever grounds can be trumped up. Democratic voters of this district should see to it that there is no ground for a contest. If every man will but do his individual duty there will be no room for any question as to the will of the majority of qualified voters who return Mr. Catchings to congress.[9]

A September 1898 editorial in the *Mayersville Spectator*, under the headline "Voters, Listen!" read,

On the 8th of next November we will be called upon to elect a member of Congress to represent this district. It is of vital importance to go to the polls. It is true that the Republicans are largely in minority in this district, but it is too true that after nominations are made our people are indifferent and do not turn out and vote. But it is our duty this time to come to the front and vote for General Catchings, who is the party nominee. We cannot afford to let a negro be elected in this district, and if we do not turn out and vote, there is danger of such a thing … Let us do our duty to the grand old party that delivered us from the clutches of negro rule years ago. Let us prove to the world that they may slander our county, but they will never weaken our Democracy.[10]

Despite these dire portents, few Democrats felt any sense of urgency, and voter turnout remained low. Catchings received only 2,486 votes, all cast on ballots that did not contain the levee amendment. Jones, whose official vote total was less than 250—all also on the disputed ballot—secured more than 1,000 certified statements, although it was likely that many were submitted by adult black males who had been disqualified as voters under the provisions of the 1890 constitution.

Jones then filed his appeal. Unlike after the previous election, Jones on this occasion hired two attorneys to prepare and file his brief, in which he specifically attacked not the constitutionality of the 1890 Mississippi Constitution, but simply the legality of the 2,486 ballots cast for his opponent. The brief stated, "The law is plain, and there remains no excuse for its violation, and the 2,486 votes cast for Representative, and the 2,212 votes cast for the levee amendment on the 8th of last November, 1898, in this district, must, in compliance with the express command of the sovereign people of Mississippi, be declared illegal."[11]

Mississippi's secretary of state freely admitted that Jones was correct, but claimed the dual ballots were due merely to oversight and should not void an election in which voters had freely and overwhelmingly expressed their preference. In any event, as an editorial in the *Vicksburg Commercial Herald* pointed out, even if the ballots for the levee amendment were voided, the ballots for Congress were legal.

> It seems, however, that in drawing up his notice of contest, Jones discovered and has disclosed a grave error in the manner of the submission of the levee amendment to the constitution. Through a process of reasoning, which is all his own, it is contended in the notice that this error vitiates the regular election for Congressman, and validates the performance. How this conclusion is reached is too absurd for consideration; it is not worthwhile to state. This is not so, we fear, as to the constitutional amendment; that seems to have been fatally marred.[12]

But it was not. The levee amendment passed, and Thomas Catchings was once more seated as the representative for Mississippi's third congressional district. Cornelius Jones did not run for Congress again.

Between his jousts with Mississippi Democrats for a congressional seat, Jones brought Henry Williams's appeal to the Supreme Court.

★ ★ ★

At the original trial in June 1896 in state circuit court, Jones had moved to quash the indictment on Fourteenth Amendment grounds, based on the systematic exclusion of blacks from the voting rolls on which grand jury participation was based. His petition specifically cited the 1890 Mississippi constitutional convention, which, according to Jones:

> was composed of 134 members, only one of whom was a negro. That under prior laws, there were 190,000 colored voters and 69,000 white voters. The makers of the new constitution arbitrarily refused to submit it to the voters of the state for approval, but ordered it adopted, and an election to be held immediately under it, which election was held under the election ordinances of the said constitution in November, 1891, and the legislature assembled in 1892, and enacted the statutes complained of for the purpose to discriminate ... and but for that the defendant's race would have been represented impartially on the grand jury which presented this indictment.[13]

Without citing it as precedent, Jones also alluded to the *Yick Wo* decision. The Mississippi Constitution, he insisted, "is but a scheme ... to abridge the suffrage of the colored electors in the State of Mississippi on account of the previous condition of servitude by granting a discretion to the said officers as mentioned in the several sections of the constitution of the state and the statute of the state adopted under the said constitution."[14]

The petition to the grand jury was rejected, and the trial and subsequent sentence of death proceeded to its foregone conclusion.

Jones then appealed Williams's case on a writ of error to federal circuit court, claiming that "the laws by which the grand jury was selected, organized, summoned, and charged, which presented the said indictment, are unconstitutional and repugnant to the spirit and letter of the Constitution of the United States of America, Fourteenth Amendment." When this appeal was also denied, Jones brought the case to the Supreme Court.

Jones claimed in his Supreme Court petition that the exclusionary effect of the property tax and literacy clauses of the Mississippi Constitution had made it impossible for his client to be judged by a jury of his peers. As a citizen of the United States, Jones went on, Henry Williams was entitled to federal constitutional guarantees. Once again, he could produce no documentary records—he claimed Mississippi officials refused to make them available—but accompanied his motion only with four affidavits, two of which were from Williams himself.

On April 25, 1898, the Court issued its decision in a unanimous opinion written by the recently appointed Joseph McKenna. McKenna, after a brief stint as attorney general, had been on the Court only three months, replacing Stephen Field, who had retired after thirty-four years.[15] But where Field had been universally respected as a brilliant legal scholar and either lauded or loathed for his role in assuring the ascension of the American corporation, McKenna was widely perceived as an intellectual mediocrity and distrusted as only the third Catholic ever appointed to the Court.[16] McKenna, during his confirmation hearings, had become so sensitive to charges that he was, in fact, ignorant of many aspects of the law that he had sat in on classes at Columbia University Law School before taking the bench.

McKenna's most compelling credential seemed to have been that, like Field, he came from California, the son of Irish immigrants who had migrated west. There, although he started a law practice, he soon went into politics, working his way from elective office to an appointment to federal circuit court, where he spent an undistinguished six years. His supporters attempted to paint the opposition to his nomination as religious bigotry. One claimed to "have no patience with men who held the opinion that Catholics necessarily must consult the Pope or some other high functionary of the Catholic Church in every important transaction of their lives." But even that supporter was lukewarm, admitting "he did not contend that Mr. McKenna was a giant in his legal attainments." Equally damning to his opponents was the charge by the California bar association "that large corporations had been instrumental in securing his nomination."[17]

Although McKenna had dealt with few African Americans in California, his racial attitudes might be tentatively discerned by his attitudes toward the Chinese. "As a politician and legislator on both state and national levels, McKenna consistently and enthusiastically advocated various types of anti-Chinese legislation, and as a federal judge in California he construed the law rigorously to enforce the exclusion of Chinese, including even those who presented evidence of American citizenship."[18]

Chief Justice Melville Fuller assigned McKenna *Williams v. Mississippi* for his first opinion. There was little doubt as to the outcome, and so it would provide the new associate an opportunity to demonstrate to a dubious legal community that he could write a lucid, persuasive, straightforward opinion. And so McKenna, who doubtless took exceptional care, mirrored his predecessors by beginning with a lofty pronouncement.

> [The Fourteenth Amendment] and its effect upon the rights of the colored race have been considered by this Court in a number of cases, and it has been uniformly held that the Constitution of the United States, as amended, forbids, so far as civil and political rights are concerned, discriminations by the general government or by the states against any citizen because of his race.[19]

Then, also as in previous opinions, McKenna retreated to the narrow, strict reading of the amendment. "But it has also been held [that] to justify a removal from a state court to a federal court of a cause in which such rights are alleged to be denied, that such denial must be the result of the constitution or laws of the state, not of the administration of them." This, of course, was not at all true, given the *Yick Wo* decision a dozen years earlier. Still, McKenna was aware enough of the precedent to acknowledge that if Williams could *prove* that the law had been administered in a discriminatory fashion, he would then have grounds for his action.

Although Jones had been unable to obtain reams of documentary evidence of specific incidents, for most laymen looking at the Mississippi voting rolls, it would have been all too obvious that some chica-

nery had been afoot, certainly as obvious as the plaintiffs had supplied in
Yick Wo. After implementation of the 1890 constitution, virtually none
of Mississippi's 907,000 black residents remained eligible to go to the
polls, whereas tens of thousands of its 563,000 white residents were. In
addition, Mississippi state officials, unlike San Francisco city fathers, had
boasted of their intention to disfranchise black voters. As such, the Court
could easily have ruled that the "interpretation clause" of the Mississippi
Constitution was not, in fact, used to test literacy, but simply as a ruse to
deny the vote to African Americans.

But McKenna and his fellows refused to see past their own prejudices, and granted wide discretion to Mississippi's administering officers
(all of whom also were white) on their choices of what an applicant to
vote should read and "interpret." Even Justice Harlan joined the cho-
rus. If Mississippi officials chose a short simple phrase for whites—or
even no phrase at all—and long, complex phrases for blacks; even if they
had publicly proclaimed that those phrases had been inserted in the state
constitution simply to foil potential black voters, the burden remained
on Williams to prove that these choices of phrase had been made intentionally, on a case-by-case basis, to deny blacks the right to register. And
then, to raise the bar yet higher, even if a certain officer was discriminatory in the manner in which he administered the test, it was the fault of
the man, not the constitution under which he was operating.

The opinion was also openly racist. McKenna cited a South Carolina
Supreme Court ruling that declared "the negro race had acquired or ac-
centuated certain peculiarities of habit, of temperament, and of character
which clearly distinguished it as a race from the whites; a patient, docile
people, but careless, landless, migratory within narrow limits, without
forethought, and its criminal members given to furtive offenses, rather
than the robust crimes of the whites," to conclude that the Mississippi
Constitution did not in itself discriminate. "Nor," he added incredibly,
"is there any sufficient allegation of an evil and discriminating administration of [it]."

In the end, the decrease of black registrants in Mississippi to almost zero did not prove that potential black voters had been dealt with in a discriminatory fashion. "The Constitution of Mississippi and its statutes do not on their face discriminate between the races, and it has not been shown that their actual administration was evil; only that evil was possible under them."[20]

Unwilling to simply dismiss McKenna's opinion and the acquiescence of his fellow justices as mere racism, some contemporary analysts have cast about, without a great deal of success, for some appropriate legal underpinning. Michael Klarman, for example, in defending the decision, wrote that "the Court drew on a dominant tradition in constitutional law that held legislative motive to be irrelevant," and cited John Marshall's opinion in *Fletcher v. Peck* as precedent. But Klarman is then forced to admit that "this tradition rejecting judicial inquiries into legislative motive was not the only one available to the Court," and that Marshall's opinion in *McCulloch v. Maryland* "sounds suspiciously like a motive inquiry." Then, of course, there was *Yick Wo*, technically decided on application, which by any reasonable understanding must be bound inextricably to motive. And in *Ah Kow*, which Klarman also cites, Stephen Field "expressly employed motive analysis."[21]

Like *Plessy*, *Williams* was accepted without criticism by the press, the public, and in legal journals. The case was not subject to critical analysis until many decades later and was, in fact, cited in a number of articles in the *Harvard Law Review* as perfectly sound precedent. And so it remains. *Williams* was never overturned by the Court at all, but rather was rendered moot by the Voting Rights Act of 1965.

Cornelius Jones never gave up the fight for equal rights. In 1915, he initiated the first ever lawsuit to gain reparations for former slaves. He sued the Treasury Department for $68 million, the proceeds from the sale of raw cotton seized from slave states during the Civil War. The suit was dismissed in 1917 because the judges ruled "the real defendant is the United States, which cannot be sued without its consent."[22] The following year, Jones was indicted for attempting to defraud former slaves by allegedly asking them to contribute $1.75 each to be a plaintiff. That case was thrown out as well.

17

Refining Redemption

WITH BOTH THE MISSISSIPPI AND SOUTH CAROLINA Constitutions unqualified successes as instruments of disfranchisement, there was little question that other Southern states would follow along. Infighting among black belt and white county Democrats remained a problem, but with a goal as clear-cut and universally accepted as white monopoly at the ballot box, no family spat was going to derail the process.

Yet, considering the acquiescence of the Supreme Court on publicly announced plans to remove black citizens from voting rolls—and on civil rights violations of African Americans in general—most Southern states, even in the wake of *Smith* and *Gibson*, remained surprisingly queasy about the prospect of these plans being overturned. The "understanding test" adopted by Mississippi and South Carolina had elicited significant criticism among white supremacists in other states, who thought it so transparent as to ultimately fail to clear even the ankle-high bar of *Strauder*. Something more deft was needed, something that would disqualify blacks but not whites, while allowing the courts to continue to pretend that a rigged game was being fairly played.

Louisiana was the next state to take a run at a new constitution, and its aims were ambitious. Sixteen years later, a law professor at the University of Mississippi wrote,

> On February 11th, 1898, Louisiana, with the blacks forming 43 per cent of the population, encouraged by the success of the franchise laws of Mississippi and South Carolina, called a constitutional convention which, says *The Times-Democrat*, 'Aimed at placing every white voter on the poll list and keeping out nearly every negro, without violating the Federal Constitution.' No scheme half so bold as this had ever before been seriously considered by any state since the adoption of the Fourteenth and Fifteenth Amendments to the Constitution of the United States.[1]

Louisianans, like their Redeemer brethren, thought of purging black Americans from the political process as a higher calling. When convention president Ernest B. Kruttschnitt addressed his fellow delegates during the convention's opening session on February 8, 1898, in the Mechanics Institute in New Orleans, he intoned, "May this hall, where, thirty-two years ago the negro first entered upon the unequal contest for supremacy, and which had been reddened with his blood"—referring to an 1866 riot at which thirty-four freedmen had been murdered—"now witness the elevation of our organic law which will establish the relation between the races upon an everlasting foundation of right and justice."[2] In case his message had not been clear enough, he added, "We are all aware that this convention has been called by the people of the state of Louisiana principally to deal with one question . . . to eliminate from the electorate the mass of corrupt and illiterate voters who have during the last quarter of a century degraded our politics."[3]

Kruttschnitt was on record as declaring that Louisiana "could do better than the state of Mississippi," and he felt similarly about South Carolina.[4] The Mississippi and South Carolina Constitutions "lost their popularity when it became known that they would also disfranchise 20,000 white voters in the state. Louisiana was determined to go a step further and disfranchise the negro without sacrificing her white citizens who had the misfortune of being illiterate."[5]

Illiterate or not, those white citizens wielded a good bit of power. In the mid-1890s, even more than in the other two constitutionally Redeemed states, the Louisiana Democratic Party was "split asunder," largely due to low crop prices, with many small farmers deserting the Democrats for the Populists. These farmers were suspicious of a new constitution, and so the conservatives would need to make certain that the poorer and less educated were confident that they would remain a part of the political process. As in North Carolina, some had joined with Republicans in a Fusionist movement that, for a time, seemed a genuine threat to Democratic rule. As a result, *The Times-Democrat* had for years opposed calling a constitutional convention "with the wildest Populist ideas so prevalent." Although most of the active rebellion had faded when the convention met in early February, simmering discontent had hardly disappeared.[6]

To mollify white farmers who suspected that black belt Democrats were targeting them as much as black voters, the convention came up with the "grandfather clause."

"Grandfathering" as a legal concept was not new or particularly controversial, meaning simply that a new rule or law would apply only to those who come under its jurisdiction after passage and would exempt those who were in a certain situation before the rule or law existed. A fee or a price increase, for example, might be charged only to those who wished to access a service after the fee or price increase was instituted, exempting anyone who had accessed the service before.

Nor did the "grandfather clause," when applied to voting—exempting certain members of the electorate from certain qualifications—have a malevolent history. In Delaware's 1792 constitution, for example, men twenty-one or twenty-two years old who were sons of eligible voters could vote even if they had not paid taxes. In 1818, Connecticut enacted a constitution that grandfathered anyone eligible to vote under the previous constitution, with an additional exemption to the property-owning requirement for those who had previously served one year in the militia. Massachusetts had a provision that exempted older voters from a literacy requirement instituted in 1857. New Hampshire, Pennsylvania, and many other states had certain grandfather provisions written into their laws as well.

But in each of those cases, the grandfather clause had been inserted to ensure that certain classes of potential voters were not shut out of the process. Louisiana intended to turn the principle on its head and use a grandfather clause to ensure that a certain class of potential voter could not help but be shut out of the process.

To achieve their objective, Louisiana delegates became the first to insert actual grandfathers into the grandfather clause. Along with the now standard literacy and property requirements, the Louisiana convention inserted,

> No male person who was on January 1st, 1867 (the date of the first Reconstruction Act) or at any date prior thereto, entitled to vote under the Constitution or statutes of any State of the United States, wherein he then resided, and no son or grandson of any such person not less than twenty-one years of age at the date of the adoption of this Constitution . . . shall be denied the right to register and vote in this State by reason of his failure to possess the educational or property qualifications prescribed by this Constitution.[7]

The grandfather clause was not universally popular among whites, any more than the understanding clause had been, and for the same reason. Louisianans knew full well how transparent they had been, and many were convinced the Supreme Court would finally see through the artifice and throw the rule out.

Also, unlike the understanding clause, which could be applied subjectively, the fate of the grandfather clause in the courts had far more potent consequences. It was the only feature in significantly more stringent suffrage requirements that protected poor, illiterate whites from suffering the same fame as almost all blacks. Registrars could always cheat, of course, and dummy up records to allow poor, illiterate whites to register anyway, and then give them help marking their ballots, but Southern states wanted very much to move away from obvious fraud. The grandfather clause, then, represented the sort of high risk/high reward strategy that made even the staunchest opponents of black suffrage fear to include it. But no one could think of anything better, so it stayed in.

Speaking to that point, Ernest Kruttschnitt closed the convention as succinctly as he had opened it.

> We have not drafted the exact constitution that we should like to have drafted; otherwise we should have inscribed in it, if I know the popular sentiment of this state, universal white manhood suffrage, and the exclusion from the suffrage of every man with a trace of Negro blood in his veins. We could not do that on account of the fifteenth amendment to the Constitution of the United States . . . What care I whether the test we have put be a new one or an old one? What care I whether it be more or less ridiculous or not? Doesn't it meet the case? Doesn't it let the white man vote, and doesn't it stop the Negro from voting, and isn't that what we came here for?[8]

After the convention concluded, *The Times-Democrat* editorialized the result. Without a hint of irony, the editor wrote,

> The convention was called (1) to secure white supremacy for all time in Louisiana, and (2) to assure honest elections and put an end to the frauds which have so long debauched the public sense of the State. The frauds have been excused heretofore on the ground that they were necessary to white supremacy. With that supremacy secure by means of a new honest suffrage, all trickery becomes unnecessary, and we can have honest elections.[9]

As in Mississippi and South Carolina, Louisiana African Americans did not sit by and passively accept what was happening. As they would in all the states that would alter their constitutions, blacks fought furiously to maintain their right to vote. The problem was not will; it was weaponry. They had no allies—not the president; not Congress; and certainly not the courts. They were fighting an enemy with vastly more resources, virtually all the power to employ them at will, an unbreakable belief in their own righteousness, and determination to succeed that would not be mitigated by morality, pity, or even religious dogma.

So African Americans were reduced to futile attempts to influence the registration process and even more futile attempts to influence the white supremacists who controlled it. During the convention, Booker T. Washington, likely the most respected black man in the nation—at least among whites—wrote an open letter to the convention that was published in newspapers across Louisiana.

> The Negro does not object to an educational or property test, but let the law be so clear that no one clothed with state authority will be tempted to perjure and degrade himself by putting one interpretation upon it for the white man and another for the black man . . . I beg of you, further, that in the degree that you close the ballot box against the ignorant that you open the school house. More than half of the population of your State are Negroes. No state can long prosper when a large part of its citizenship is in ignorance and poverty and has no interest in the government. I beg of you that you do not treat us as an alien people. We are not aliens.[10]

But, as Washington seemed to realize, to the white supremacists who were meeting at the Mechanics Institute, black people were precisely that.

By the time the Louisiana convention ended in early May, *Williams v. Mississippi* was a matter of record, which meant also that while the justices were deliberating the case, Louisiana was flouting the Fifteenth Amendment right under their noses. A legal challenge to Louisiana, not a promising prospect to begin with, then became that much more difficult. One would be undertaken—a lawsuit on behalf of a sixty-year-old illiterate, propertyless black man—but it went nowhere. Booker T.

Washington was urged by some to support the action, but he, and an African American lawyer he had recently met, Wilford H. Smith, thought the case too weak to be pursued. Both would feel quite differently about a different challenge in a different state a few years later.

★ ★ ★

After Wilmington, North Carolina had all the motivation it needed, but it chose a different route. The election of 1898, which had been as race-baiting as Daniel Schenck had predicted, went overwhelmingly for Democrats—with Republicans terrorized across the state and their votes destroyed, the result could hardly have been otherwise—and the new governor and state legislature set to work on ensuring that they never had to resort to such distasteful tactics again.

To try to determine the best way to proceed, the state Democratic Committee dispatched Josephus Daniels to Washington. Daniels, whose white supremacist credentials were unquestioned, was editor of the state's largest newspaper, *The News and Observer*. During the run-up to the Wilmington coup, the newspaper, with Daniels at the helm, "led a campaign of prejudice, bitterness, vilification, misrepresentation, and exaggeration to influence the emotions of whites against the Negro." They published such articles as "Negro Control in Wilmington," "Greenville Negroized," "Arrested By A Negro: He Was Making No Resistance," "Negroes Have Social Equality," and "The Negro In Power In New Hanover."[11]

Daniels's job in Washington was to speak with Southern congressmen as to the best way to purge African Americans from the voting rolls without running afoul of either Congress or the courts. (Daniels would return to the nation's capital in 1913 to become Woodrow Wilson's secretary of the navy, where he would serve for eight years, which remains the longest tenure of anyone in that post. He would also serve as Franklin Roosevelt's ambassador to Mexico.) When Daniels had gotten what he needed, he traveled to Louisiana to see for himself how their recently enacted plan was working. "Upon returning to North Carolina, his report was most favorable; the 'Grandfather Clause' was proving quite effective in caring for the illiterate white 'Cajans,' while most of the Negroes were being disfranchised by the educational tests."[12]

Leading Democrats quickly made a decision. Rather than rewrite its constitution entirely, which would involve a convention and a level of uncertainty as to the demands its delegates might bring to the table, Democrats in North Carolina's legislature would draft amendments to the constitution it already had. There was an unknown here as well—rather than adopting what a convention had drawn up, the state would be forced to place the amendments before the voters for approval. Still, as in Louisiana, there did not seem to be a better way to go about it, and after the 1898 elections, black, Republican, or even Fusion voting did not seem much of a threat.

The suffrage amendment was drafted within weeks. It contained the usual residency and poll tax requirements and barred from voting anyone who had served a term in state prison. (It also barred anyone "who shall deny the being of Almighty God" from holding public office.) The amendment also contained a literacy and a grandfather clause that mimicked Louisiana's, with a couple of added wrinkles. Section Four required that "every person presenting himself for registration shall be able to read and write any section of the Constitution in the English language," but Section Five stated, "No male person, who was on January 1, 1867, or at any time prior thereto, entitled to vote under the laws of any State in the United States wherein he then resided, and no lineal descendant of any such person; shall be denied the right to register and vote at any election in this State by reason of his failure to possess the educational qualifications prescribed in section 4 of this Article: Provided, he shall have registered in accordance with the terms of this section prior to Dec. 1, 1908." Making the clause temporary, it was argued, would make it less likely to be vulnerable to a successful court challenge.

The haste with which North Carolina legislators had produced the amendment did not necessarily work in its favor. The referendum on its acceptance would not take place until a special election scheduled for August 1900. It faced opposition from white populists who were convinced that they were every bit as much targets as blacks. At the People's Party convention in Raleigh in April 1900, the delegates included in their official platform:

> We denounce the machine leaders of the Democratic party for laying the whip on the backs of the Democratic Legislature and forcing them into enacting and submitting a disfranchising constitutional amendment in violation of the solemn pledges of the party ... We denounce them not only for doing this in violation of their pledges, but also for submitting a measure most odious in form and dangerous in effect. That General Assembly being composed of some of the best lawyers of the party, must have known, or at least had a reasonable doubt, not only as to the unconstitutionality of the monstrous provision of Section 5, known as the "grandfather clause" in said amendment, but also of the great danger of that unconstitutional section failing, leaving the remainder of the amendment to stand, thus disfranchising by an educational qualification fifty or sixty thousand white voters of North Carolina, who in 1898 gave the Democratic party power in the Legislature, and whose ignorance is no fault of their own but is chargeable to the neglect of the Democratic party, which now seeks to disfranchise them and make their ignorance a crime alongside that of the felon.[13]

But North Carolina whites, like their brethren in other states, were more than willing to take a risk with black disfranchisement as the reward. With almost no African Americans allowed to vote and many white Republicans too terrified to cast ballots, the amendment passed by approximately 50,000 votes. North Carolina newspapers reported that "the negro vote was very light. Thousands of them had not registered and thousands that were registered failed to vote." The reports added, "A considerable number of negroes in the towns voted for the amendment."[14] While it is likely that the ballots of those black voters favored the amendment, it remains questionable whether those black voters actually cast them.

The result was generally trumpeted as a triumph of government. The *Semi-Weekly Messenger* proclaimed,

A fair analysis of the vote of Thursday would astonish the North Carolina enemies and slanderers in the northern press. It is almost certain that the state has gone for white government by from a 50,000 to 60,000 majority. It is known that thousands of the best and most intelligent Republicans voted for white government because they tired of negro rule. It is thought that more than half possibly three-fourths of the original populists voted for freeing the whites from bad bossing and negro control.[15]

★ ★ ★

And so the spotlight shifted to Alabama, the next stage on which "legal" disfranchisement of black voters would be played out. "We cannot afford to live with our feet upon fraud," exclaimed an Alabama Democrat in 1900. "We will not do it. We have disfranchised the African in the past by doubtful methods, but in the future we will do so by law."[16]

But Alabama faced the same two problems as had the other secessionist states—fear that the new constitution would not survive a test in federal court, and the more significant fear that it would not survive an assault by white populists who saw the new constitution as a power grab by the elites. In 1893, those elitist Democrats, called "Bourbons," had forced through the Sayre Act, which empowered the Alabama governor to appoint election officials; restrict voter registration to May, the busiest month for farmers; list candidates on the ballot alphabetically, with no party; and require voters to display registration certificates. Although Alabama also gerrymandered election districts to limit the impact of black voters, the Sayre Law infuriated white farmers so much that "they flirted with civil insurrection, even threatening in 1894 to seat their candidate by Winchester rifle and shotgun."[17]

A Fusionist movement sprang up, similar to North Carolina's, which

advocated a reformist platform that promised to protect the voting rights of Negroes, regulate trusts, end the convict lease system, inaugurate labor reforms, expand the supply of currency with silver coins, abolish national banks, enact a graduated income tax, and nominate political candidates in a direct statewide primary rather than in a closed party convention, the insurgents fundamentally threatened Conservative Democratic control.[18]

Unlike in North Carolina, however, the movement was beaten back statewide by fraud and ballot box stuffing in the black belt, although the reformers did win control in some hill country counties. In addition, white racism was more intense in Alabama, which rendered any coalition with blacks short-lived.

Still, the split in the white electorate made it possible that black voters, those that remained, could play a key role. "The emotionalism surrounding the insurgents' frank appeal for black votes was not lost on white voters. If whites divided politically, they invited black voters to control the balance of power. If freely allowed to vote, blacks could not themselves govern, but they could decide which of the two white factions would rule."[19] Whites, however, had no intention of sitting idly by. "To prevent such racial assertiveness during the disruptive 1890s and keep blacks 'in their place,' whites turned to violence and committed 177 lynchings during the decade—more than in any other state."[20]

Suppressing the black vote, however, had not healed the rift among the whites, and so calling a constitutional convention remained a very risky proposition. The Bourbons could not be certain to what degree they would be forced to make concessions to the agrarians. By 1900, however, the direct populist threat had largely faded, and there did not seem to be much of a choice. Also, Alabama whites had been able to watch a similar process play out in other states, and could employ whatever refinements they chose in fashioning the document.

Early the following year, the Alabama legislature passed a resolution calling for a referendum on whether or not to call a convention. Proponents were surprised at the degree of resistance that remained among populists, and so felt forced to include in the resolution a unique proviso—

the draft document would not be adopted by a vote either by the delegates or by the state legislature, but rather would be submitted to the electorate in a second referendum. In April 1901, the state voted 70,000–45,000 to hold the convention, although rumors of fraud were rife.

When the delegates were chosen, there was a clear tilt toward the Bourbons. Of the 155 delegates, ninety-six were lawyers and twelve were bankers. All were white men, of course, and 141 were Democrats. They were to meet in Montgomery on May 21 and would sit until September, working every day except Sunday and the Fourth of July. The constitution those delegates would draft would prove to be perhaps the most important document of the post-Reconstruction era, not because it was in any way unique or a departure from prevailing trends, but rather because it would be the vehicle by which white supremacy in the Redeemed South was irrevocably assured.

From the first speech, convention president John B. Knox left no doubt as to why these men had assembled. He opened the convention with these remarks:

> In my judgment, the people of Alabama have been called upon to face no more important situation than now confronts us, unless it be when they, in 1861, stirred by the momentous issues of impending conflict between the North and the South, were forced to decide whether they would remain in or withdraw from the Union. Then as now, the negro was the prominent factor in the issue.
>
> The Southern people, with this grave problem of the races to deal with, are face to face with a new epoch in Constitution-making, the difficulties of which are great, but which, if solved wisely, may bring rest and peace and happiness. If otherwise, it may leave us and our posterity continuously involved in race conflicts, or, what may be worse, subjected permanently to the baneful influences of the political conditions now prevailing in the State.[21]

Morality was to play a big part in their deliberations.

But if we would have white supremacy, we must establish it by law—not by force or fraud. If you teach your boy that it is right to buy a vote, it is an easy step for him to learn to use money to bribe or corrupt officials or trustees of any class. If you teach your boy that it is right to steal votes, it is an easy step for him to believe that it is right to steal whatever he may need or greatly desire. The results of such an influence will enter every branch of society; it will reach your bank cashiers, and affect positions of trust in every department; it will ultimately enter your courts, and affect the administration of justice.[22]

Knox also expounded on the nation's racial attitudes, which, sadly, were not misplaced:

So long as the negro remains in insignificant minority, and votes the Republican ticket, our friends in the North tolerate him with complacency, but there is not a Northern State, and I might go further and say there is not an intelligent white man in the North, not gangrened by sectional prejudice and hatred of the South, who would consent for a single day to submit to negro rule.

If the negroes of the South should move in such numbers to the State of Massachusetts, or any other Northern State, as would enable them to elect the officers, levy the taxes and control the government and policy of that State, I doubt not they would be met, in spirit, as the negro laborers from the South were met at the State line of Illinois, with bayonets, led by a Republican Governor, and firmly but emphatically informed that no quarter would be shown them in that territory.[23]

Finally, Knox sought to reassure delegates representing poor whites that whatever the product of the convention, it would not be aimed at them.

There is a difference it is claimed with great force, between the uneducated white man and the ignorant negro. There is in the white man an inherited capacity for government which is wholly wanting in the negro. Before the art of reading and writing was known, the ancestors of the Anglo-Saxon had established an orderly system of government, the basis, in fact, of the one under which we now live. That the negro, on the other hand, is descended from a race lowest in intelligence and moral perception of all the races of men.[24]

A record of the convention proceedings was published verbatim in an Alabama newspaper, and Knox knew he was not speaking only to his fellow delegates. Disfranchisement had become important news, and the Alabama convention was widely covered by newspapers across the nation. Some took issue with disfranchisement of black Americans. *The Vermont Watchman* called it "bare-faced violations of right and justice," and the *Sacramento Evening Bee* wrote, "Alabama is About to Wrong the Negro." The *Duluth News Tribune* called grandfather clauses "dishonest" and "odious."[25]

But the most important newspaper in the United States took a different view of the proceedings. *The New York Times* devoted two columns on the front page of its June 9, 1901, Sunday edition to the convention. After noting that "the intelligence of the people of the State is represented in its composition, and it has thus far shown a disposition to approach the performance of the delicate and difficult task intrusted [sic] to it with judgment and deliberation," the article continued, "it is understood that the people of Alabama will not ratify its work if the political status of the negro is not so well defined as to remove him from his present position as a menace to the supremacy of the white citizen in the control of State and local affairs."[26]

The *Times* reporter, whose initials were J. C. B.—this was a "Special to *The New York Times*"—did not make much of an attempt to disguise whose side he was on.

As to the restriction of the franchise to exclude from the right to vote the mass of ignorant and mercenary negroes who cannot be trusted

with the privileges of full citizenship, and who showed their inca-
pacity for the proper use of the ballot when they had it, a Constitutional amendment was necessary ... Some idea of the difficulty which
confronts members of the Alabama convention may be gained from
the fact that they are expected and pledged to do what is practically
impossible—to take away from the negro the voting privilege without
depriving any white man of the ballot.

The reporter did acknowledge that there was a serious impediment
that these serious and upright Alabamans were forced to overcome—the
United States Constitution. "Congress has the unquestioned power not
only to reduce representation in a State which, in contravention of the
Fifteenth Amendment, denies the negro as a negro the right to vote,
but to declare that such State has not a republican form of government."
Remedies might even include "overthrowing the existing State Government and displacing from office those elected under void suffrage provisions." Significantly, the reporter did not mention the Supreme Court,
although the delegates to the convention were well aware that the judiciary was a more likely battleground than the legislature. John Knox, in
fact, had mentioned *Williams v. Mississippi* in his opening remarks.

What the delegates settled on, which was agreed to by a 122–12 vote
in the Alabama legislature on September 3, 1901, was the most complex
disfranchisement scheme ever undertaken by any state. In addition to the
usual residency and poll tax requirements, it consisted of two separate
plans, a "temporary plan"—which made registration permanent—and "a
permanent plan"—which made registration temporary.

The temporary plan, Section 180, introduced the "fighting grandfather clause." It granted permanent voting rights to any male over twenty-
one years of age who registered before December 20, 1902, *and* had

honorably served in the land or naval forces of the United States in the
war of 1812, or in the war with Mexico, or in any war with the Indians,
or in the war between the States, or in the war with Spain, or who hon-

orably served in the land or naval forces of the Confederate States, or of the State of Alabama in the war between the States; or, the lawful descendants of persons who honorably served in the land or naval forces of the United States in the war of the American Revolution, or in the war of 1812, or in the war with Mexico, or in any war with the Indians, or in the war between the States, or in the land or naval forces of the Confederate States, or of the State of Alabama in the war between the States.

To make certain that those few whites whose ancestors hadn't fought anywhere would not be shut out, an additional category was included: "All persons who are of good character and who understand the duties and obligations of citizenship under a republican form of government."

What made the plan "temporary" was its expiration date. After January 1, 1903, the permanent plan kicked in. For these men, registration would not be permanent—they would need to reregister personally for each election in which they wished to vote. In addition to paid-up poll taxes, each would need to prove that he or his wife owned at least forty acres of land with paid-up property taxes of at least $300. Those who owned no property needed to be able to "read and write any article of the Constitution of the United States in the English language" and, unless "physically unable to work," must have "worked or been regularly engaged in some lawful employment, business, or occupation, trade or calling, for the greater part of the twelve months next preceding the time they offer to register." Low-end workers were paid in cash, so whether or not to accept the word of a black man who claimed to have been employed was left to the discretion of the registrar.

Section 182 listed conditions under which a man could be denied registration, which again included a laundry list of crimes of which black men were regularly convicted, or could be convicted if a local sheriff was of a mind to arrest him:

All idiots and insane persons . . . those who shall be convicted of treason, murder, arson, embezzlement, malfeasance in office, larceny, receiving stolen property, obtaining property or money under false pretenses, perjury, subornation of perjury, robbery, assault with intent to rob, burglary, forgery, bribery, assault and battery on the wife, bigamy, living in adultery, sodomy, incest, rape, miscegenation, crime against nature, or any crime punishable by imprisonment in the penitentiary, or of any infamous crime or crime involving moral turpitude; also, any person who shall be convicted as a vagrant or tramp.

So proud were the delegates in fashioning an electorate committed to "good government" and "traditional values" that they began their new constitution, with total seriousness, by mimicking the Declaration of Independence: "All men are equally free and independent; that they are endowed by their Creator with certain inalienable rights; that among these are life, liberty and the pursuit of happiness."

The date for the ratification referendum was November 11, 1901. As in South Carolina and Louisiana, opposition was intense. Many white farmers in northern Alabama were unconvinced by the fighting grandfather clause, which, if it was struck down, left them in the position of passing a literacy test. They were also none too pleased about the poll tax requirement, which was made cumulative. So much opposition surfaced that the black belt Bourbons, who most favored the new plan, thought rejection was a genuine possibility. To avoid it, they resorted to the same sort of fraud and dishonesty that John B. Knox had condemned when he opened the convention.

With egregiously shoddy journalism, *The New York Times* reported on the result. "The instrument has carried by a majority ranging between 25,000 and 35,000"—it was actually 108,000 to 82,000, so they at least got the vote count correct—and although "the negroes voted in much larger numbers than expected [they] were unable to control the result."[27] In fact, it was black votes that provided victory for the Bourbons—or to be more precise, the presence, for the last time, of a sizable number of African Americans on the voting rolls. In the state's black belt, where all those black men had supposedly voted, the totals reported out were 36,224 for ratification and 5,471 against, which was larger than the ratification majority of the entire state.[28] So, unless African Americans voted by a 7–1 margin to enact a constitution that would strip away their right to vote, that ballot fraud had been responsible would seem to have been undeniable.

Giving a sense of why the *Times*, and most Northern newspapers, refused to even hypothesize the obvious, the newspaper ran another article in the next column, this one taken from the *New Orleans Picayune*. It opened: "Nothing could be more false than that there is any general hostility, or any hostility at all, on the part of the white people of the Southern States of the Union toward the negroes who live among them. On the contrary, the most complete kind feeling and friendliness are the rule." For proof, the article cited the one million white babies and small children, "every one of whom is in the care of a negro woman nurse." There could never be political or social equality, of course, but "negroes who obey the laws and perform their ordinary duties are never disturbed unless it be by some individual criminal and they have all the protection that the laws and enlightened public sentiment, expressed in force when needed, can give them."[29] This, while dozens if not hundreds of innocent black Americans were beaten, raped, and murdered every year by whites who were never called to account for their crimes.

The only real denunciations of the vote came from erstwhile allies, white populists and African Americans. The former restricted their activities to voicing outrage, but the latter, under two unlikely leaders, would do far more, and would force the Supreme Court to once and for all decide if the United States Constitution meant what it said.

18

Forging an Attack

O N SEPTEMBER 18, 1895, JUST AS SOUTH CAROLINA'S constitutional convention was entering its second week and the South's disfranchisement campaign was gaining momentum, the Cotton States and International Exposition in Atlanta, Georgia, celebrated its opening day. The South's answer to the great Columbian Exposition in Chicago two years before, this gala trade fair was billed as the largest and most important event in the Georgia capital since the end of the Civil War, an ostentatious display of progress and prosperity in the Redeemed South. The exposition featured 6,000 exhibits and had cost $2 million to produce. John Philip Sousa had composed a special march, "King Cotton," to greet the crowds. The fair was expected to attract as many as one million visitors from across the nation and around the world.

Peace and reconciliation were two of the themes. "It is a great day for Atlanta and a great day for the South," extolled the *New-York Tribune*. "Atlanta has again been captured, not this time by fire and sword, but by a peaceful army, of fellow-citizens and friends. Old feuds are forgotten, the old lines of suspicion and hate are obliterated, the old soldiers who once faced each other in hostile camps are clasping hands together, while the Stars and Stripes grandly float over the union of hearts and hands."[1]

Among the featured string of luminaries, albeit from a distance, was President Grover Cleveland himself. Via wiring that had been installed specifically for this event, the president threw an electric switch, a "golden button," at his home in Buzzards Bay, Massachusetts, and "the wheels of the machinery . . . leaped into life," officially inaugurating the proceedings.[2] In his welcoming speech, Judge Emory Speer proclaimed, "This is indeed a happy day for the country. Cold and dull must be the nature of that man who is insensible to these convincing proofs gathered that the world may see the advancement of our people on all the paths trending toward a more perfect civilization."[3]

Selling the rehabilitation of the South and portraying it as a bastion of racial harmony were unmistakably the organizers' major goals. If they were not, Judge Speer would have been the last man chosen to open the event. Although a Confederate war veteran, he had switched to the Republican Party during Reconstruction and been elected to Congress as a proponent of integration and equal rights. He had moved on to be a United States attorney, known for his vigorous prosecution of violent white supremacists, and had aroused the fury of many Georgians by obtaining a conviction of eight white men accused of brutalizing African Americans to deny them the right to vote. He had even been able to get the conviction upheld in the Supreme Court.[4] Speer had been appointed to the federal bench in 1888, and had further made himself a pariah to white supremacists with a series of decisions that upheld the civil rights of blacks.

But commerce overwhelmed personal animosity. To convince investors from both the North and across the Atlantic that the new, redeemed, racially tolerant South was a land of opportunity, Emory Speer seemed to be the perfect choice as a host. To further demonstrate to skeptics that the South harbored no ill to black people, and that racial policies were based in practicality, and even charity, the fair had sponsored a "Negro

Building" and designated December 26, five days before the fair closed, as "Negro Day." It is fitting, then, albeit not without irony, that with all the hoopla, the Cotton States Exposition is primarily remembered for a speech by a Negro.

As a final validation of their good will, the organizers had invited a black man to the opening ceremonies to address the assembled throng— tens of thousands, virtually all of them white. For this honor, they had chosen a forty-year-old educator named Booker T. Washington, de- scribed as the "principal of the Tuskegee Alabama Normal and Industrial School," which was devoted to training young black men and women in teaching and the mechanical arts. Little was known about Washington outside Alabama, but Americans soon learned that he had been born a slave and, through education and hard work, had risen to lead a respected institution and become what white people liked to term "a credit to his race."

The reaction in the Northern press to this unique invitation was everything Southern Democrats could have hoped for.

> The selection of Booker T. Washington . . . to make an address at the opening of the Atlanta Exposition, is an almost unparalleled tribute to Mr. Washington personally, and to the negro race of which he is such a distinguished representative. Had any one predicted twenty- five years ago that the South would so honor a negro he would have been looked upon as a madman.[5]

Washington was the third to speak, following Judge Speer and Mrs. Joseph Thompson, president of the Women's Board. He would need a deft hand, for Speer, who had fully embraced the spirit in which he had been invited, had stated unequivocally,

> There was never the slightest danger of continued negro control in the local affairs of a Southern State. Those who apprehended it had done well to consider that of all the American Union, the Southern people

present the largest percentage of old Anglo-Saxon stock. I here declare the so-called 'race question' does not exist. There are millions of colored people who live and who will live among many more millions of white people. Why shall anyone forge a race issue?[6]

It is unclear whether or not the organizers had cleared the text of Washington's remarks in advance, but he hit precisely the right balance between conciliatory and proud, deferential and challenging. He was willing, he conceded, to accept whites' assertions that black Americans, only thirty years removed from slavery, were not ready for full equality, or even in most cases the right to vote. He also accepted segregation as a path to prosperity for both races. "In all things that are purely social we can be as separate as the fingers, yet one as the hand in all things essential to mutual progress."[7]

He counseled black Americans to stop thinking in grandiose terms but rather to focus on building themselves up from the bottom to share in "a new era of industrial progress."

> The wisest among my race understand that the agitation of questions of social equality is the extremest folly, and that progress in the enjoyment of all the privileges that will come to us must be the result of severe and constant struggle rather than of artificial forcing . . . It is important and right that all privileges of the law be ours, but it is vastly more important that we be prepared for the exercise of these privileges. The opportunity to earn a dollar in a factory just now is worth infinitely more than the opportunity to spend a dollar in an opera-house . . . Our greatest danger is that in the great leap from slavery to freedom we may overlook the fact that the masses of us are to live by the productions of our hands, and fail to keep in mind that we shall prosper in proportion as we learn to dignify and glorify common labor, and put brains and skill into the common occupations of life.

Washington's main goal, however, and one that is rarely mentioned, was to convince Southern whites to choose African Americans rather than white immigrants for these agrarian and industrial jobs, and thus provide a pathway to economic self-sufficiency. Speer, in his speech, had emphasized that with slavery over, the South was seeking that very sort of competitive labor. "Slavery was here and the toiling masses from other lands could not or would not compete with slaves," but now, "the world should awaken to the fact that no other land lighted by the sun in its diurnal progress around the world affords such attractions as a home for men with lives before them as do these Southern States of the Union."

For black citizens in a society in which they could not vote, could not affect discriminatory legislation, cheap foreign labor could doom any small chance they had of improving their position in society, so Washington countered with the only tools he had, a plea that is often incorrectly seen as supplication.

> To those of the white race who look to the incoming of those of foreign birth and strange tongue and habits for the prosperity of the South, were I permitted, I would repeat what I say to my own race. 'Cast down your bucket where you are.' Cast it down among the eight millions of Negroes whose habits you know, whose fidelity and love you have tested in days when to have proved treacherous meant the ruin of your firesides. Cast down your bucket among these people who have, without strikes and labor wars, tilled your fields, cleared your forests, built your railroads and cities, and brought forth treasures from the bowels of the earth, and helped make possible this magnificent representation of the progress of the South . . . As we have proved our loyalty to you in the past, in nursing your children, watching by the sick-bed of your mothers and fathers, and often following them with tear-dimmed eyes to their graves, so in the future, in our humble way, we shall stand by you with a devotion that no foreigner can approach.

The reaction was resoundingly positive. The *New-York Tribune* wrote, "When [men] think of American freedom, they can do no better than to think of Booker T. Washington's oration at Atlanta."[8] Even African

Americans were almost universal in their praise, although that would soon change. W. E. B. Du Bois wrote, "Let me heartily congratulate you upon your phenomenal success at Atlanta—it was a word fitly spoken."[9]

Within months, Washington's apparent retreat from militancy and embrace of the American ideal of hard work had made him a national celebrity, at least in white society. He would become a favorite of wealthy white industrialists—such as Andrew Carnegie, John D. Rockefeller, Sears, Roebuck's Julius Rosenwald, and George Eastman of Eastman Kodak—and would be the beneficiary of their philanthropy, including $150,000 as a personal gift from Carnegie; in 1901, he would publish an autobiography, *Up from Slavery*, to almost universal acclaim and booming sales; he would lecture to white audiences across the nation; he would help found the National Negro Business League, to promote entrepreneurship and financial independence; he would have tea with Queen Victoria; and he would even eventually, to the rage of James K. Vardaman and Ben Tillman, be invited to the White House for dinner with President Theodore Roosevelt.

As his acceptance by whites increased, however, he began to arouse the enmity of some blacks. They resented not only Washington being singled out as essentially the only acceptable black man in America, but also his unwillingness to challenge a rising tide of white oppression. "His militant black critics deeply believed that his efforts at appeasement had led the whites to the very aggressions he was trying to check."[10]

Du Bois was among the disenchanted. He called Washington's approach "the Atlanta Compromise," and accused him of "practically accepting the alleged inferiority of the Negro races." He added, "There is among educated and thoughtful colored men in all parts of the land a feeling of deep regret, sorrow, and apprehension at the wide currency and ascendancy which some of Mr. Washington's theories have gained."[11]

Although "his public utterances were limited to what whites approve," Washington was a good deal more subversive than either white admirers or black detractors gave him credit for, nowhere more so than when it came to voting rights.[12] Publicly, Washington made a point of accepting limited suffrage for African Americans, although he was less forthcoming about insisting that the same limitations that were in place for blacks be applied to whites as well. As such, he did not oppose literacy, property, or poll tax requirements, per se, even though they would hit blacks harder, but he found grandfather clauses anathema. In 1899, with his national fame assured and money available, he privately cast about for the best way to test the Louisiana Constitution in court.

After *Williams* and *Mills*, however, it was clear that in order to win a voting rights case, three things would be required: a plaintiff with impeccable credentials, a ream of supporting material to leave no doubt of the discriminatory nature of the state constitution, and, most of all, a superb lawyer to present arguments that even nine white men would be forced to accept. Washington made a secret visit to New Orleans, but after some abortive attempts at fund-raising and putting a plan of action together, he was forced to conclude that a Louisiana challenge lacked all three. Washington, who had made certain that his name had never been associated with the Louisiana partisans, returned home discouraged.

But then his private secretary, Emmett J. Scott, reminded him of Scott's fellow Texan, Wilford H. Smith, who was making quite a name for himself in Galveston. Smith had been born in a backwater town in the Mississippi Delta in 1860, almost certainly the son of slaves, but somehow had worked his way to Boston University Law School, where he had graduated in 1883. He first returned to Mississippi to begin a practice, but eventually moved to Galveston, where he achieved success in both law and business. Scott had first introduced Smith to Washington in 1897, during a conference at Tuskegee, and Smith may well have analyzed the Louisiana case and advised Washington of its flaws.[13]

The following year, Wilford Smith would achieve a milestone in African American law in the case of Seth Carter, a twenty-three-year-old black man and convicted murderer.

On November 24, 1897, according to news accounts, Carter, from Galveston, pumped four bullets into his girlfriend, Alberta Brantley, then tried to shoot himself, but somehow missed. Carter then threw away his gun and cut his throat with a razor. "After this, he walked from the scene of the tragedy to the police station, almost a mile, and surrendered. His appearance at the station caused a sensation. He was one mass of blood, with a racing gash in the right side of his neck, extending around under the chin, partially severing the windpipe. He made signs for paper and ink and scrawled out a confession that he had murdered his sweetheart because she was untrue to him."[14] In spite of his wound, Carter did not die, but Alberta Brantley did. Carter, who "healed up nicely," was in-dicted by a grand jury two days after the murder, and a court date was set for the following March.

In the months leading up to the trial, Carter seemed to have had a change of heart about wanting to die. He hired Emmanuel Hewl-ett, Cornelius Jones's co-counsel in *Gibson* and *Smith* and, like Wilford Smith, a Boston University Law School alumnus. Hewlett lost and Car-ter was convicted. Hewlett asked Smith to handle the appeal, and Smith succeeded in winning a new trial on technical grounds.

At the retrial, when court convened, "before he had been arraigned or had pleaded to the indictment, [Smith] presented and read to the court a motion to quash the indictment."[15] Smith's motion stated that no black men had served on the grand jury, although they represented one-fourth of the registered voters of Galveston County, and that they had been specifically excluded because of their race, as they had been for many years. Smith offered to submit exhibits and call witnesses to testify to the systematic exclusion of blacks on Galveston's grand juries. The trial judge overruled the motion and refused to hear testimony or view exhibits on the matter. Carter was tried again for first-degree murder before an all-white jury, convicted, and sentenced to hang.

Smith's appeals in state court were rejected, and so he brought the case before the United States Supreme Court. He had an advantage over Cornelius Jones in *Williams* because the trial judge had refused to allow him to present evidence of racial bias. And that was what Horace Gray, speaking for a unanimous Court, homed in on. After noting that the

Texas appeals court ruled against Carter because he had presented no evidence of his claim of bias, Gray wrote:

> It thus clearly appears by the record that the defendant, having duly and distinctly alleged in his motion to quash that all persons of the African race were excluded because of their race and color from the grand jury which found the indictment, asked leave of the court to introduce witnesses, and offered to introduce witnesses, to prove and sustain that allegation, and that the court refused to hear any evidence upon the subject, and overruled the motion without investigating whether the allegation was true or false . . . the assumption in the final opinion of the state court that no evidence was tendered by the defendant in support of the allegations in the motion to quash is plainly disproved by the statements in the bill of exceptions of what took place in the trial court.[16]

His conviction overturned, Seth Carter got a new trial—unclear to what end—the right of black Americans to serve on juries was reaffirmed, and Wilford Smith gained the distinction of being the first African American to win a case in the United States Supreme Court. Any lingering doubts that Washington or anyone else might have harbored about Smith's competence were brushed away by Horace Gray's opinion.

For all the accolades, however, the victory was largely symbolic. The Court had not ruled on systematic exclusion of African Americans from juries for non-statutory reasons, only that in this specific case, a trial judge had pushed discrimination just a bit too far. In a real sense, *Carter v. Texas* was simply a rehash of *Strauder*, which did not help the overall problem of jury exclusion. But whatever its shortcomings, a decision had been rendered by the United States Supreme Court in favor of a case made by an African American attorney.

It might be time, Booker T. Washington decided, to try another.

19

The Window Slams Shut

Giles v. Harris

O N MARCH 13, 1902, WITH ALABAMA'S NEW CONSTI-
tution by then in force, Jackson W. Giles walked into the
courthouse in Montgomery, Alabama, to once again register
to vote. Giles, who worked as a janitor at the post office, had voted in
Montgomery for more than twenty years, but like every other adult male,
he now had to reregister. Giles's qualifications seemed excellent. He was
employed, literate, owned his home, had no criminal record, and had
paid his poll tax of $1.50. He was also black.

Alabama registrars had been extremely aggressive in applying the
new voting regulations, but with an eye to the court battles to come, they
had been careful to not shut out every black voter. Lifetime voting rights
were granted to a trickle of African American veterans of the army or
navy who presented valid discharge papers, although many more were
turned away. Booker T. Washington, of course, received lifetime registration, as did a handful of other prominent African Americans. As
Governor William Dorsey Jelks noted, registrars "would carry out the

spirit of the Constitution, which looks to the registration of all white men not convicted of crimes, and only a few Negroes."[1] (Jelks was also widely known for his advocacy of lynching as an appropriate punishment for African Americans accused of attacking a white woman.)

Jackson Giles was not Booker T. Washington, however, and so his application to register to vote was denied, as were those of many of his fellow employees at the post office. Rather than simply accept the refusal, Giles and some of the others formed the Colored Men's Suffrage Association of Alabama specifically to protest the voting rules of the 1901 Alabama Constitution. Giles was elected president and the group expressed determination to mount a legal challenge that they were willing to press all the way to the United States Supreme Court. Giles chose to create the case in his own name because he was unwilling to expose any of his fellow members to the risks that would accrue to any black man who took on whites—loss of employment, property, or even life. But in addition to his own claim, Giles would also represent 5,000 other qualified African Americans similarly denied the right to register.

Lawsuits were expensive, however, and at the group's first meeting they raised only $200, a tenth of the sum they thought necessary to begin. They used some of that to take out ads in African American newspapers under the heading "AN APPEAL: To the Colored Citizens of Alabama." They claimed, "The requirements of the Board of Registrars are altogether out of harmony with law and justice," and that "the workings of the new constitution are in conflict with the Federal constitution" and that "the grandfather clause was unconstitutional." They asked for donations to raise the $2,000 to begin a lawsuit.[2]

Giles was no lawyer, but still, in preparing his case for federal court, he knew he must present all the proof that Cornelius Jones in *Williams v. Mississippi* had not. He set to compiling reams of statistics, newspaper reports, and affidavits, all to demonstrate that the law was being employed solely to discriminate against a specific class of individual, in this case black voters. It was an enormous task.

To Giles's surprise, soon afterward, a prominent African American attorney from New York named Wilford H. Smith suddenly appeared in Montgomery, claiming to represent something called the "Citizens Protective League," and offered to step in and supply the appropriate resources, and then handle the case in court. A stunned but happy Jackson Giles gratefully accepted, unsure how his case had become known to an attorney in New York.

★ ★ ★

During the four months that the Alabama constitutional convention met, Booker T. Washington had campaigned vigorously against the grandfather clause and for equal application of the law. With white state leaders, such as Governor Jelks, he attempted to use his national fame to buttress fawning communications, seeking concessions that would at least provide the same voter registration standards to blacks and whites. He had also met secretly with black leaders to urge them to use all their resources to register protests against this provision. This was all a fruitless exercise, of course, since the whole point of drafting a new constitution was to make voting standards different for blacks and whites, and black leaders had no resources that actually mattered.

That left the courts as the only avenue to pursue. Washington was savvy enough politically to realize how slim were his chances, so he used his influence with President Roosevelt to try to pry out a bit of an advantage. Roosevelt had taken to consulting Washington on appointments in the South, and as it happened, there was a key federal judgeship available in the very court where any challenge to the Alabama Constitution would be heard. The incumbent, John Bruce, a Ulysses Grant appointee, had died in October 1901, and the president asked Washington who he would like to see as a replacement. Local black leaders had urged Washington to recommend a Republican, but Washington thought a Democrat—if it was the right Democrat—would give him a better shot at attacking the voter registration provisions of the new constitution. He chose Thomas Jones, a former Confederate officer, Alabama governor, and constitutional convention delegate, because Jones, whom Washington knew personally, had been a fierce opponent of the grandfather clause. Roosevelt accepted the recommendation and Jones was seated on December 17, 1901.

Even with Thomas Jones on the bench, Wilford Smith had no illusions as to the odds against pressing a successful action. He would write later,

> With the population of the South distinctly divided into two classes, not the rich and poor, not the educated and ignorant, not the moral and immoral, but simply whites and blacks, all negroes being generally regarded as inferior and not entitled to the same rights as any white person, it is bound to be a difficult matter to obtain fair and just results when there is any sort of conflict between the races.[3]

In the meantime, Washington and Smith were forced to sit and watch while Alabama registrars applied the temporary plan in a transparently discriminatory fashion, as Smith described:

> Under the Alabama Constitution, a soldier in the Civil War, either on the Federal or Confederate side, is entitled to qualification. When a negro goes up to register as a soldier he is asked for his discharge. When he presents it he is asked, "How do we know that you are the man whose name is written in this discharge? Bring us two white men whom we know and who will swear that you have not found this paper, and that they know that you were a soldier in the company and regiment in which you claim to have been." This, of course, could not be done, and the ex-soldier who risked his life for the Union is denied the right to vote.
>
> The same Constitution provides that if not a soldier or the legal descendant of one, an elector must be of good character and understand the duties and obligations of citizenship under a Republican form of government. When a negro claims qualifications under the

good character and understanding clauses he is put through an examination similar to the following:

"What is a republican form of government?"

"What is a limited monarchy?"

"What islands did the United States come into possession of by the Spanish-American War?"

"What is the difference between Jeffersonian Democracy and Calhoun principles, as compared to the Monroe Doctrine?"

"If the Nicaragua Canal is cut, what will be the effect if the Pacific Ocean is two feet higher than the Atlantic?"

Should these questions be answered satisfactorily, the negro must still produce two white men known to the registrars to testify to his good character.[4]

Inability to answer some of these seemed to have been the reason Jackson Giles had been disqualified. He was not alone. Black lawyers, schoolmasters, decorated war veterans, business owners, and even public officeholders were not allowed to register because they could not answer the quiz-show-caliber questions put to them by registrars—who certainly would have been unable to answer them either—or find whites willing to take the risk of vouching for a black man. In the end, the new constitution worked exactly as planned. Of the 181,000 African Americans eligible to vote in Alabama, only 3,000 would be registered under the new system.[5]

Still, a legal challenge could not be undertaken precipitously—finding the right plaintiff was crucial. The Louisiana endeavor had come to naught largely because the only plaintiff proponents could find was illiterate and without property. After Booker T. Washington heard of the appeal for funds by the Colored Men's Suffrage Association and did a bit of checking, he got in touch with Wilford Smith in New York and told him to come to Montgomery without delay. Their search for a plaintiff was over—Jackson Giles was perfect.

And so, unbeknownst to both Giles and those he intended to sue,

Smith had been hired with great secrecy by the very same man that Alabama whites had tried so hard to bring to their side and that other black leaders accused of being a sellout.

It was a secret that Washington intended to be kept, since his ability to have any influence at all depended on whites believing he accepted both segregation and the phony restrictions—except the grandfather clause—that Southerners had placed on African American voting. To hide his true intentions, he directed that all correspondence between him and Smith be handled by Emmett Scott. They used code names for important messages, with Washington himself at first referred to with a series of false names, such as "His Nibs" or "the Wizard." Smith seems to have been called "Filipino." When Washington realized that anyone reading the letters would know immediately to whom those names referred, he instructed Emmett Scott to switch to the aliases R. C. Black (for Scott) and J. C. May (for Smith) and leave references to himself out altogether.

In early May, Wilford Smith filed suit against E. Jeff Harris and the other members of the Board of Registrars of Montgomery County in Alabama Supreme Court. Both Smith and the judges he faced were aware that the game being played out had little or nothing to do with words in Smith's petition. Smith, as the judges knew, wanted the case removed to federal court, so he had included Fourteenth and Fifteenth Amendment grounds in his argument, while the judges wanted to avoid removal, and in fact to avoid ruling on the merits at all. So they dodged the issue by denying jurisdiction, ruling that Smith should have filed his suit in Montgomery city court, not at the state supreme court.

The last thing Smith wanted was to have the case plod its way through the Alabama judicial system. There was no chance of winning there, certainly not in any way that would alter the behavior of state officials, and a protracted process would be too costly to pursue. He wrote Washington that the ruling had been "purely political, with the sole purpose, in my opinion, to delay, and thus discourage the further effort to bring the case before the U.S. Supreme Court."[6] Still, he filed three separate lawsuits in city court, including one for monetary damages, in which he "included a thick stack of evidence, including convention speeches and newspaper articles, census tables, preliminary registration figures, and affidavits, which showed intent, opportunity, and discriminatory results. He was not asking to have the entire suffrage plan set aside, only those elements he believed had produced a discriminatory result. The registrars' discretion was the real target here."[7] These were precisely the parameters under which the Supreme Court had invalidated the brick laundry law in *Yick Wo*, a precedent Smith would cite repeatedly, where the question of unbridled discretion had been the crux of the majority opinion.

With his city court filings likely to be beset by foot-dragging, and with funds tightening by the week, Smith also filed a separate action in federal court before Judge Jones. Although Jones had been willing to oppose his fellow delegates in the convention, he was now being asked to express that opposition in practical terms to the disadvantage of his fellow whites. Washington had hoped Jones would at some point be in this very position and that the combination of his own public statements and the fact that he owed a black man his seat on the federal bench would yield a favorable decision.

And, in what might have been a surprise, Washington got one.

Jones did not rule for Giles, nor did Smith and Washington intend him to. But he did agree to be party to a legally hazy agreement, dismissing the suit on jurisdictional grounds, thus allowing Smith to bypass circuit court and appeal directly to the Supreme Court. This required the attorney representing Alabama to cooperate as well, which he did, likely pleased to get the case out of Alabama and confident that nine white justices were not going to invalidate his state's constitution.

And so, on February 24, 1903, *Giles v. Harris* was filed with the United States Supreme Court. In his brief, Wilford Smith presented the same overwhelming evidence as he had in the state action, demonstrating that discrimination against his client sprung directly from the 1901 Alabama Constitution—no matter how even-handedly it pretended to be worded—and therefore met all the requirements the Court had established to strike down a law as a violation of the Fourteenth and Fifteenth Amendments.

Smith wrote, "If the suffrage provisions of the constitution of Alabama bore equally upon the whites and blacks alike, no matter what the standard of property or education required might be, no cause of complaint would be urged here against them; but they sought to restrict the suffrage of the blacks without depriving a single white man of his right to vote." Cognizant of the "political question" issue, he added, "This is not a suit brought to enforce a political right, but a civil right guaranteed by the Constitution of the United States. Nor is it sought in this action to control the exercise of any political functions of the State of Alabama."[8]

Smith's documentation was so persuasive that the attorney for Alabama, William Gunter Sr., did not contest it, but rather restricted himself to questions of jurisdiction. For this, he was forced to defend the Alabama Constitution as facially neutral, which was all the United States Constitution required, and avoid at all costs discussing how the provisions were implemented.

It cannot be said, that giving the privilege to soldiers and sailors and their descendants was a denial or abridgment of the right to vote on account of color, race or previous condition of servitude . . . The objection, then, if any can be made, must rest on the third provision extending the privilege to all persons of good character understanding the duties and obligations of citizenship. It is evident that there can be no valid objection to the terms of this clause. It is clear that persons of the negro race may have in the highest degree good characters, and understand the duties and obligations of citizenship under a republican government, and thus that they are not excluded. On the other hand, it is equally obvious that white persons are liable to be excluded as not possessing these qualifications. Therefore, the clause is unobjectionable in its terms.[9]

Liberally citing *Williams* and *Reese*, and calling voter registration a "purely political function" and part of the "ordinary operations of government," he asked that the suit be dismissed.

To anyone who thought that the law should actually apply to people it had been implemented to protect, the case could not have been clearer. Unless blacks indeed were lower on the evolutionary scale than whites—and Social Darwinists, of which there were many, believed just that—there could be no doubt that the new Alabama Constitution was being applied in a discriminatory fashion and that black American citizens were being denied the right to vote solely because of their race. One need look no further than the failure to deny discriminatory application by the defendant's attorney. As such, whether or not voter registration was normally a political function was irrelevant. There was a constitutional amendment on the books that forbade such activity, whether political or not. In submitting such powerful documentation, Wilford Smith, who had assured Booker T. Washington that "the case would win itself," seemed to have provided sufficient evidence to achieve that very outcome.

Only, of course, if five of the nine justices agreed, and the Court had undergone an important change since *Williams*. To replace Horace Gray, who had retired due to illness in 1902, President Theodore Roosevelt had appointed to the high bench a man of towering reputation, a celebrated legal philosopher and former war hero, a man destined to become almost as famous as the court on which he served.

Oliver Wendell Holmes Jr. was born in Boston in March 1841. His father, Oliver Wendell Holmes Sr., was a famed physician, as well as a sparkling writer, poet, philosopher, and bestselling author. Among his closest friends were Emerson, Longfellow, and James Russell Lowell. He was one of the founders of *The Atlantic Monthly*, a magazine of ideas that survives to this day. The elder Holmes was known for rational thinking and deductive reasoning, and is generally thought to have lent his name to Arthur Conan Doyle, when Doyle was considering writing a series of detective stories.

It is rare that a son could outshine such a famed and celebrated father, but Holmes Jr. did. After fighting in some of the most famous battles of the Civil War, including Chancellorsville, Fredericksburg, and Antietam—and being wounded three times—Holmes left the army and studied law at Harvard. (His father had studied law as well, but had never practiced.) While working as an attorney for fifteen years, Holmes wrote articles about the philosophy of law, some of which were published in a book, *The Common Law*, that is still read by law students more than 125 years later. He served on the Massachusetts Supreme Judicial Court as both associate and chief justice, all the while watching his reputation soar. His successor on the Supreme Court, Benjamin Cardozo, praised him as "probably the greatest legal intellect in the history of the English-speaking world."

Holmes would serve on the Supreme Court for thirty years and, after his death in 1935, would be acclaimed in a best-selling biography, *Yankee from Olympus*, and become the subject of an Oscar-nominated film, *The Magnificent Yankee* (Louis Calhern lost for Best Actor to José Ferrer playing Cyrano de Bergerac). In another Oscar-winning film, *Judgment at Nuremberg*, the very film that was interrupted to show news reports of the violence in Selma, Holmes would be portrayed as the personification of American fairness.

To this day, Oliver Wendell Holmes Jr. is widely thought of as a great champion of civil liberties and an unwavering defender of democratic ideals.

If that were the Oliver Wendell Holmes who sat as an associate justice of the Supreme Court, he, along with Jackson Giles, Wilford Smith, and Booker T. Washington, might have changed the course of American history.

But Holmes was far more complex than Hollywood, flattering biographers, or even fellow justices portrayed. He was a committed Social Darwinist who believed in the superiority of the white race, and in religion his views were equally intolerant. In 1916, when Louis Brandeis was finally confirmed as an associate justice after a bitter floor fight in the Senate—the notion of a Jew on the Court disgusted many senators—Holmes observed that he would rather "see power in the hands of the Jews than the Catholics," although he really did not "want to be run by either."[10] In 1927, he would write the notorious opinion in *Buck v. Bell*, which upheld the forced sterilization of a nineteen-year-old woman judged—incorrectly, as it turned out—to be mentally retarded. "Three generations of imbeciles is enough," he wrote. Holmes was so obsessed with his image that, shortly before his death, he destroyed any personal papers that might reflect poorly on his reputation, retaining only those that painted him in a favorable light.

This was the Oliver Wendell Holmes Jackson Giles was up against.

Holmes had taken his seat in December 8, 1902, and *Giles v. Harris* would be his first major case. Chief Justice Melville Fuller chose him to write the opinion. On April 27, 1903, the case was decided. The vote was 6–3.

Holmes's opinion was brief, only six pages. Bowing to the weight of Wilford Smith's evidence, Holmes agreed that the voting rights provisions of the Alabama Constitution did indeed discriminate against the state's black citizens. And Holmes was certainly cognizant of the application argument. "According to the allegations of the bill, this part of the constitution, as practically administered and as intended to be administered, let in all whites and kept out a large part, if not all, of the blacks, and those who were let in retained their right to vote after 1903, when tests which might be too severe for many of the whites as well as the blacks went into effect."[11]

Nor would Alabama be able to sidestep judgment as South Carolina had in *Mills v. Green*. "The bill was filed in September, 1902, and alleged the plaintiff's desire to vote at an election coming off in November. This election has gone by, so that it is impossible to give specific relief with regard to that. But we are not prepared to dismiss the bill or the appeal on that ground, because to be enabled to cast a vote in that election is not . . . the whole object of the bill. It is not even the principal object of the relief sought by the plaintiff. The principal object of that is to obtain the permanent advantages of registration as of a date before 1903."

And finally, despite arguments to the contrary, Holmes ruled that no jurisdictional issue should prevent the Court from rendering judgment. "The plaintiff had the right to appeal directly to this Court . . . the case properly is here."

For four of the six pages of his opinion, Holmes had written everything black Americans could have hoped for. But neither the Supreme Court of the United States nor Oliver Wendell Holmes personally had any intention of compelling Southern states to grant African Americans the right to vote, no matter what the Fifteenth Amendment said.

In the last two pages of his opinion, despite a mountain of unquestioned evidence, without mentioning or accounting for *Yick Wo* at all, Holmes denied Giles's claim. More significant, however, were the ridiculous lengths to which he was forced to go to justify his judgment. Holmes's reasoning was such a distortion of constitutional principles that legal scholar Richard Pildes called *Giles v. Harris* "the one key moment, one decisive turning point . . . in the bleak and unfamiliar saga . . . of the history of anti-democracy in the United States."[12]

To begin with, Holmes acknowledged, "We cannot forget that we are dealing with a new and extraordinary situation." And to deal with it, he claimed that since Giles insisted "the whole registration scheme of the Alabama Constitution is a fraud upon the Constitution of the United States, and asks us to declare it void," Giles was suing to "to be registered as a party qualified under the void instrument." If the Court then ruled in Giles's favor, Holmes concluded, it would become "a party to the unlawful scheme by accepting it and adding another voter to its fraudulent lists."

Holmes's elaboration is almost comically circular:

If we accept the plaintiff's allegations for the purposes of his case, he cannot complain. We must accept or reject them. It is impossible simply to shut our eyes, put the plaintiff on the lists, be they honest or fraudulent, and leave the determination of the fundamental question for the future. If we have an opinion that the bill is right on its face, or if we are undecided, we are not at liberty to assume it to be wrong for the purposes of decision. It seems to us that, unless we are prepared to say that it is wrong, that all its principal allegations are immaterial, and that the registration plan of the Alabama Constitution is valid, we cannot order the plaintiff's name to be registered. It is not an answer to say that, if all the blacks who are qualified according to the letter of the instrument were registered, the fraud would be cured.

Leaving aside that if Giles and his fellow African Americans were indeed registered under the instrument, it would no longer be a "fraud," by Holmes's reasoning, *any* law that was discriminatory would be a fraud, and the Court would become party to that fraud by protecting the plaintiff's right as a citizen. It would follow that the Supreme Court could never protect *any* citizen from *any* state law, which was precisely what the Fourteenth and Fifteenth Amendments said the Court *must* do. Even using Joseph Bradley's strangled view of the Fifteenth Amendment, here it was clear, as Holmes had admitted, that "citizens of the United States" were being denied the right to vote in Alabama "on account of race, color, or previous condition of servitude."

In addition, adding the Supreme Court's imprimatur to a "fraudulent instrument" was not the Court's only alternative. If he had chosen to, Holmes could simply have declared Sections 180 and 181 void, and any state provision that, in word or application, prevented equal access to the ballot box would also be void. Alabama would then have had the choice of either eliminating the offending provisions from its constitution, desisting in using them as a means to disfranchise black voters, or cease conducting elections for national office. (For statewide offices, Holmes was correct in his later assertion that the Court had no standing to enforce its ruling.)

If he had chosen this route, Holmes would hardly have been committing a judicial transgression. Justices dating from John Marshall had regularly voided specific sections of a law, as Marshall did with Section 13 of the Judiciary Act of 1789 in the case that established judicial review, *Marbury v. Madison*, while leaving the remainder intact. Holmes, however, did not mention that alternative at all.

Holmes's second objection, that the Court "cannot undertake . . . to enforce political rights," followed Melville Fuller's lead in *Mills v. Green* and accepted Alabama's ludicrous claim that the state had been conducting voter registration as a "purely political function." As things stood, this would only have been the case if the systematic removal of its black citizens fell under the "political" umbrella. Here again, "political rights" proved to be one of those hazy concepts whose definition could change depending on who was doing the defining. But whatever position one takes on whether or not the Court should ensure political rights, or even what political rights are, Holmes's reasoning was tortured and disingenuous:

> The court has as little practical power to deal with the people of the state in a body. The bill imports that the great mass of the white population intends to keep the blacks from voting. To meet such an intent, something more than ordering the plaintiff's name to be inscribed upon the lists of 1902 will be needed. If the conspiracy and the intent exist, a name on a piece of paper will not defeat them. Unless we are prepared to supervise the voting in that state by officers of the court, it seems to us that all that the plaintiff could get from equity would be an empty form. Apart from damages to the individual, relief from a great political wrong, if done, as alleged, by the people of a state and the state itself, must be given by them or by the legislative and political department of the government of the United States.

In other words, since the Court could not enforce its ruling, it should make no ruling at all.

But the Court has no power of enforcement for *any* ruling. It has no dedicated police force, no power over Congress. The Court gains its authority *only* from the willingness of the parties to adhere to its rulings and to the Constitution. If one of the parties refuses, force of arms, a tool of the other branches of government, may be used to ensure compliance. (As was the case sixty years later, when the government used federal troops and marshals to enforce school integration and the 1965 Voting Rights Act.)

And so, in a few paragraphs, Jackson Giles was turned away and the Alabama Constitution, created specifically to remove black Americans from the political process, was approved by the highest court in the land. Holmes's opinion cut away the last hope citizens of color had of being able to have a voice in their government in the South. Previous court decisions had limited the reach of the Fourteenth and Fifteenth Amendments to actions by a state, and then further restricted the amendments to actual state laws, rather than the actions of state employees. Now, it seemed, even state laws acknowledged to be discriminatory would be allowed to stand.

The decision was not unanimous. Justices Brown, Brewer, and Harlan dissented. Brown, who had authored the *Plessy v. Ferguson* decision, did not file an opinion, but later that year, he wrote, "In some criminal cases against negroes, coming up from the Southern States, we have adhered to the technicalities of the law so strictly that I fear injustice has been done to the defendant."[13]

But ten years later, after he had left the bench, he also wrote,

> There is a large class of people in our country who love change for the sake of change, or who think they may profit by it individually. These ideas are a perpetual source of trouble, but, of course, all wrong. There are always a few in the District who are clamoring for a change to a popular government, but the phantom of negro suffrage stands inexorably in their path. No suffrage without the nigger—no suffrage, no nigger.[14]

Harlan and Brewer did write opinions, each focusing more on the jurisdictional gymnastics by which the case came to the Court, and less on the merits. Still, Harlan wrote, "To avoid misapprehension, I may add that my conviction is that, upon the facts alleged in the bill . . . the plaintiff is entitled to relief in respect of his right to be registered as a voter."

Brewer's dissent was more substantive. He stated plainly, "The plaintiff was entitled to a place on the permanent registry, and was denied it by the defendants, the board of registrars in the county in which he lived."

As to Holmes's contention that Giles's disfranchisement could only be reversed in the legislature, Brewer replied,

> Neither can I assent to the proposition that the case presented by the plaintiff's bill is not strictly a legal one, and entitling a party to a judicial hearing and decision. He alleges that he is a citizen of Alabama, entitled to vote; that he desired to vote at an election for representative in Congress; that, without registration, he could not vote, and that registration was wrongfully denied him by the defendants. That many others were similarly treated does not destroy his rights or deprive him of relief in the courts. That such relief will be given has been again and again affirmed in both national and state courts.[15]

Holmes's opinion, as with many of the equal rights decisions, passed into American jurisprudence largely without comment. For decades, neither politicians, legal scholars, nor journalists expressed indignation or rebuke.[16] No one in the white mainstream seemed to notice or care that Holmes had, as had Justices Bradley, Field, Brown, and others before him, simply aligned the law with his own belief in white racial superiority.[17] A Holmes biographer wrote, "As for race . . . Holmes' opinions were not only driven into intolerance by his social Darwinism, but were driven beyond the general intolerance of the age."[18]

But Holmes was just one of many Supreme Court justices who abdicated their responsibility to protect an abused class of citizens simply because they seemed to decide that those citizens did not deserve protection. Further, if the Constitution seemed to disagree, then the Constitution must somehow be wrong. In the end, what is most sad is that *Giles v. Harris* was in no way an exception in the Supreme Court's commitment to allowing—even encouraging—voting rolls to remain white. Rather, the decision is remarkable precisely because it was so unremarkable.[19]

Stolen Justice

W ITHOUT THE RIGHT TO VOTE, NO OTHER RIGHT IS secure. That was precisely what white supremacists in the South desired, and that is what they achieved.

When Georgia became the last of the secessionist states to draft a new constitution in 1908, each of the eleven had instituted a poll tax, generally assessed on a running total, and most in combination with a grandfather clause. Seven demanded literacy tests. Each constitution was facially neutral, but each managed to become the vehicle by which only African Americans were stricken from the voting rolls. By 1908, 83 percent of white males in the South were registered to vote, compared to 2 percent of black men. As the South sank into one-party Democratic rule, laws mandating white primaries became widespread, so votes in general elections by the few African Americans who had slipped through the net were certain to be meaningless. Although the grandfather clause was finally struck down in 1915 in *Guinn v. United States*, and the white primary in *Smith v. Allwright* in 1944—the Court very belatedly beginning to rouse itself to the obvious—by that point black Americans had been so frozen out of the political process that white supremacists had little difficulty replacing the grandfather clause with some equally transparent and discriminatory rule, or relying on some contrivance other than the white primary to achieve the same end.

With voting rights denied, Southern state governments proceeded to segregate virtually every aspect of public life. Georgia passed a Public Park Law in 1905, and within a few years people of color were excluded from virtually all park facilities throughout the South. Forced segregation was soon mandated at factory entrances, pay windows, movie theaters, restaurants, on streetcars and railroads, in grocery stores, taverns, and especially schools, cemeteries, and public toilets. By 1910, African Americans had been effectively herded out of the white South into decrepit, slum-ridden ghettos called "Darktowns." To postulate that the Jim Crow restrictions were as severe as those for slaves would not be an exaggeration.

As all this transpired, and while politicians such as Ben Tillman and James Vardaman were extolling their achievements, the justices of the Supreme Court contented themselves with taking refuge in parsing language, debating the meaning of this clause or that, or deciding whether or not a definition of a term meant what it said or something else. They pretended not to notice that in the nation for which they were the highest authority on what the Constitution meant and how it was administered, their fellow citizens were being brutalized and murdered. Between 1890 and 1903, 1,889 lynchings were conducted in the United States. In 1,405 of those cases, the victims were black. According to records compiled by Booker T. Washington's Tuskegee Institute, 70 to 80 percent of those lynchings occurred in the South.

One of the most important tools for those who analyze the law, either from the bench or in the classroom, is logic. Sometimes directly, sometimes tortuously, they wend their way through the densest rhetoric, examining arguments for logical flaws, from which they may then base a decision to arrive at, to quote John Marshall, "what the law is." But there is a flaw in formal logic that is not often cited in legal analysis—*reductio ad absurdum*, an argument that appears to follow all the rules but leads to an absurd conclusion. And the conclusion that the Fourteenth and Fifteenth Amendments had no power to prevent the horrors of Jim Crow, that the Supreme Court of the United States had no choice but to allow tens of millions of qualified citizens to be deprived of the most basic rights of citizenship, especially the right to have a voice in their destiny, is just that—absurd.

All this leads to the biggest question of all—is the law merely language or is it also an idea? Is the American Constitution only a series of articles, sections, and clauses, or is it something larger than that, an attempt to devise a government that will guarantee fundamental justice? Will there be times when simply breaking down language to try to come to a definition will defeat that goal of equal justice for all? The Constitution has been amended for more than two centuries, but was it to better define language or to better define justice?

Those who believe that the law must be based in language, often referred to these days as "textualists," insist the objectivity of the words on the page is the only fair way to administer justice. Once subjectivity is introduced, the standards of justice can change from person to person, from moment to moment. As the late Justice Antonin Scalia noted in a 1996 speech, "I take the words as they were promulgated to the people of the United States, and what is the fairly understood meaning of those words."

But "fairly understood meaning" is subjective in itself. The Constitution, as every textualist knows but few will admit, is notoriously and often deliberately vague. For example, in Article I, Section 8, which grants explicit powers to Congress, the final clause reads, "To make all Laws which shall be necessary and proper for carrying into Execution the foregoing Powers, and all other Powers vested by this Constitution in the Government of the United States, or in any Department or Officer thereof." How could there possibly be a "fairly understood meaning," a quantifiable, objective meaning, of "necessary and proper"? The phrase defies objectivity, as language often does.

False objectivity, however, is precisely what the nine justices relied on to allow white supremacists to rob African Americans of their rights, to allow the United States to become the land of quasi-slavery, to permit the oppression of United States citizens as if they were still property. What Americans should never forget is that the right to vote should never be taken for granted, never assumed to be "just there," because it is never "just there." Remaining a nation that values freedom and justice requires that all Americans insist that their fellow citizens, no matter what their race, gender, religion, or political belief, be allowed to participate in choosing the nation's leaders.

It is a simple rule, one ordinary citizens, elected officials, and especially Supreme Court justices should not forget.

ACKNOWLEDGMENTS

I am deeply grateful to Counterpoint for the enthusiasm with which they embraced a piece of American history that I thought very much needed to be aired. To Jack Shoemaker, Alisha Gorder, Megan Fishmann, Jordan Koluch, Jennifer Alton, Yukiko Tominaga, my thanks. And also to my agent, Michael Carlisle, who found the perfect home for this book.

I would also like to thank Adam Winkler, Henry Louis Gates Jr., Leon Friedman, Marsha Darling, and Ronald King for careful reads, excellent suggestions, and gratifying support.

In previous books, I've expressed appreciation to my wife, Nancy, and daughter, Lee, who have the thankless job of putting up with me. I'm happy to say that they still do.

NOTES

Introduction

1. "Introduction to Federal Voting Rights Laws," Electronic Privacy Information Center, epic.org/privacy/voting/register/intro.html.
2. "The Effects of Shelby County v. Holder," Brennan Center for Justice, August 6, 2018, www.brennancenter.org/analysis/effects-shelby-county-v-holder.
3. P. R. Lockhart, "This is Voter Suppression: Black Seniors in Georgia Ordered Off Bus Taking Them to Vote," *Vox*, October 17, 2018, www.vox.com/identities/2018/10/17/17990110/georgia-senior-citizens-bus-removal-black-voters-matter-suppression.
4. Senators were initially appointed by state legislatures, but that was changed to popular vote in 1913 with ratification of the Seventeenth Amendment.

Prologue: Overthrow

1. Richard Wormser, *The Rise and Fall of Jim Crow* (New York: St. Martin's Press, 2003) 84.
2. *The Daily Record*, August 18, 1898.
3. Reprinted in the Wilmington, NC, *The Semi-Weekly Messenger*, September 6, 1898, 8.
4. "The Ghosts of 1898: Wilmington's Race Riot and the Rise of White Su-

premacy," *News and Observer*, November 17, 2006, media2.newsobserver
.com/content/media/2010/5/3/ghostsof1898.pdf.

5. "The Ghosts of 1898," *News and Observer*, November 17, 2006, media2
.newsobserver.com/content/media/2010/5/3/ghostsof1898.pdf.

6. "Rev. Charles S. Morris Describes the Wilmington Massacre of 1898," Black
Past.org, January 28, 2007, www.blackpast.org/african-american-history
/1898-rev-charles-s-morris-describes-wilmington-massacre-1898.

7. Harry Hayden, *The Story of the Wilmington Rebellion* (Privately printed,
1936), www.1898wilmington.org/hayden.shtml.

8. "The Life of Alexander L. Manly," Goin' North, goinnorth.org/exhibits
/show/milo-manly/manly-family.

Chapter 1: Who Votes?

1. Max Farrand, *Records of the Federal Convention* (New Haven, CT: Yale University Press, 1937) Vol. 2, 203–4.

2. Jonathan Elliot, *The Debates in the Several State Conventions on the Adoption of
the Federal Constitution* (Philadelphia: J. B. Lippincott & Co., 1839) Vol. 5, 243.

3. "From John Adams to James Sullivan, 26 May 1776," National Ar-
chives, Founders Online, founders.archives.gov/documents/Adams/06-04
-02-0091.

4. Harold C. Syrett, ed., *Papers of Alexander Hamilton* (New York: Columbia
University Press, 1961–79) Vol. 1, 106.

5. Farrand, *Records*, Vol. 1, 299.

6. Julian P. Boyd, ed. *Papers of Thomas Jefferson* (Princeton, NJ: Princeton University Press, 1950) Vol. 1, 504.

7. "Thomas Jefferson to Richard Price," Library of Congress, January 8, 1789,
www.loc.gov/exhibits/jefferson/60.html.

8. Quoted in Alexander Keyssar, *The Right to Vote: The Contested History of
Democracy in the United States* (New York: Basic Books, 2000), 3.

Chapter 2: Two Amendments . . .

1. Congressional Globe, 40th Congress, 2nd Session, (1867) 2. The message
was delivered in an attempt to ward off impeachment. Johnson was successful that time. Two days after his message was read in Congress, the House
of Representatives voted 108–57 against reporting a bill of impeachment.
He would not be so fortunate two months later.

2. Congressional Globe, 40th Congress, 2nd Session, (1867) 2.

3. George P. Smith, "Republican Reconstruction and Section Two of the

Fourteenth Amendment," *The Western Political Quarterly*, Vol. 23, No. 4 (December 1970): 829–853.

4. Mildred Bryant-Jones, "The Political Program of Thaddeus Stevens, 1865," *Phylon*, Vol. 2, No. 2 (2nd Qtr., 1941): 149.

5. Bryant-Jones, "Political Program," 150.

6. Statutes at Large, 14 Stat. 27 (1866).

7. Quoted in C. Vann Woodward, "The Political Legacy of Reconstruction," in "The Negro Voter in the South," *The Journal of Negro Education*, Vol. 26, No. 3 (Summer 1957), 231.

8. Gerard N. Magliocca, *American Founding Son: John Bingham and the Invention of the Fourteenth Amendment* (New York: NYU Press, 2013), 125.

9. *New York Times*, June 15, 1866, 4.

10. *Hartford Courant*, June 14, 1866, 2. The article referred to Stevens's proposal of a section bluntly barring disfranchisement of blacks.

11. William W. Van Alstyne, "The Fourteenth Amendment, the 'Right' to Vote, and the Understanding of the Thirty-Ninth Congress," *The Supreme Court Review*, Vol. 1965 (1965).

12. Statutes at Large, 39th Congress, 2nd Session, 428.

13. Statutes at Large, 39th Congress, 2nd Session, 429.

14. Eric Foner, *Reconstruction: America's Unfinished Revolution, 1863–1877* (New York: Harper and Row, 1988), 276.

15. *New York Times*, March 25, 1867, 4.

16. *New York Times*, July 10, 1868, 4.

17. Eric Foner, *Freedom's Lawmakers: A Directory of Black Officeholders during Reconstruction*, revised ed. (Baton Rouge: Louisiana State University Press, 1996), xi–xxxii.

Chapter 3: Power in Black and White

1. Eddy W. Davison and Daniel Foxx, *Nathan Bedford Forrest: In Search of the Enigma* (Gretna, LA: Pelican Publishing, 2007) 246.

2. Mary Polk Branch, *Memoirs of a Southern Woman* (Chicago: Joseph E. Branch Publishing Company, 1912).

3. Thomas W. Burton, *What Experience Has Taught Me: An Autobiography of Thomas William Burton* (Cincinnati: Press of Jennings and Graham, 1910).

4. Frank Alexander Montgomery, *Reminiscences of a Mississippian in Peace and War* (Cincinnati: Robert Clarke Company, 1901), 268–70.

5. James Wilford Garner, *Reconstruction in Mississippi* (New York: MacMillan, 1901), 338.

6. William A. Dunning, "The Undoing of Reconstruction," *The Atlantic Monthly*, vol. 88, 1901, 440–1.

7. Foner, *Reconstruction*, 343.

8. Garner, *Reconstruction*, 341.

Chapter 4: . . . and a Third

1. Congressional Globe, 39th Congress, 1st Session (1866), 362.

2. Congressional Globe, 39th Congress, 1st Session (1866), 1287.

3. Congressional Globe, 37th Congress, 3rd Session (1863), 2766.

4. "Amendments to the Constitution: a brief legislative history. Prepared for the use of the Subcommittee on the Constitution, Committee on the Judiciary, United States Senate." Washington, D.C.: U.S. G.P.O., 1985, 36.

5. Congressional Globe, 40th Congress, 3rd Session (1868–1869), 378.

6. Edward McPherson, *The Political History of the United States of America During the Period of Reconstruction (from April 15, 1865 to July 15, 1870)* (Washington, D.C.: Philp and Solomons, 1871), 402–3.

7. Congressional Globe, 40th Congress, 3rd Session (1868-9), 727.

8. Garrison, of course, had also warned that such "coercion would gain nothing," words that proved prophetic in the decades to come.

9. Xi Wang, "The Making of Federal Enforcement Laws, 1870–1872—Freedom: Political," *Chicago-Kent Law Review*, vol. 70 (1995), 1015.

10. *New York Times*, March 31, 1870, 5. Grant did "call the attention . . . of our newly enfranchised race to the importance of their striving in every honorable manner to make themselves worthy of their new privilege."

11. Quoted in Foner, *Reconstruction*, 449.

12. Quoted in Foner, *Reconstruction*, 446.

13. Quoted in the *Hartford Courant*, February 2, 1870, 2.

Chapter 5: A Fragile Illusion

1. *Washington Evening Star*, March 4, 1869, 1.

2. 16 Stat. 140 (1870).

3. Wang, "Federal Enforcement Laws," 1033. He writes, "The Republican party's loss in New York during the 1868 presidential election was still a fresh memory. Not only did New York fail to give its electoral votes to Grant and Colfax, but the Democratic Party also won thirteen of the state's thirty-one seats in Congress."

4. The office of Attorney General had existed since the Judiciary Act of 1789. It was originally a part-time position, manned by an attorney who main-

tained a private practice to supplement his salary. He didn't even have a clerk until 1818. Only after the start of the Civil War was the Attorney General given authority over United States attorneys. After the war, there were some nascent efforts to establish an executive department, but only after Andrew Johnson was out and Ulysses Grant was in did the bill authorizing its creation pass Congress.

5. Robert Kaczorowski, *The Politics of Judicial Interpretation: The Federal Courts, Department of Justice and Civil Rights, 1866–1876* (New York: Fordham University Press, 2005), 65.

6. J. Morgan Kousser, "Response to Commentaries," *Social Science History*, 24:2 (Summer 2000): 18.

7. Ulysses S. Grant, *The Papers of Ulysses S. Grant: November 1, 1870–May 31, 1871* (Carbondale: Southern Illinois University Press, 1998), 259.

8. Grant, *Papers*, 261.

9. Kaczorowski, 99.

10. Congressional Globe, 42nd Congress, 1st Session (1875), 135.

11. Richard Zuczek, "The Federal Government's Attack on the Ku Klux Klan: A Reassessment," *The South Carolina Historical Magazine* 97, no. 1 (1996), 50.

12. Quoted in Kaczorowski, 66.

13. Quoted in Kaczorowski, 76.

14. Kousser, 18.

Chapter 6: Any Way You Slice It

1. "Report of the Special Joint Committee on Levees to the Legislature of the State of Louisiana," Baton Rouge, 1859, 35.

2. Quoted in Jonathan Lurie, "Reflections on Justice Samuel F. Miller and the *Slaughter-House Cases*: Still a Meaty Subject," *NYU Journal of Law & Liberty*, Vol. 1 (2005), 357.

3. There are those who insist the opposition by Democrats was not racially motivated; that complaints that the new corporation was just a money grab were sincere. Still, in a city and state famed for graft and corruption that knew no party boundaries, Democrats' indignation would seem suspect, especially since they would be getting a tangible and long-demanded benefit.

4. Michael A. Ross, "Justice Miller's Reconstruction: The *Slaughter-House Cases*, Health Codes, and Civil Rights in New Orleans, 1861–1873," *The Journal of Southern History*, Vol. 64, No. 4 (November 1998), 21.

5. Quoted in Charles Lane, *The Day Freedom Died: The Colfax Massacre, the*

Supreme Court, and the Betrayal of Reconstruction (New York: Henry Holt & Company, 2009), 120.

6. Michael A. Ross, "Obstructing Reconstruction: John Archibald Campbell and the Legal Campaign Against Louisiana's Republican Government, 1868–1873," *Civil War History*, Vol. 49, No. 3, 235–53 (2003), 241–2.

7. 83 U.S. 36 (1873).

8. The *Slaughter-House Cases* are among the most widely dissected Supreme Court decisions. The most common slant, and the most obvious, is that Samuel Miller erred horribly, and in excising the privileges and immunities clause opened the door to rampant discrimination in the Redeemed South. Agreeing with conventional wisdom, however, is not the road to academic publication, and so a revisionist view has been taking shape. For example, David S. Bogen wrote, "Justice Miller used federalism in order to protect Reconstruction legislatures where significant numbers of African-Americans participated fully for the first time. His recital of the history and purpose of the Civil War Amendments centered on the Amendments' design to protect African-Americans, and suggested sweeping federal power to accomplish that end. Gutting the Privileges and Immunities Clause compelled the Court to read the Equal Protection Clause broadly, and was indirectly responsible for the reapportionment decisions of the Warren Court." (David S. Bogen, "Slaughter-House Five: Views of the Case." *Hastings Law Journal*, Vol. 55, No. 2 (December 2003), 1130.

There are also those who argue, a good deal more persuasively, that voting, because of the many limitations that have traditionally been put on it—gender, property ownership, even age—cannot be considered a "privilege" of citizenship *per se*; it is a "political" rather than a "constitutional" right, and therefore must be left to political departments of government rather than the judiciary.

Certainly, that voting was a political act, not strictly a civil right, was supported by the prohibitions on certain classes of citizens, especially women, as the Court would unanimously rule in *Minor v. Happersett* in 1875. But the Fourteenth and Fifteenth Amendments seemed to have been intended to eliminate race as a legitimate barrier to the right to vote, to in fact create a "civil right" for African Americans who otherwise could have been barred from voting by criteria not applied to other races. It would then have been made a privilege of national citizenship not susceptible to being overturned by state law.

But once again, that interpretation would only become operative if the courts, and especially the Supreme Court, chose to rule that way. If not, after the *Slaughter-House* ruling, with federal privileges of citizenship no longer binding on the states without appended qualifications, unless the Court was willing to apply different reasoning in subsequent cases, discrimination and disfranchisement were certain to follow.

As they did.

Chapter 7: Equality by Law

1. Four seats, two on each side of the aisle, were held by splinter parties.
2. Congressional Globe, 41st Congress, 2nd session (May 13, 1870), 3,434.
3. Congressional Globe, 41st Congress, 2nd session (May 13, 1870), 767.
4. Congressional Globe, 41st Congress, 2nd session (May 13, 1870), 772.
5. 18 Stat. 335 (1875).
6. *New York Times*, March 2, 1875, 6.
7. *Chicago Daily Tribune*, March 1, 1875, 4.

Chapter 8: The Uncertainty of Language

1. 16 Stat. 141 (1870).
2. 16 Stat. 140–6 (1870).
3. Kaczorowski, 163.
4. Kaczorowski, 163.
5. Charles Warren, *The Supreme Court and United States History* (Boston: Little, Brown and Company, 1923), 275.
6. Warren, *Supreme Court*, 275.
7. *Brooklyn Daily Eagle*, April 21, 1875, 2. Quoted in the *New York Herald*, December 8, 1873, 1.
8. John S. Goff, "The Rejection of United States Supreme Court Appointments," *The American Journal of Legal History*, Vol. 5, No. 4 (October 1961): 365.
9. George H. Williams, "Reminiscences of the United States Supreme Court," *The Yale Law Journal*, Vol. 8, No. 7 (April 1899): 299.
10. William H. Rehnquist, *Centennial Crisis: The Disputed Election of 1876* (New York: Alfred A. Knopf, 2004), 132.
11. Widely quoted. See, for example, Lane, *The Day Freedom Died*, 231.
12. Quoted in Anthony Champagne and Dennis Pope, "Joseph P. Bradley: An Aspect of a Judicial Personality," *Political Psychology*, Vol. 6, No. 3 (September 1985): 485.
13. Champagne and Pope, "Joseph P. Bradley," 481, 485–6.

14. Champagne and Pope, "Joseph P. Bradley," 485.

15. *New Orleans Republican*, June 28, 1874, 1.

16. 92 U.S. 542 (1875).

17. 92 U.S. 214 (1875).

18. L. C. Northrop to Charles Devens, January 14, 1879. Quoted by C. Peter Magrath, *Morrison R. Waite: The Triumph of Character* (New York: The Macmillan Company, 1963) 132.

Chapter 9: Rutherfraud Ascends, but Not Equal Rights

1. John Copeland Nagle, "How Not to Count Votes," *Columbia Law Review*, Vol. 104, No. 6 (October 2004): 1734.

2. *New York Times*, November 6, 1876, 1.

3. Nagle, "How Not to Count Votes," 1736.

4. *New York Times*, November 8, 1876, 1; November 9, 1876, 1.

5. Roy Morris Jr., *Fraud of the Century. Rutherford B. Hayes, Samuel Tilden and the Stolen Election of 1876* (New York: Simon and Schuster, 2003), 218.

6. Allan Peskin, "Was There a Compromise of 1877?" *The Journal of American History*, Vol. 60, No. 1 (June 1973): 63.

Chapter 10: A Slight Case of Murder

1. *Wheeling Daily Intelligencer (WDI)*, April 19 1872, 4. *Wheeling Daily Register (WDR)*, April 19, 1872, 4. Each newspaper was four pages long and, unlike contemporary newspapers, featured the major local news on the back page.

2. *WDR*, April 22, 1872, 2.

3. *WDR*, May 9, 1873, 4.

4. *WDR*, July 22, 1873, 4.

5. *WDI*, August 29, 1873, 4.

6. According to statute, the case needed to be put before county court as an examining court before it could be tried in circuit court, and that had not been done.

7. *WDR*, March 3, 1875, 4.

8. *WDI*, December 23, 1876, 4.

9. *WDI*, November 19, 1877, 4.

10. *WDI*, April 3, 1878, 4.

11. *WDI*, January 24, 1880, 4.

12. 80 U.S. 581 (1871).

13. 14 Stat. 27. Italics added.

14. 100 U.S. 303–312 (1880).
15. *WDI*, May 3, 1881, 4.
16. *WDI*, April 27, 1898, 5.
17. *WDI*, June 21, 1898, 6.

Chapter 11: Tightening the Knot

1. William Eleazar Barton, *Pine Knot: A Story of Kentucky Life* (New York: D. Appleton and Co., 1900).
2. Details of the crime from *Richmond Daily Dispatch*, December 2, 1878, 1.
3. Virginia G. Pedigo and Lewis G. Pedigo, *History of Patrick and Henry Counties, Virginia* (Baltimore: Genealogical Publishing Com, 1933).
4. Philip Alexander Bruce, *History of the University of Virginia, 1819–1919: The Lengthened Shadow of One Man*, Vol. III (New York: The Macmillan Company: 1920–22).
5. Bruce, *University of Virginia*, 112.
6. "Alexander Rives to James Madison, December 28, 1832," Library of Congress, Manuscript Division, www.loc.gov/resource/mjm.23_1167_1169/?st =gallery.
7. Gaillard Hunt, ed., *The Writings of James Madison*, Vol. 9 (New York: G. P. Putnam's Sons, 1903), 495.
8. *Richmond Daily Dispatch*, November 22, 1878, 3.
9. *Staunton Spectator*, December 17, 1878, 2.
10. *Richmond Daily Dispatch*, November 30, 1878, 3.
11. *Richmond Daily Dispatch*, December 10, 1878, 2.
12. *New Orleans Daily Democrat*, November 30, 1878, 4.
13. *Richmond Daily Dispatch*, December 5, 1878, 2.
14. *Brooklyn Daily Eagle*, Monday, October 20, 1879, 2.
15. *New York Times*, January 18, 1879, 4.
16. *Chicago Daily Tribune*, March 20, 1879, 2.
17. 100 U.S. 313, 314.
18. *Richmond Daily Dispatch*, June 25, 1880, 3.
19. Jed Rubenfeld observed: "For me *Strauder v. West Virginia*, in which the Court held that the Fourteenth Amendment prohibited states from excluding blacks from jury service, is an easy case and a strong, clear example of the kind of paradigm-case reasoning I advocate." Patrick Foley of Catholic University wrote: "By reversing the lower court, the Supreme Court incisively recognized that the protection offered by the Fourteenth Amendment included an assurance of Federal protection from legislation

unfriendly to the Negroes as a class in order that they might enjoy the civil rights enjoyed by the white race . . . That the equal protection clause guarantees protection by the Federal Government against State denial thereof is clear." Michael Klarman added: "[The Court's] ruling in *Strauder v. West Virginia* that juries because of their race, either by statute or through the deliberate exercise of administrative discretion, violated the Fourteenth Amendment." In fact, when *Rives* is added in, it is apparent that the Court did no such thing.

20. 103 U.S. 401 (1881).
21. 103 U.S. 401 (1881).

Chapter 12: Strangling the Constitution

1. 109 U.S. 3 (1883). The New York plaintiff, William R. Davis, was a twenty-six-year-old employee of a black weekly newspaper, the *Progressive American*, who had been born a slave in South Carolina.
2. Horatio Seymour, "The Political Situation," *The North American Review.* Volume 136, Issue 315 (February 1883): 155.
3. C. Vann Woodward, *Origins of the New South, 1877–1913* (Baton Rouge: Louisiana State University Press, 1951), 216. Hayes had left office in 1880 and been replaced by James Garfield. But Garfield had been assassinated, and Roscoe Conkling associate Chester Arthur was president.
4. Quoted in Alan F. Westin, "John Marshall Harlan and the Constitutional Rights of Negroes: The Transformation of a Southerner," *The Yale Law Journal*, Vol. 66, No. 5 (April 1957).
5. Quoted in Westin, "John Marshall Harlan," 653.
6. Quoted in Westin, "John Marshall Harlan," 660.
7. Quoted in Westin, "John Marshall Harlan," 666.
8. 109 U.S. 10 (1883).
9. 109 U.S. 24–5 (1883).
10. Oliver Wendell Holmes Jr., *The Common Law* (Boston: The Little, Brown & Company, 1881) 35.
11. Italics added.
12. Italics added.
13. *New York Times*, October 16, 1883, 4.
14. *Brooklyn Daily Eagle*, October 16, 1883, 2.
15. *The Atlanta Constitution*, Oct 16, 1883, 1.
16. *Hartford Courant*, October 16, 1883, 2.
17. All quoted in Valeria W. Weaver, "The Failure of Civil Rights 1875–1883

and Its Repercussions," *The Journal of Negro History*, vol. 54, no. 4 (Oct. 1969): 371–2.

18. Quoted in Westin, "John Marshall Harlan," 668.

Chapter 13: The Curious Incident of the Chinese Laundry and Equal Protection

1. Sutter never did make any money on the find. Eventually, he transferred ownership of what remained of his land to his son, who laid out a city he called Sacramento. Sutter was furious—he had wanted it to be called Sutterville. The elder Sutter moved east to Pennsylvania and, while engaged in an unsuccessful fifteen-year crusade to persuade Congress to pay him restitution for his stolen land, died in a Washington, D.C., hotel in 1880.

2. Previous pacts, such as the Treaty of Tianjin in 1858, gave the United States and some European powers access to Chinese ports, allowed Christian missionaries to operate freely, and legalized the import of opium, giving the Chinese nothing in return, except the promise not to overrun their country.

3. 43rd Congress, 2nd Session, Ch. 141 (1875).

4. Paul Kens, *Justice Stephen Field: Shaping Liberty from the Gold Rush to the Gilded Age* (Lawrence: University Press of Kansas, 1997) 205.

5. Kens, *Justice Stephen Field*, 212.

6. Ah Kow v. Nunan. 12 F. Cas. at 253, 256–57.

7. He also asserted that the law violated the provisions of the Burlingame Treaty.

8. The law was tested, but in a unanimous 1889 decision, authored by Stephen Field, the Court ruled that the United States was within its rights to enact legislation that abrogated provisions of previously negotiated treaties.

9. A Caucasian woman named Mary Meagles was also turned down for reasons never made explicit.

10. *New York Times*, December 2, 1888, 4.

11. Douglas S. Watson, "The San Francisco McAllisters," *California Historical Society Quarterly*, Vol. 11, No. 2 (June 1932): 124–8.

12. Roughly $3 million today. *New York Times*, December 2, 1888, 4.

13. Others in the family achieved notoriety of their own. Sam Ward eventually did do a spot of mining and made a bit of money, but not nearly as much as when he returned east and married the eldest daughter of John Jacob Astor. His sister Julia married an abolitionist physician, Samuel Gridley Howe, became a noted poet, advocated for women's suffrage, and eventually wrote "Battle Hymn of the Republic."

14. *In re* Wo Lee, 26 E 471, 476 (C.C.D. Cal. 1886).
15. *United States Supreme Court Reports*, volume 59, 1013–15.
16. 111 U.S. 703 (1885), italics added. Willingness to take public statements, sociological factors, or motivation into account when judging the constitutionality of a law has been inconsistently applied by the Court. In some cases, *Brown v. Board of Education* being among the most prominent, the Court did so, but on other occasions, *Hawaii v. Trump*, for example, the Court ignored public pronouncements as to a law's intent.
17. 118 U.S. 356 (1886).
18. Although not entirely. There is currently a Yick Wo Alternative Elementary School in San Francisco. Their school mascot is a panda.
19. Hall McAllister died on December 1, 1888. As reported in *The New York Times*: "He had been suffering from nervous prostration brought on by overwork for the past six months and his death has been expected for some time." On April 15, 1905, 1,000 people stood in the rain to see a statue of McAllister unveiled near San Francisco City Hall and hear him praised as the "foremost advocate" of the city's bar. The statue was mounted on a granite pedestal, which held the inscription LEARNED, ELOQUENT, UNTIRING. A FEARLESS ADVOCATE, A COURTEOUS FOE. The statue still stands.
20. *United States Supreme Court Reports*, Volume 118 (1885), 409.
21. 118 U.S. 394 (1886). Waite later confirmed in correspondence with the court reporter that the transcript was correct.
22. See, for example, Gabriel J. Chin, "Unexplainable on Grounds of Race: Doubts About *Yick Wo*," *University of Illinois Law Review*, 2008, and David Bernstein, "Revisiting *Yick Wo v. Hopkins*," *George Mason University Law and Economics Research Paper Series*, 2008.

Chapter 14: Mississippi Leads the South

1. Jerrold M. Packard, *American Nightmare: The History of Jim Crow* (New York: Macmillan, 1992), 41.
2. Thomas B. Reed, "The Federal Control of Elections," *The North American Review*, Vol. 150, No. 403 (June 1890): 677.
3. Reed, "Federal Control," 671.
4. Reed, "Federal Control," 675.
5. William Alexander Mabry, "Disenfranchisement of the Negro in Mississippi," *The Journal of Southern History*, Vol. 4, No. 3 (August 1938).
6. Earl M. Lewis, "The Negro Voter in Mississippi," in "The Negro Voter in

the South," special issue, *The Journal of Negro Education*, Vol. 26, No. 3, (Summer 1957), 330.

7. Mabry, 319.

8. S. S. Calhoon, "The Causes and Events that Led to the Calling of the Constitutional Convention of 1890," in Mississippi Historical Society, Publications (Oxford, etc., 1897–1914; Centenary Series, 1916–1925), vol. VI (1902), 107. Quoted in Mabry, "Disenfranchisement," 319.

9. Quoted in Mabry, "Disenfranchisement," 319.

10. Mabry, "Disenfranchisement," 320.

11. Woodward, *Origins*, 72–3.

12. "Report of the Annual Meeting of the Mississippi Bar Association" (Jackson, MS: Clarion Steam Printing, 1888), 14–15.

13. Timothy S. Huebner, "Emory Speer and Federal Enforcement of the Rights of African Americans, 1880–1910," *American Journal of Legal History*, Vol. 54 (January 2015): 47–8.

14. *The North American Review*, Vol. 151, No. 406 (September 1890), 258.

15. Michael Perman, *Struggle for Mastery: Disfranchisement and the South 1888–1908* (Chapel Hill: University of North Carolina Press, 2001), 74.

16. *The Magnolia Gazette*, August 2, 1890, 2.

17. Woodward, *Origins*, 72.

18. Quoted in Packard, *American Nightmare*, 69.

19. Jackson *Daily Clarion-Ledger*, August 7, 1890, 4.

20. *Natchez Daily Democrat*, August 12, 1890, 2.

21. Perman, *Struggle for Mastery*, 80.

22. Mabry, "Disenfranchisement," 326.

23. *Collier's*, July 6, 1946, 18.

24. J. W. Sumers, "The Grandfather Clause," *Lawyer & Banker & Southern Bench & Bar Review*, Vol. 7 (1914): 39.

25. Perman, *Struggle for Mastery*, 86.

Chapter 15: The First Test

1. W. Lewis Burke, "Killing, Cheating, Legislating, and Lying: A History of Voting Rights in South Carolina after the Civil War," *South Carolina Law Review*, Vol. 57 (2006): 869.

2. Daniel M. Robison, "From Tillman to Long: Some Striking Leaders of the Rural South," *The Journal of Southern History*, Vol. 3, No. 3 (August 1937): 295.

3. Robison, "From Tillman to Long," 297.

4. Stephen Kantrowitz, "Youngest Living Carpetbagger Tells All: Or, How Regional Myopia Created 'Pitchfork' Ben Tillman," *Southern Cultures*, Vol. 8, No. 3 (Fall 2002): 19.

5. Burke, 867.

6. Burke, 870.

7. Burke, 870.

8. Perman, 104.

9. R. Volney Riser, *Defying Disfranchisement* (Baton Rouge: Louisiana State University Press, 2010).

10. 67 *Federal Reporter*, 822.

11. Riser, 24.

12. 67 *Federal Reporter*, 831.

13. 67 *Federal Reporter*, 832.

14. *Yorkville* (South Carolina) *Enquirer*, May 15, 1895, 2.

15. Riser, 27.

16. *New York Times*, May 1, 1888, 5; *Brooklyn Daily Eagle*, April 30, 1888, 6. The *Daily Eagle* was somewhat more praising of Fuller's qualifications than was the *Times*.

17. *New-York Tribune*, May 1, 1888, 1.

18. Michael J. Klarman, *From Jim Crow to Civil Rights: The Supreme Court and the Struggle for Racial Equality* (New York: Oxford University Press, 2004), 16.

19. Green v. Mills. U.S. Courts of Appeals Reports, v. 25 (1894–1896), 383–406.

20. Riser, 29.

21. Quoted in Perman, 100.

22. Quoted in Perman, 100.

23. (Sumter, South Carolina) *Watchman and Statesman*, October 16, 1895, 1.

24. 159 U.S. 651 (1895).

25. Riser, 33.

Chapter 16: Peer Review

1. "Anselm J. McLaurin (late a senator from Mississippi)" (Washington, D.C.: U.S. Government Printing Office, 1911), 10. Senators were not elected by popular vote until 1914.

2. 162 U.S. 567 (1895).

3. 162 U.S. 574 (1895).

4. Washington D.C. *Evening Star*, October 31, 1895, 16.

5. *Washington Bee*, December 21, 1895, 1.

6. 162 U.S. 565.

7. 163 U.S. 537.

8. *Greenville Times*, December 12, 1896, 2.

9. *Greenville Times*, November 5, 1898, 2.

10. Quoted in "Contested election case of Cornelius J. Jones vs. T. C. Catchings in House of Representatives of 56th Congress of the United States: brief of contestant" (Washington, D.C.: U.S. Government Printing Office, 1894), 18–19.

11. "Contested election case of Cornelius J. Jones," 17.

12. *Vicksburg Commercial Herald*, January 5, 1899, 4.

13. 170 U.S. 213 (1898).

14. 170 U.S. 213 (1898), 214.

15. Field retired December 1, 1897. Despite encroaching senility, he had refused to resign until his tenure exceeded that of John Marshall, a display of hubris that aroused the enmity of his fellows, but since senility does not constitute a violation of "good behavior," neither they nor anyone else who disapproved of Field's stubbornness could do anything about it.

16. Roger Brooke Taney and Edward Douglass White were the previous two.

17. *New York Times*, January 15, 1898, 4.

18. Edward Purcell, "The Particularly Dubious Case of *Hans v. Louisiana*: An Essay on Law, Race, History, and Federal Courts," *North Carolina Law Review* (June 2003): 2010.

19. 170 U.S. 213 (1898).

20. 170 U.S. 213 (1898).

21. Michael J. Klarman, "The Plessy Era," *The Supreme Court Review*, Vol. 1998, 362–3.

22. *Reports of Cases Adjudged in the Court of Appeals of the District of Columbia*, Vol. 45 (1917): 440–1.

Chapter 17: Refining Redemption

1. Sumers, 40.

2. Quoted in George E. Cunningham, "Constitutional Disenfranchisement of the Negro in Louisiana, 1898," *Negro History Bulletin*, Vol. 29, No. 7 (April 1966): 147.

3. Quoted in Mabry, 299.

4. Riser, 77.

5. Sumers, 40.

6. Mabry, 292.

7. "State Constitution of Louisiana, 1898, Suffrage and Elections," Yale University, Gilder Lehrman Center, glc.yale.edu/state-constitution-louisiana-1898-suffrage-and-elections.

8. Mabry, 309.

9. *New Orleans Times-Democrat*, March 22, 1898, 2.

10. *The Daily Picayune* (New Orleans), Feb. 21, 1898, 2.

11. Helen G. Edmonds, *The Negro and Fusion Politics in North Carolina, 1894–1901* (Chapel Hill: University of North Carolina Press, 1951), 141.

12. Mabry, 3.

13. *The Caucasian* (Clinton, N.C.), April 26, 1900, 3.

14. *Winston* (N.C.) *Progressive Farmer*, August 7, 1900, 3.

15. *Wilmington* (N.C.) *Semi-Weekly Messenger*, August 7, 1900, 4.

16. Perman, 18.

17. Wayne Flynt, "Alabama's Shame: The Historical Origins of the 1901 Constitution," *Alabama Law Review*, Vol. 53 (2001): 69.

18. Flynt, 69.

19. Flynt, 70.

20. Flynt, 70.

21. *Journal of the Proceedings of the Constitutional Convention* (1901), 8–9.

22. *Journal*, 12.

23. *Journal*, 9.

24. *Journal*, 9.

25. Quoted in Riser, 115–6.

26. *New York Times*, June 9, 1901, 1.

27. *New York Times*, November 12, 1901, 2.

28. Riser, 136.

29. *New York Times*, November 12, 1901, 2

Chapter 18: Forging an Attack

1. *New-York Tribune*, September 18, 1895, 1.

2. *New York Times*, September 19, 1895, 1.

3. *New York Times*, September 19, 1895, 1.

4. See Timothy S. Huebner, "Emory Speer and Federal Enforcement of the Rights of African Americans, 1880-1910," *American Journal of Legal History*, Vol. 54 (January 2015).

5. *Indianapolis Sunday Journal*, September 15, 1895, part 2, 12.

6. *New York Times*, September 19, 1895, 1.

7. *New York Times*, September 19, 1895, 5.

8. *New-York Tribune*, September 19, 1895, 6.
9. "Letter from W. E. B. Du Bois to Booker T. Washington, September 24, 1895," Columbia College, www.college.columbia.edu/core/content /letter-web-du-bois-booker-t-washington-september-24-1895.
10. Louis R. Harlan, "The Secret Life of Booker T. Washington," *The Journal of Southern History*, vol. 37, no. 3 (August 1971): 396.
11. W. E. B. Du Bois, *Souls of Black Folk: Essays and Sketches* (Chicago: A. C. McClurg, 1903), 45.
12. Harlan, 394.
13. Riser, 102–3.
14. *Wichita Daily Eagle*, November 25, 1897, 1.
15. 177 U.S. 442 (1900).
16. 177 U.S. 448–9.

Chapter 19: The Window Slams Shut

1. Perman, 318.
2. Riser, 151.
3. Wilford H. Smith, "The Negro and the Law," *The Negro Problem: A Series of Articles by Representative American Negroes of Today* (New York: James Pott and Company, 1903), 144.
4. Smith, *The Negro Problem: A Series of Articles by Representative American Negroes of Today*, 151–2.
5. Richard Pildes, "Democracy, Anti-Democracy and the Canon," *Constitutional Commentary* (University of Minnesota Law School, 2000), 303.
6. Riser, 165.
7. Riser, 167.
8. 189 U.S. 475–6 (1903).
9. 189 U.S. 480–1 (1903).
10. Gary Aichele, *Oliver Wendell Holmes, Jr.: Soldier, Scholar, Judge* (Woodbridge, CT: Twayne Publishing, 1989), 155.
11. 189 U.S. 475 (1903).
12. Pildes, "Democracy," 296.
13. Charles A. Kent, *Memoir of Henry Billings Brown* (New York: Vail-Ballou Company, 1915), 92.
14. Kent, 113.
15. In view of jurisdictional issues, Smith tried again, this time suing for damages, but in *Giles v. Teasley* lost once more, with only Justice Harlan dissenting.

16. In 2000, Richard Pildes wrote: "*Giles* has been airbrushed out of the constitutional canon. It is surely one of the most momentous decisions in
United States Supreme Court history and one of the most revealing. Yet,
as far as I can tell, it receives nary a mention in four of the leading Constitutional Law casebooks. A fifth, the most historically oriented, notices the
case but in an uncharacteristically legalistic footnote that hardly conveys
the stakes. Professor Tribe's magisterial treatise does not cite it. *Giles* permits the virtual elimination of black citizens from political participation in
the South. Yet while extensive attention is devoted to judicial validation of
separate but equal segregation, none is devoted to this." He added, "*Giles*
reflected and shaped a constitutional culture in which the large issues of
democratic governance and institutional structure were, like unknown territories on a medieval map, cast as threatening monsters and placed outside
the known domains of constitutional law." ("Democracy, Anti-Democracy,
and the Canon," *Constitutional Commentary* [University of Minnesota Law
School, 2000], 297.)

Primarily because of Professor Pildes, who described Holmes's opinion as "wedding legalism with realpolitik into one of the most fascinat-
ingly repellant analyses in the Court's history," *Giles* has since received
more notice, and many recent characterizations have been more critical.
One scholar called *Giles* "an especially noteworthy feat of judicial leger-
demain . . . silently condoning states that had adopted new voting rules
to deny blacks the vote at the end of the nineteenth century" and "cynical
and disingenuous." (Daniel P. Tokaji, "The Sordid Business of Democracy," *Ohio Northern University Law Review*, Vol. 34, No. 2 [2008], 344.)
Another wrote that Holmes "framed the case . . . as being about political
rights as opposed to race. [He] suggested that political rights cases are not
justiciable and that the political process itself must supply the remedy to
political wrongs. If race cases are truly political rights cases, and political rights cases are not justiciable, then *Giles* clearly imports that claims
alleging racial discrimination in the political process are also nonjusticia-
ble." (Guy-Uriel E. Charles, "Democracy and Distortion," *Cornell Law Review*. Vol. 92 [May 2007], 626.) Others claimed claimed Holmes's opinion
"ingeniously evaded reaching the merits of the allegations that the African American electorate had been disenfranchised." (Gabriel J. Chin and
Randy Wagner, "The Tyranny of the Minority: Jim Crow and the Counter-Majoritarian Difficulty," *Harvard Civil Rights-Civil Liberties Law Review* [Winter 2008], 294.)

But analyzing Holmes's opinion in legalisms is largely beside the point. *Giles* should be viewed, as Holmes thought, as a political question.

17. Two Holmes critics later wrote, "This case represents a clear example of Justice Holmes allowing his racist views to shade his constitutional decision-making ... [his] performance is nothing short of appalling ... Even aside from his atrocious eugenics opinion, Justice Holmes's deprivation of the right of African-Americans to vote is an egregious constitutional error. As in *Buck v. Bell*, Justice Holmes was judicially restrained in *Giles v. Harris* when the law called for judicial activism to enforce a real legal right conferred by the Fifteenth Amendment." (Steven G. Calabresi and Hannah M. Begley, "Justice Oliver Wendell Holmes and Chief Justice John Roberts's Dissent in *Obergefell v. Hodges*," *Elon Law Review*, Vol. 8, No.1 [2016], 30.)

18. Morris B. Hoffman, "Reviewed work: *Law without Values: The Life, Work and Legacy of Justice Holmes* by Albert W. Alschuler," *Stanford Law Review*, Vol. 54, No. 3 (December 2001): 612.

19. To Holmes's point about the inability to enforce a decision in Giles's favor, Michael Klarman, although speaking in this instance about *Plessy v. Ferguson*, wrote: "Given the background state of race relations at the turn of the century and the limited capacity of the Supreme Court generally to frustrate dominant public opinion, it may be implausible to think that the Justices realistically could have reached different results in these cases ... it may be fanciful to expect the Justices to have defended black civil rights when racial attitudes and practices were as abysmal as they were at the turn of the century."

But Professor Klarman and others who make that argument are missing an important point. The same criticism has been leveled at *Brown v. Board of Education*, in which not only did the justices unanimously take a position with which many Americans profoundly disagreed—and in the South that is a vast understatement—but it did not seem to have any positive impact, since segregation actually got worse in its wake. (It is unclear whether or not 1954 Americans, in the North at any rate, thought *Brown* was the right thing to do, although it is likely that most thought the Court had no business deciding who should go to what school.)

But *Brown* announced that, for the first time, the United States viewed segregation as wrong, even though the decision was confined to schools. And that mattered—as it turned out, it mattered a great deal. The following year, the Interstate Commerce Commission outlawed segregation on buses that traveled from one state to another, for the first time repealing the separate-but-equal doctrine. Five years later the ICC outlawed segregation in waiting rooms, and the year after in all interstate travel. Eventually, all forms of legal segregation slowly vanished—too slowly perhaps, but at least it got done. In other words, while the Court could not change behavior immediately, by ruling as it did, it set a tone that eventually moved the country in the direction it had mandated. Although one cannot know for certain, if the Court had ruled differently in *Giles*, it is possible that the impact of Jim Crow might have been mitigated.

BIBLIOGRAPHY

—The American Law Register (1852–1891)

—Congressional Globe: memory.loc.gov/ammem/amlaw/lwcg.html

—Statutes at Large: memory.loc.gov/ammem/amlaw/lwsl.html

—United States Reports: www.loc.gov/law/help/us-reports.php

—Historic newspapers: chroniclingamerica.loc.gov

—*New York Times*: www.nytimes.com

—*Brooklyn Daily Eagle*: bklyn.newspapers.com

—*Journal of the Proceedings of the Constitutional Convention*. Montgomery, AL: Brown Printing Company, 1901.

—*The North American Review*, Vol. 151, No. 406 (September 1890).

—*Report of the Annual Meeting of the Mississippi Bar Association*. Jackson, MS: Clarion Steam Printing, 1888.

—"The Alabama Franchise Case." *Harvard Law Review*, Vol. 17, No. 2 (December 1903).

—"Amendments to the Constitution: a brief legislative history. Prepared for the use of the Subcommittee on the Constitution, Committee on the Judiciary, United States Senate." Washington, D.C.: U.S. Government Printing Office: 1985.

—"Anselm J. McLaurin (late a senator from Mississippi)." Washington, D.C.: U.S. Government Printing Office, 1911.

—"Constitutionality of the Grandfather Clauses." *Columbia Law Review*, Vol. 14, No. 4 (April 1914).

—"Contested election case of Cornelius J. Jones vs. T.C. Catchings in House of Representatives of 56th Congress of the United States: brief of contestant." Washington, D.C.: U.S. Government Printing Office, 1894.

—"Report of the Special Joint Committee on Levees to the Legislature of the State of Louisiana." Baton Rouge, 1859.

—"The Strange Career of 'State Action under the Fifteenth Amendment.'" *The Yale Law Journal*, Vol. 74, No. 8 (July 1965).

Abraham, Harry J. "John Marshall Harlan: A Justice Neglected." *Virginia Law Review*, Vol. 41, No. 7 (November 1955).

Aichele, Gary. *Oliver Wendell Holmes, Jr.: Soldier, Scholar, Judge*. Woodbridge, CT: Twayne Publishing, 1989.

Alschuler, Albert W. *Law Without Values: The Life, Work and Legacy of Justice Holmes*. Chicago: University of Chicago Press, 2000.

Amar, Akhil Reed, and Jed Rubenfeld. "A Dialogue." *The Yale Law Journal*, Vol. 115, No. 8 (June 2006).

Aynes, Richard L. "Constricting the Law of Freedom: Justice Miller, The Fourteenth Amendment, and the *Slaughter-House Cases*—Freedom: Constitutional Law." *Chicago-Kent Law Review*, Vol. 70 (1994).

Barton, William Eleazar. *Pine Knot; a Story of Kentucky Life*. New York: D. Appleton and Co., 1900.

B. E. H. and J. J. K. Jr. "Federal Protection of Negro Voting Rights." *Virginia Law Review*, Vol. 51, No. 6 (October 1965).

Benedict, Michael Les. "Preserving Federalism: Reconstruction and the Waite Court." *The Supreme Court Review*, Vol. 1978 (1978).

David Bernstein. "Revisiting *Yick Wo v. Hopkins.*" *George Mason University Law and Economics Research Paper Series*, 2008.

Bilbo, *Collier's*, July 6, 1946.

Bogen, David S. "Slaughter-House Five: Views of the Case." *Hastings Law Journal*, Vol. 55, No. 2 (December 2003).

Boyd, Julian P., ed. *Papers of Thomas Jefferson*. Princeton, NJ: Princeton University Press, 1950.

Borchard, Edwin. "The Supreme Court and Private Rights." *The Yale Law Journal*, Vol. 47, No. 7 (May 1938).

Branch, Mary Polk. *Memoirs of a Southern Woman*. Chicago: Joseph E. Branch Publishing Company, 1912.

Brenner, Samuel. "Airbrushed out of the Constitutional Canon: The Evolving Understanding of *Giles v. Harris*, 1903–1925." *Michigan Law Review*, Vol. 107, No. 5 (March 2009).

Bruce, Philip Alexander. *History of the University of Virginia, 1819–1919: the lengthened shadow of one man*. Vol. III. New York: The Macmillan Company, 1920–22.

Bryant-Jones, Mildred. "The Political Program of Thaddeus Stevens, 1865." *Phylon*, Vol. 2, No. 2 (2nd Qtr., 1941).

Burke, W. Lewis. "Killing, Cheating, Legislating, and Lying: A History of Voting Rights in South Carolina after the Civil War." *South Carolina Law Review*, Vol. 57 (2006).

Burton, Thomas W. *What Experience Has Taught Me: An Autobiography of Thomas William Burton*. Cincinnati: Press of Jennings and Graham, 1910.

Calabresi, Steven G., and Hannah M. Begley. "Justice Oliver Wendell Holmes and Chief Justice John Roberts's Dissent in *Obergefell v. Hodges.*" *Elon Law Review*, Vol. 8 (2016).

Calhoon, S. S. "The Causes and Events that Led to the Calling of the Constitutional Convention of 1890." *Mississippi Historical Society*, *Centenary Series*, Vol. VI (1902).

Champagne, Anthony, and Dennis Pope. "Joseph P. Bradley: An Aspect of a Judicial Personality." *Political Psychology*, Vol. 6, No. 3 (Sep. 1985).

Charles, Guy-Uriel E. "Democracy and Distortion." *Cornell Law Review*, Vol. 92 (May 2007).

Chin, Gabriel J. "Unexplainable on Grounds of Race: Doubts About *Yick Wo*." *University of Illinois Law Review* (2008).

Chin, Gabriel J., and Randy Wagner. "The Tyranny of the Minority: Jim Crow and the Counter-Majoritarian Difficulty." *Harvard Civil Rights-Civil Liberties Law Review* (Winter 2008).

Corwin, Edward S. "The Supreme Court and the Fourteenth Amendment." *Michigan Law Review*, Vol. 7, No. 8 (June 1909).

George E. Cunningham. "Constitutional Disenfranchisement of the Negro in Louisiana, 1898." *Negro History Bulletin*, Vol. 29, No. 7 (April 1966).

Davison, Eddy W., and Daniel Foxx. *Nathan Bedford Forrest: In Search of the Enigma*. Gretna, LA: Pelican Publishing, 2007.

Du Bois, W. E. B. *Autobiography of W.E.B. Dubois: A Soliloquy on Viewing My Life from the Last Decade of Its First Century*. New York: International Publishers, 1968.

—"Reconstruction and its Benefits." *The American Historical Review*, Vol. 15, No. 4 (July 1910).

—"Reconstruction, Seventy-Five Years After." *Phylon*, Vol. 4, No. 3 (3rd Qtr., 1943).

—*Souls of Black Folk: Essays and Sketches*. Chicago: A. C. McClurg, 1903.

Dunning, William A. "The Undoing of Reconstruction." *The Atlantic Monthly*. Vol. 88 (1901).

Edmonds, Helen G. *The Negro and Fusion Politics in North Carolina, 1894–1901*. Chapel Hill: University of North Carolina Press, 1951.

Elliot, Jonathan. *The Debates in the Several State Conventions on the Adoption of the Federal Constitution*. Philadelphia: J. B. Lippincott & Co., 1839.

Epps, Garrett. *Democracy Reborn: The Fourteenth Amendment and the*

Fight for Equal Rights in Post–Civil War America. New York: Henry Holt, 2006.

Farrand, Max. *Records of the Federal Convention*. New Haven: Yale University Press, 1937.

Flynt, Wayne. "Alabama's Shame: The Historical Origins of the 1901 Constitution." *Alabama Law Review*, Vol. 53 (2001).

Foley, Patrick J. "Class Discrimination in Selection of Jurors." *Catholic University Law Review*, Vol. 5.

Foner, Eric. *Freedom's Lawmakers: A Directory of Black Officeholders during Reconstruction*, revised ed. Baton Rouge, LA: Louisiana State University Press, 1996.

—*Reconstruction: America's Unfinished Revolution, 1863–1877*. New York: Harper and Row, 1988.

Franklin, John Hope. "'Legal' Disfranchisement of the Negro" in "The Negro Voter in the South," special issue, *The Journal of Negro Education*, Vol. 26, No. 3 (Summer 1957).

Garner, James Wilford. *Reconstruction in Mississippi*. New York: MacMillan, 1901.

Goff, John S. "The Rejection of United States Supreme Court Appointments." *The American Journal of Legal History*, Vol. 5, No. 4 (October 1961).

Grant, Ulysses S. *The Papers of Ulysses S. Grant: November 1, 1870–May 31, 1871*. Carbondale: Southern Illinois University Press, 1998.

Hamm, Walter C. "The Three Phases of Colored Suffrage." *North American Review*, Vol. 168, No. 508 (March 1899).

Harlan, Louis R. "The Secret Life of Booker T. Washington." *The Journal of Southern History*, Vol. 37, No. 3 (August 1971).

Hayden, Harry. *The Story of the Wilmington Rebellion*. Privately printed, 1936. www.1898wilmington.org/hayden.shtml.

Hoffman, Morris B. "Reviewed work: *Law without Values: The Life, Work and Legacy of Justice Holmes* by Albert W. Alschuler." *Stanford Law Review*, Vol. 54, No. 3 (December 2001).

Huebner, Timothy S. "Emory Speer and Federal Enforcement of the

Rights of African Americans, 1880–1910." *American Journal of Legal History*, Vol. 54 (January 2015).

Hoeveler, J. David, Jr. "Reconstruction and the Federal Courts: The Civil Rights Act of 1875." *The Historian*, Vol. 31, No. 4 (August 1969).

H. M. J. "Federal Jurisdiction: The Civil Rights Removal Statute Revisited." *Duke Law Journal*, Vol. 1967, No. 1 (Feb., 1967).

Holmes, *The Common Law*. Boston: Little, Brown and Company, 1881.

Hunt, Gaillard (ed). *The Writings of James Madison*, Vol. 9. New York: G. P. Putnam's Sons, 1903.

Kaczorowski, Robert. *The Politics of Judicial Interpretation: The Federal Courts, Department of Justice and Civil Rights, 1866–1876*. New York: Fordham University Press, 2005.

Kantrowitz, Stephen. "Youngest Living Carpetbagger Tells All: Or, How Regional Myopia Created 'Pitchfork' Ben Tillman." *Southern Cultures*, Vol. 8, No. 3 (Fall 2002).

Kens, Paul. *Justice Stephen Field: Shaping Liberty from the Gold Rush to the Gilded Age*. Lawrence: Kansas University Press, 1997.

Kent, Charles A. *Memoir of Henry Billings Brown*. New York: Vail-Ballou Company, 1915.

Keyssar, Alexander. *The Right to Vote: The Contested History of Democracy in the United States*. New York: Basic Books, 2000.

Klarman, Michael J. *From Jim Crow to Civil Rights: The Supreme Court and the Struggle for Racial Equality*. New York: Oxford University Press, 2004.

—"How Brown Changed Race Relations: The Backlash Thesis." *The Journal of American History*, Vol. 81, No. 1 (June 1994).

—"The Plessy Era." *The Supreme Court Review*, 1998.

Kousser, J. Morgan. "Response to Commentaries." *Social Science History*, 24:2 (Summer 2000).

—*The Shaping of Southern Politics: Suffrage Restriction and the Establishment of the One-Party South, 1880–1910*. New Haven: Yale University Press, 1974.

—*Colorblind Injustice: Minority Voting Rights and the Undoing of the Sec-

ond Reconstruction. Chapel Hill: University of North Carolina Press, 1999.

Kurland, Philip B., and Ralph Lerner, eds. *The Founders' Constitution.* Chicago: University of Chicago Press, 1987.

Kutler, Stanley I. "Reconstruction and the Supreme Court: The Numbers Game Reconsidered." *The Journal of Southern History*, Vol. 32, No. 1 (February 1966).

—*Judicial Power and Reconstruction Politics*. Chicago: University of Chicago Press, 1968.

Lane, Charles. *The Day Freedom Died: The Colfax Massacre, the Supreme Court, and the Betrayal of Reconstruction.* New York: Henry Holt & Company, 2009.

Levy, Leonard W. *Original Intent and the Framers' Constitution.* New York: Macmillan, 1988.

Lewis, Earl M. "The Negro Voter in Mississippi." *The Journal of Negro Education*, Vol. 26, No. 3 (Summer 1957).

Lurie, Jonathan. "Reflections on Justice Samuel F. Miller and the *Slaughter-House Cases*: Still a Meaty Subject." *NYU Journal of Law & Liberty*, Vol. 1 (2005).

Mabry, William Alexander. "Disenfranchisement of the Negro in Mississippi." *The Journal of Southern History*, Vol. 4, No. 3 (August 1938).

—"Louisiana Politics and the Grandfather Clause." *The North Carolina Historical Review*, Vol. 13, No. 4 (October 1936).

—"The Negro in North Carolina Politics Since Reconstruction." *The Journal of Negro History*, Vol. 25, No. 4 (October 1940).

—"Negro Suffrage and Fusion Rule in North Carolina." *The North Carolina Historical Review*, Vol. 12, No. 2 (April 1935).

—"White Supremacy and the North Carolina Suffrage Amendment." *The North Carolina Historical Review*, Vol. 13, No. 1 (January 1936).

McPherson, Edward. "The political history of the United States of America during the period of reconstruction, (from April 15, 1865, to July 15, 1870,) including a classified summary of the legislation of the Thirty-ninth, Fortieth, and Forty-first congresses. With the votes thereon; together with the action, congressional and state, on the fourteenth and fifteenth amendments to the Constitution of the United States, and the other important executive, legislative, politico-military, and judicial facts of that period." Washington, D.C.: Philp and Solomons, 1871.

McPherson, James M. "Abolitionists and the Civil Rights Act of 1875." *The Journal of American History*, Vol. 52, No. 3 (December 1965).

Magliocca, Gerard N. *American Founding Son: John Bingham and the Invention of the Fourteenth Amendment*. New York: NYU Press, 2013.

Magrath, C. Peter. *Morrison R. Waite: The Triumph of Character*. New York: The Macmillan Company, 1963.

Montgomery, Frank Alexander. *Reminiscences of a Mississippian in Peace and War*. Cincinnati: Robert Clarke Company, 1901.

Morris, Roy, Jr. *Fraud of the Century: Rutherford B. Hayes, Samuel Tilden and the Stolen Election of 1876*. New York: Simon and Schuster, 2003.

Nagle, John Copeland. "How Not to Count Votes." *Columbia Law Review*, Vol. 104, No. 6 (October 2004).

Nimmer, Melville B. "A Proposal for Judicial Validation of a Previously Unconstitutional Law: The Civil Rights Act of 1875." *Columbia Law Review*, Vol. 65, No. 8 (December 1965).

Packard, Jerrold M. *American Nightmare: The History of Jim Crow*. New York: Macmillan, 1992.

Pedigo, Virginia G., and Lewis G. Pedigo. *History of Patrick and Henry Counties, Virginia*. Baltimore: Genealogical Publishing Co., 1933.

Peek, Ralph L. "Curbing of Voter Intimidation in Florida, 1871." *The Florida Historical Quarterly*, Vol. 43, No. 4 (April 1965).

Perman, Michael. *Struggle for Mastery: Disfranchisement and the South 1888–1908*. Chapel Hill: University of North Carolina Press, 2001.

Peskin, Allan, "Was There a Compromise of 1877?" *The Journal of American History*, Vol. 60, No. 1 (June 1973).

Pildes, Richard. "Constitutional and Political Competition." *Nova Law Review*, Vol. 30 (2006).

—"Democracy, Anti-Democracy, and the Canon." *Constitutional Commentary*. University of Minnesota Law School, 2000.

—"Keeping Legal History Meaningful." *Constitutional Commentary*. University of Minnesota Law School, 2002.

—"What Kind of Right is the Right to Vote?" *Virginia Law Review*, Vol. 93 (April 2007).

Purcell, Edward. "The Particularly Dubious Case of *Hans v. Louisiana*: An Essay on Law, Race, History, and Federal Courts." *North Carolina Law Review* (June 2003).

Reed, Thomas B. "The Federal Control of Elections." *The North American Review*, Vol. 150, No. 403 (June 1890).

Rehnquist, William H. *Centennial Crisis: The Disputed Election of 1876*. New York: Alfred A. Knopf, 2004.

Riser, R. Volney. *Defying Disfranchisement*. Baton Rouge: Louisiana State University Press, 2010.

Robison, Daniel M. "From Tillman to Long: Some Striking Leaders of the Rural South." *The Journal of Southern History*, Vol. 3, No. 3 (August 1937).

Ross, Michael A. "Justice Miller's Reconstruction: The *Slaughter-House Cases*, Health Codes, and Civil Rights in New Orleans, 1861–1873." *The Journal of Southern History*, Vol. 64, No. 4 (November 1998).

—"Obstructing Reconstruction: John Archibald Campbell and the Legal Campaign Against Louisiana's Republican Government, 1868–1873." *Civil War History*, Vol. 49 (2003).

Russ, William A., Jr. "The Negro and White Disfranchisement During Radical Reconstruction." *The Journal of Negro History*, Vol. 19, No. 2 (April 1934).

Seymour, Horatio. "The Political Situation." *The North American Review*, Vol. 136, Issue 315 (February 1883).

Smith, George P. "Republican Reconstruction and Section Two of the Fourteenth Amendment." *The Western Political Quarterly*, Vol. 23, No. 4 (December 1970).

Smith, Wilford H. "The Negro and the Law." *The Negro Problem: A Se-*

ries of Articles by Representative American Negroes of Today. New York: James Pott and Company, 1903.

Spackman, S. G. F. "American Federalism and the Civil Rights Act of 1875." *Journal of American Studies*, Vol. 10, No. 3 (December 1976).

Steelman, Joseph F. "Republican Party Strategists and the Issue of Fusion with Populists in North Carolina,1893–1894." *The North Carolina Historical Review*, Vol. 47, No. 3 (July 1970).

Sumers, J. W. "The Grandfather Clause." *Lawyer & Banker & Southern Bench & Bar Review* 39 (1914).

Syrett, Harold C., ed. *Papers of Alexander Hamilton.* New York: Columbia University Press, 1961–79.

Tokaji, Daniel P. "The Sordid Business of Democracy." *Ohio Northern University Law Review,* Vol. 34, No. 2 (2008).

Van Alstyne, William W. "The Fourteenth Amendment, the 'Right' to Vote, and the Understanding of the Thirty-Ninth Congress." *The Supreme Court Review*, 1965.

Walter, Marilyn R. "The Ku Klux Klan Act and the State Action Requirement of the Fourteenth Amendment." *58 Temp. L.Q. 3* (1985).

Wang, Xi, "The Making of Federal Enforcement Laws, 1870–1872—Freedom: Political." *Chicago-Kent Law Review*, Vol. 70 (1995).

Warren, Charles. *The Supreme Court and United States History.* Boston: Little, Brown and Company, 1923.

Washington, Booker T. *Up From Slavery.* New York: Doubleday, Page & Company, 1901.

Watson, Douglas S. "The San Francisco McAllisters." *California Historical Society Quarterly*, Vol. 11, No. 2 (June 1932).

Weaver, Valeria W. "The Failure of Civil Rights 1875–1883 and its Repercussions." *The Journal of Negro History*, Vol. 54, No. 4 (Oct. 1969).

Weinberg, Louise. "Holmes' Failure." *Michigan Law Review*, Vol. 96, No. 3 (December 1997).

Westin, Alan F. "John Marshall Harlan and the Constitutional Rights of Negroes: The Transformation of a Southerner." *The Yale Law Journal*, Vol. 66, No. 5 (April 1957).

Wiecek, William M. "The Emergence of Equality as a Constitutional Value: The First Century." *Chicago-Kent Law Review*, Vol. 82 (2007).

Williams, George H. "Reminiscences of the United States Supreme Court." *The Yale Law Journal*, Vol. 8, No. 7 (April 1899).

Woodward, C. Vann. *The Burden of Southern History*. Baton Rouge: Louisiana State University Press, 1968.

—*The Strange Career of Jim Crow*. Second ed. New York: Oxford University Press, 1966.

—*Origins of the New South, 1877–1913*. Baton Rouge: Louisiana State University Press, 1951.

—"The Political Legacy of Reconstruction" in "The Negro Voter in the South," special issue, *The Journal of Negro Education*, Vol. 26, No. 3 (Summer 1957).

Wormser, Richard. *The Rise and Fall of Jim Crow*. New York: St. Martin's Press, 2003.

Wyatt-Brown, Bertram. "The Civil Rights Act of 1875." *The Western Political Quarterly*, Vol. 18, No. 4 (December 1965).

Zuczek, Richard. "The Federal Government's Attack on the Ku Klux Klan: A Reassessment." *The South Carolina Historical Magazine*, Vol. 97, No. 1 (1996).

INDEX

© Nancy Goldstone

LAWRENCE GOLDSTONE is the author of five books and numerous articles on constitutional law. His reviews and opinion pieces have appeared in, among other publications, *The Wall Street Journal*, *Los Angeles Times*, *Chicago Tribune*, *Miami Herald*, *The New Republic*, and *Tablet*. His wife is the noted medieval and Renaissance historian Nancy Goldstone. Find out more at lawrencegoldstone.com.